WHAT ARE WE TO DO?

WHAT ARE WE TO DO?

by

JOHN STRACHEY

You must rise or you must fall. You must rule
and win, or serve and lose, you must suffer or
triumph, you must be anvil or hammer. *Goethe*

*Quoted by Dimitrov in his concluding speech
from the dock at the Reichstag fire trial*

LONDON
VICTOR GOLLANCZ LTD
1938

PRINTED IN GREAT BRITAIN BY PURNELL AND SONS, LTD. (T.U.
PAULTON (SOMERSET AND LONDON

CONTENTS

PART I

WHAT IS A LABOUR MOVEMENT?

PART II

THE NEW MODEL

CONTENTS

PART III

TOWARDS A UNITED LEFT

INTRODUCTION

THIS BOOK IS a study of the Labour movement. The object of undertaking such a study is to discover whether, and if so under what conditions and circumstances, the Labour movement may be an instrument of desirable social change.

It is in this sense that the book is an attempt at a contemporary answer to the question what are we to do? Behind the asking and answering of that question lie the assumptions that something ought to be done, and that something can be done.

The second of these assumptions, especially, is often questioned to-day. Weary with unfulfilling years, many may be tempted to suppose that once again, as so often before in human history, misery and violence are failing to stir men to social reconstruction.

The truth is that misery has never been more than the mother of social change. Social change itself must be begotten by events which make it impossible to carry on society in the old way. Hence we must not be surprised because in Britain the tens of millions who must act if society is to be reconstructed, as yet feel no sufficient urge to do so. It is impossible for the immense majority of us, cut off from all effective knowledge of what is happening in the world, or, worse still, provided only with a pseudo-knowledge which can do no more than confuse, to *foresee* events. Whole peoples can learn from experience alone. It is only when they are faced, not with signs that it will soon be impossible to sustain the existing social system, but with that impossibility itself, that the millions are driven to act. That situation will arise, however, in Britain just as it has arisen already in large parts of continental Europe and of Asia. And it will arise all too soon.

There is not the slightest danger that we shall not be forced to do something. On the contrary our whole danger is that we shall not have learnt in time what to do and how to do it.

For decisive social action can be successful or unsuccessful, fruitful or barren, constructive or destructive, progressive or regressive. A heavy responsibility now rests upon those who foresee the coming impasse. They must not claim the slightest superiority over the still unconscious millions. Their greater foresight is due, in almost every case, to chance alone. A certain number of people have been forced by the circumstances of their lives to understand what is happening in the world to-day. But this accident imposes upon them the duty of achieving a clear understanding, not only of what is going to *happen*, but of what to *do*.

This book is an attempt to answer that question. Some of its readers, under the pressure of contemporary events, may feel impatience with its opening chapters, which discuss the character and historical origins of the British Labour movement. But it is only by the study of what *has happened* in the past, that we can hope to discover what to *do* now. Unless we devote the most careful and serious attention to that interplay of human and economic forces which has created the social complex in which we live, we shall have no hope, even, of finding the right answers to the life and death questions which contemporary events thrust upon us.

NOTE.—The title of this book asks the same question which Lenin asked in 1902 in his famous work *What is to be Done?* It may be said that in so doing I am comparing myself to Lenin. But no, what is compared is the situation which confronted the members of the Russian Labour movement at the beginning of this century, with the situation which confronts us all to-day. Nor does anything in our situation excuse us from the imperative task of asking this same question, and answering it as best we may.

WHAT IS A LABOUR MOVEMENT?

CHAPTER I

THE ORIGIN OF LABOUR MOVEMENTS

WHENEVER AND WHEREVER the capitalist system has been established, a new social phenomenon appears. This phenomenon is universally called "the Labour movement". The original form of the British and American Labour movements consisted of combinations of workmen engaged in particular trades.

As soon as, that is to say, the land, the factories and the mines of a country have become the property of a distinct class of persons, and, as a necessary consequence, most of the rest of the population finds itself in the employment of this class, a new and peculiar type of organisation, now universally called *Trade Unions*, appears upon the social scene. The workers form themselves into groups the primary purpose of which is to bargain with their employers over hours, wages and conditions of work.

Now no one went and told the workers to form Trade Unions. Trade Unions were in existence long before anyone outside the wage-workers had begun to take the slightest interest in them.[1] In Britain, for example, Trade Unions have been in existence since about 1700. Now in 1700 the land, factories and mines—the means of

---

[1] But after the establishment of Trade Unions discussion of them has been continuous. The spokesmen of the owners of the means of production at first tirelessly denounced them, then grudgingly admitted them as a necessary evil, and are now (in Britain) seeking to use them for their own ends. The lawyers and the judges have both outlawed them and, simultaneously, subjected them to meticulous legal restrictions. On the other hand writers and thinkers within the working-class movement have extolled, criticised, theorised upon, and admonished the Unions, also without cease. Below we shall examine this mass of theory and speculation about the Trade Unions. Here we are making the simple point that all this had nothing to do with the origin, and little to do with the growth, of the Trade Unions. These have everywhere appeared as the reflex action of the working class to its condition of life in capitalist societies.

production—of Britain had not passed by any means completely into the hands of a special, limited class. There was
still a great deal of individual, scattered ownership of means
of production (such as the farms of the yeomen, the looms
of the handloom weavers, and the tools of numerous independent artisans). Such people employed themselves.
Hence the very idea of Trade Unions to bargain for them
with an outside employer could not occur to them. It was
only amongst those relatively few workers who were
already working for wages in other men's factories, or on
other men's farms, that the eighteenth century Trade
Unions could arise.

Thus Trade Unions could only develop as and when
there developed a capitalist system of the ownership of
the means of production by a limited class of persons.
And capitalism developed gradually, unevenly, over a
period of nearly four hundred years. We must not, then,
suppose that first capitalism established itself, the means
of production were concentrated in a few hands, the mass
of the population were converted into wage-workers, and
then Trade Unions appeared amongst these wage-workers.
History is never so simple as that. In fact the two things
happened simultaneously. Long before anything like all
the means of production had passed into the hands of a
particular class, Trade Unions had appeared amongst the
relatively small class of wage-workers. But Trade Unions
could not and did not become general until work for
wages had become the inescapable way of life of the pre-
ponderant part of the population.

Nor must we suppose that this major social development took place earlier than it did. It is true that in Britain
work for wages has now been the staple form of existence
for the largest single group of the population for some
hundred years. But in this respect Britain is unique. In
America, capitalism on the great scale began to develop
only a little later than in Britain. But the vast and virgin
continent in which that development took place allowed
the process to be a very long one. Although the *pace* of

capitalist development in America was incomparably swift, yet the *distance* which that development had to go —the sheer ground it had to cover—was so immense that it is scarcely too much to say that the structure of American capitalism, as a finished system which has fully overcome all earlier systems of production, has only been completed in the present generation. Above all, so long as free land existed within the United States as it did until forty years ago, American capitalism was not a closed, completed system which might be expected to exhibit the typical social consequences of vesting a monopoly of the means of production in the hands of a limited class.

In particular, general and stable Trade Unionism could not grow up in such conditions. For American workers, dissatisfied with the status and condition of wage-workers, had before them, as an alternative to the arduous and desperate course of challenging the will of their employers by means of Trade Union organisation, the prospect of leaving work for wages altogether and setting up for themselves as farmers, or as independent artisans, in the West. So long, to put the point in economic terms, as an earlier economic system, commonly called *small commodity production*, existed as something approaching an equal partner with capitalism in the economic life of America, American workers were not likely to be driven to universal, or even very widespread, combination for bargaining with their employers. For it is the characteristic of small commodity production that under it the worker owns his own means of production (as the farmer his farm, or the artisan his tools) and so, as it were, employs himself.

It is necessary to distinguish exactly between small commodity production and capitalist production, for the argument of this chapter rests upon this distinction. Small commodity production is production carried on by people who both do the actual work and own the raw materials and the tools with which they work. A typical example of the small commodity producer is a peasant farmer; another example is a doctor in private practice, for it makes no difference whether the commodity produced is a good or a service. Another, though virtually extinct, example, is that of the hand-loom weaver. These kinds of workers produce their respective commodities, either to use themselves (as when a peasant eats the potatoes he has raised) or more often to exchange for other commodities which they want (as when a doctor buys a motor-car with the money his patients have paid him for his medical attention).

Now many people half-consciously assume that most of our economic life is still carried on in this way. But this is not so. To-day most people do not produce commodities from their own raw materials with their own tools. On the contrary, they work upon raw materials and with tools owned by other people. A typical factory worker, clerical employee, or miner, works upon raw materials, and with tools, owned by the shareholders of the company which employs him. Hence when he has produced something it does not belong to him but to these shareholders. He is, of course, paid wages for his work, or else he could not live. And it is true that the payment of wages is a kind of process of exchange. But what the wage-worker has exchanged for his wages is not anything which he has produced, but his ability to work; for this is the only thing he has.

This latter type of economic arrangement is called capitalist production. Capitalist production has developed out of small commodity production, and both are forms of production for exchange. The two forms of production can exist simultaneously in the same community. But it is clear that a community will be of a very different character according to whether small commodity production or capitalist production is the dominant, typical economic arrangement within it. For example, a community in which small commodity production is dominant will have no Trade Unions—or will have them only in that small field of production in which the distinctive relationship of employer and employed has established itself. On the other hand, a community in which capitalist relations of production predominate will certainly have substantial Trade Unions. (Unless, indeed, the owners of the means of production have suppressed them by force.) It will be found, on examination, that most of the idealisations of the capitalist system in which its admirers indulge are based upon a slurring over of the above distinction between small commodity production and distinctively capitalist economic arrangements; by writing or talking as if we still lived in a world of independent producers each satisfying his needs by producing something to exchange with his fellow men.

In regard to the Britain of to-day, in which no less than over 80·0 per cent of the working population consists of dependent wage-workers, who can produce nothing on their own, and consequently have not, as a rule, anything to exchange except their capacity to work, this illusion is exceptionally misleading.[1] It is only less misleading in regard to America, where in spite of the persistence of a substantial amount of small commodity production, above all in agriculture, work for wages has now become the typical way of life of the greatest single mass of the population. Until that had happened Trade Unions, the basic form of a Labour movement, could not become general, as they have done in the last five years, amongst the American wage-earners.

It is sometimes forgotten, however (especially in the case of America), how recently it is that distinctively capitalist relations of production have become overwhelmingly

[1] Census of 1931. Of a total British working population of 21,326,000, 18,872,000, or 88·4 per cent, were in that year wage-workers, and 1,273,000, or 6·0 per cent, were "workers on their own account". That is to say they were workers owning their own means of production. This figure of 6·0 per cent gives us a good indication of the extent to which the earlier economic system of small commodity production survives in Britain. The remaining 1,180,000, or 5·5 per cent of the working population, are owners of the means of production employing wage-workers. (This category includes, however, factory, mine and shop managers who in many cases have no ownership in the means of production and are, therefore, really wage-workers. So, in spite of a certain number of professional men being included in the wage-earners, the figure probably underestimates the proportion of wage-workers.)

predominant.[1] Until 1914 American capitalism was not only an open system, constantly drained of superfluous labour by the rapidly developing small commodity production of the West; it was open at the eastward end also. It was open to a perpetual inflow of European labour pouring across the Atlantic. The effect of the inflow of this river of polyglot labour on checking the organisation of the American workers has often been described. But the technical difficulties which confronted these workers when they attempted to organise have, perhaps, been emphasised to the exclusion of more fundamental factors. Difficulties due to divisions of language, race and religion could and would in the end have been overcome by the sheer pressure of permanent wage-workers' elemental need to organise.[2]

For, after all, even after 1900, a great part of the inflow consisted not of illiterate and unskilled workers from South-Eastern Europe, but of skilled, intelligent and exceptionally sturdy British, German and Scandinavian workers. Such men would certainly have organised themselves if they had had to remain permanently in the condition of wage-workers, working for American capitalist employers. But a decisive proportion of them were on their way westwards, "to set up for themselves" as small commodity producers of one kind or another. It is true that free land became exhausted in the eighteen-nineties. But we must not think that that event ended the opportunities of escape from dependence upon work for wages. So long as a vast, *and above all, swiftly growing,* rural population of independent

---

[1] "Capitalist relations of production" have been established when the making of goods or the offering of services are carried on by a group of wage-earners employed by an individual employer or by a company owned by a group of share-holders. One of the most important distinctions of Social Science is between this way of arranging the productive system and the older form of productive relations, under which a peasant or artisan, independently of any employer, produced goods on his own account with his own tools, out of his own raw materials.

[2] For example, in the immediately pre-war period, at the height of the polyglot invasion of America, it proved possible for immigrant, foreign, non-English-speaking workers, under I.W.W. leadership, to fight and win major strikes, as at McKnee Rock in 1909 and, more famously, at Lawrence in 1912. But in neither case was it possible to establish permanent organisations, basically because these were not yet permanently established wage-workers.

farmers existed in the West, there was substantial opportunity for a dissatisfied, independently minded, energetic American worker to escape from dependent employment. For any significant number that escape was never into the class of employers of labour. The typical worker never had more than a most remote opportunity of himself becoming a capitalist; this was always the goal of fantasy rather than of fact. But the American wage-worker did have a considerable opportunity of becoming an independent small commodity producer, enjoying the fruits of his own labour.[1]

As the distinctively capitalist relations of employers and employed began to become predominant in the Western States, also, this opportunity for escape began to close. At the same time, however, the character of the immigrant flow began to change. Instead of permanent settlers an important proportion of the immigrants became little more than temporary visitors who after five or ten years of work in American industry returned to their usually peasant homes in Europe. Hence the transitory, provisional character of the status of a high proportion of American wage-workers was preserved, though now in a different form.

So long as American capitalism bore this character of *one* of the forms of economic organisation, but only one, and that barely the predominant one, in American society, the opportunity and necessity for general Trade Union organisation on the part of its wage-workers did not exist. This fact is fairly well recognised. It is not so often recognised, however, that this situation applied to a considerable extent to British capitalism also throughout the nineteenth

---

[1] Indirect ways of milking the independent American farmers and other small commodity producers were of course devised. They were steadily exploited, in the sense that a part of the values which their labour created was drawn off, by the owners of the railways, the makers of agricultural machinery and other groups of owners of means of production employing wage-labour. But such exploitation is partial compared to the direct exploitation of the wage-worker by the owners of the mine or factory in which he works. Moreover, the American small commodity producers struggled, and are still struggling, to check by political means this indirect form of exploitation. And they have had some limited successes.

century. It is true that for the past hundred years few substantial opportunities of escape from the condition of wage-workers have existed within Britain. But they existed in the world outside. And a constant flow of emigration from Britain, which in the immediately pre-war years averaged no less than a quarter of a million persons a year, provided the same outlet for British capitalism as the undeveloped West provided for American capitalism.[1] Indeed it was to a predominant extent the same outlet in an actual, physical sense. The British wage-workers who grew tired of providing profits for the masters of Manchester and Birmingham fled to the same wheatfields as the wage-workers of Philadelphia, Boston and New York. The prairies of the Western States, of Canada, and of Australia, performed much the same function for British capitalism as if they had been within the British Isles. For the relative internationalism of pre-war capitalism made the national boundary lines irrelevant.

The essential fact is that capitalism right up to 1914 was never a closed system. In Britain it appeared to be so, and in one sense it was so. During the second half of the century large-scale production, involving the ownership of the means of production by a limited class, and the

---

[1] The net emigration from the British Isles to places out of Europe since 1876 has been as follows (figures in each case are an average for the five-year period):

1876–1880	.	87,000	1901–1905 .	117,000
1881–1885	.	187,000	1906–1910 .	179,000
1886–1890	.	159,000	1911–1913 .	257,000
1891–1895	.	89,000	1921–1925 .	124,000
1896–1900	.	56,000	1926–1930 .	99,000

(After 1930 the figures drop to a few thousands a year.)

Before 1876 no exact figures are available. But the following figures give a reliable indication of the order of magnitude of emigration since 1815.

1815–20	.	20,000 (annual averages)
1831–40	.	70,000
1841–50	.	168,000
1853–60	.	164,000
1861–70	.	157,000

(The last two figures are probably appreciably too large as they take no account of immigration, which was then unrecorded but which may have amounted to anything up to 50,000 a year.)

But see *Migration from and to the United Kingdom*, a paper read by H. Leak and T. Priday to the Royal Statistical Society (Vol. XCVI, Part II, 1933) for the above figures and for a full discussion of them.

conversion of the rest of the population into wage-workers, finally conquered the small-scale production of independent men using their own tools on their own land or on their own raw materials. The independent self-employing yeomen and the hand-loom weavers were driven into the factory, or on to the farm, of an employer. But these groups of independent small commodity producers, destroyed at home, were continually being reconstituted overseas. The prairies of the world absorbed a perpetual stream of men, who, if they had had to remain wage-workers in either British or American capitalist industry, would certainly have been driven to combine for the purpose of bargaining with their employers.[1] In a word, a rapidly developing, and predominantly pre-capitalist, agricultural hinterland played a vital part in the economy of nineteenth century capitalism. Nor, of course, was the function of this hinterland confined to providing outlets for dissatisfied wage-workers. It provided an ever-growing source of raw materials and food, and in return an ever-growing market, for the goods produced by the wage-labour of the capitalists' factories. But here we are concerned with its direct effect on the wage-workers.

Moreover, emigration, or in the case of America "going West," has never been the only avenue of escape from work for wages. Although large-scale industry is now supreme in both Britain and America, and has crushed small commodity production in every considerable branch of industry, yet many small independent producers still exist (although precariously) in the interstices of the great industries. For the rise of some new, large-scale industry will often

[1] During the last century the British workers were acutely conscious that emigration offered them the possibility (though it was often an illusory possibility) of escape from work for wages for the enrichment of others. In a sense paradoxically, for the existence of mass emigration was a vital factor in preventing the appearance of mass Trade Unions, the British Trade Unions of the eighteen-forties and fifties actually turned themselves into emigration agents and devoted quite large sums (considering their resources) to Emigration Funds out of which they assisted their members to leave the country. They did this, not only as a method of providing an escape from exploitation for some of their members, but also as a way of lessening the supply of wage-workers in Britain and so of maintaining the wage rates of those who remained. But in fact they were never able to act on a scale sufficiently large to affect the situation. (See the Webbs' *History of Trade Unionism*, p. 203.)

itself open up a new sphere for small commodity producers. This is a further factor, tending to counteract the general pressure of capitalist relations of production towards the formation of working-class organisations. It has been, and still is, of importance in both Britain and America. We may instance the rise of the American motor-car producing industry, in itself the most capitalistic industry in the world. It is an industry in which two or three vast firms almost monopolise the productive field, so that the very idea of a wage-worker starting up in the business of producing motor-cars, in competition with General Motors, Ford or Chrysler, is laughable. (And this is only a little less true of the British motor-car producing industry.) But the motor-car producing industry has (in both countries) given birth to another vast industry. This is the motor-car repairing, selling and maintenance industry.

And this derivative industry was, until recently, predominantly carried on by independent small commodity producers. The typical, predominating unit of the motor repairing industry is the small garage with a working, self-employing owner, employing an apprentice or at most one or two wage-workers. The rise of the garage industry (it is to-day a very great industry in both Britain and America) is a neglected social phenomenon. For it has provided a real way of escape into independence for hundreds of thousands of skilled wage-workers. All through the last twenty years it really has been possible for a significant number of enterprising men both in Britain and America to set up for themselves as garage proprietors. And these men would undoubtedly have been precisely the types most likely to take an active and effective part in Trade Union organisation, had they found no way of escape from working for wages. The rise of a vast network of garages all over Britain and America is a striking example of how large-scale, fully developed capitalism, in . the very act of crushing small commodity production in one sphere, re-creates it, and the class of independent, small commodity producers that goes with it, in another. The contemporary garage, considered as a social phenomenon, is worth the attention of the social student. It is an example of a general tendency. To a lesser extent, but yet appreciably the rise of every great industry opens up, *though only for a time*, a new field for small commodity production. But, as will be described below, the time during which small commodity production is re-created, is becoming shorter and shorter.

Indeed it may now at long last be said that the process of closing the wage-workers' avenues of escape into independence is almost complete. Even in America free land is but a memory. Agricultural opportunities, far from growing, and thus offering possibilities of independence to wage-workers weary of working for the profit of the great corporations, are diminishing. The Middle West is returning to prairie (or to desert). The headlong growth of large-scale industry which characterised the nineteen-twenties, and which created substantial opportunities for small-scale independent producers in its interstices, or on its outskirts, has been arrested.

To-day the counter-process of the invasion of these outlying spheres of production themselves by large-scale industry, and the gradual expulsion of the small, independent owner-producers from them, has begun. The example of the garage industry is again relevant. Comparatively large, capitalistically organised garages owned by small joint-stock companies, the shareholders of which have no part whatever in the work of the garages, are becoming more and more numerous. More significant still, chains of garages (viz., The LEX Garages in Britain) have appeared. These chains of garages are owned by quite large companies in which serious amounts of capital are invested; they employ thousands of wage-workers, whose status is exactly the same as that of any other wage-workers. The result of the contest between these large capitalist garages and the small owner-worker garages is not in doubt. These latter will be, and are being, pushed out of the really profitable field, out of the big towns, off the trunk roads, into the villages and onto the by-roads. For the owner-workers cannot be in a position to resist, in the long run, the competition of the big capitalistically organised concerns.[1]

The pressure to escape from working for wages in other men's factories is so overwhelming that almost any worker who can beg, borrow or steal the barest minimum of necessary capital will attempt to set up a small independent business of his own—of which the small garage is merely a typical contemporary example. The inevitable result is that such little ventures spring up thickly wherever there is any demand for their services. The outskirts of every town are covered, to return to our example, with dozens of little garages and filling stations, one beside the other, and each offering identical goods and services. They are inevitably forced into the fiercest competition and soon each is working on the barest margin of subsistence. Their worker-owners are often forced, by the impersonal compulsion of competition, to work themselves harder, for longer hours and for no better pay, than if they were wage-workers. The independence for which they have schemed and slaved and saved and dreamed turns out, only too often, to be pathetically illusory. Thus, when the big, heavily capitalised concerns begin to appear in some new field, the small commodity producers are in no position to put up more than a lingering rear-guard action. The process is everywhere the same.[2] The traditional fields of "the small man", the one-man business and the worker-owner, such as house repairing, for example, have been, and are being, remorselessly invaded by large scale, distinctively capitalist concerns, such as the large, well-organised builders and contractors.

This is above all true of what is to-day by far the largest remaining refuge of the independent worker-owner, namely,

[1] The British census of production records that in 1931 of the 14,000 managers and owners of garages, 11,500 were described as salaried managers and only 2,500 were recorded as working on their own account.

[2] Chicken farming is another striking example of a field in which small commodity production persists as the predominant form, but persists most wretchedly. Probably because chicken farming is one of the few fields in which a new-comer can get started with little experience and small capital, it attracts a perpetual stream of new entrants, so that competition is always sufficiently fierce to keep all but the most fortunate, skilful and well-equipped chicken farmers just on the verge of bankruptcy.

retail distribution. The invasion of this vast field of economic activity by the multiple shop and the great department store, both of which are organised on the basis of the characteristically capitalist relationship of, on the one hand, owning and employing shareholders and, on the other, wage-earning workers, is one of the most striking, and most frequently discussed, social phenomena of to-day. As it reaches the point at which it becomes impossible to increase the number of small shops operated by independent worker-owners, it closes one of the few major remaining ways of escape from wage-employment. For it is evident that what is in question is not the extinction of the tens of thousands of small shops in existence, but the closing up of the avenue of escape represented by an ever-growing number of such small independent shops.

In general it is not that large numbers of small independent producers do not continue to exist in many fields; they do exist and will no doubt continue to do so. It is rather that the number of these independent producers becomes smaller rather than larger; hence these fields of production provide, on balance, no outlet for dissatisfied wage-workers. The pressure upon the wage-worker towards organisation in Trade Unions becomes ever greater.

To sum up. Capitalist industry destroys the small commodity producer in some staple sphere of production only to re-create him on the periphery of the economic life of the community. But the small commodity producers are always reconstituted in a more outlying and secondary region. Moreover this outlying, secondary sphere of production is itself sooner or later invaded by the forces of organised, centralised capital. The small, independent commodity producers are driven ever onwards until most of them have become wage-workers, whilst the remnant find refuge in the nooks and crannies of the economic system.

What concerns us here is to realise to the full, first that the distinctively capitalist relationship of employers and employed has only become dominant in one sphere of production after another; that the process has been long drawn out and uneven; that the small, independent, self-employing producer, driven out, either of one part of the world, or of one sphere of production, has appeared again in another continent or in another sphere; and finally, that in spite of all these fluctuations, the distinctively capitalist relationship of employers and employed has become predominant in every considerable sphere of economic life.

It is necessary to say all this because it is often supposed that capitalist relations of production have long been the exclusive economic arrangement of British and American society. Capitalist relations of production have, of course, long predominated in both Britain and America. But considerable avenues of escape from these relations remained open to wage-workers until much more recently than many students of contemporary society are willing to allow. Indeed, I believe that it is hardly too much to say that it was not until the nineteen-thirties that British and American capitalism finally became closed systems, which had cut off all considerable ways of escape to small-scale, independent production, and had thus made work for wages the inescapable way of life of by far the greater number of their inhabitants. This assertion will no doubt be strongly disputed. But I believe that the more it is examined the greater element of truth will be found in it. Its importance, if it is established, is that in this case it will be only now that the social and political consequences of condemning the great majority of the population to work for wages will make themselves felt. It is contended that only now have we come to that critical situation in which the objective forces driving the decisive majority of the British and American populations, now become wage-workers without possibility of escape, towards, first, organisation for self-protection in Trade Unions, and then to the development of Labour movements, have become unchecked by any considerable counter influences.

It is one of the main themes of this book that once this critical period is reached, the resultant Labour movement must either rapidly grow to a point at which it is capable of reconstructing human society, and at which it actually does reconstruct it, or be forcibly suppressed.[1]

The foundations of the modern British Trade Union movement were laid in the eighteen-fifties. But until 1870 the Trade Unions remained small and exclusive organisations of the highly skilled, relatively well-paid workers. In the eighteen-seventies a wave of Trade Unionism struck the British working class. Between 1871 and 1875, the number of British Trade Unionists more than doubled. (From about 375,000 members to about one million, but the figures are very uncertain.) Even in the eighteen-seventies, however, considerable opportunities for escape into "independence" from work for wages still remained. The rising tide of Trade Unionism was checked and for a time receded again. But in 1889 a second and larger wave of organisation struck the British working class. And this new wave of organisation differed in an essential particular from the preceding one. In the seventies men and women had poured into the Trade Unions as a direct reaction to the conditions of life which had been imposed upon them. In and after 1889 the new-comers to Trade Unionism were recruited by men and women who knew what had imposed intolerable conditions of life upon the

[1] We are here speaking of objective economic and social counter influences, such as those exercised by the existence of ways of escape into independence. It would be the reverse of the truth to suggest that conscious counter influences, intended to dissuade the wage-workers from combination, had disappeared or had decreased. On the contrary, precisely because the pressure which the economic system now exercises upon the wage-worker, driving him towards combination in all its forms, is almost overwhelming, the efforts of that class against which he is so apt to combine, to prevent him from doing so, have been redoubled. These efforts take the form of active dissuasion, of the granting of certain concessions and reforms which, it is hoped, will make the wage-worker feel that independent organisation is unnecessary, and finally, if these two former methods fail, of resolute efforts to suppress all forms of working-class combination by force. This type of counter influence, which I repeat, far from having disappeared, is ever growing, is discussed in detail in subsequent chapters.

British wage-worker. Class consciousness and Socialist consciousness had been reborn in Britain, and the new wave of Trade Unionism was, in one aspect at any rate, a direct consequence of that rebirth. For it was led by men, who, to a lesser or greater degree, had become conscious of the aims of their class. There have been many fluctuations and hesitations in the advance of British Trade Unionism since 1889. But since that time the advance itself has never stopped.

The result has been that the leading categories of British workers are now organised in large, wealthy, long-established and influential industrial organisations, which exercise a considerable influence on the terms of employment offered to their members. It is true that even now the British Trade Unions enroll only a minority of the wage-workers (some 5 millions out of a total of $13\frac{1}{2}$ million insured workers and of 18 million wage-workers). But the rates of pay, hours, and conditions of work secured by their organisations for these 5 million Trade Unionists exercise a strong influence on the wages, hours and conditions of all the other workers. Thus to a much greater extent than would at first sight seem true, the establishment of the distinctive, capitalist relationship of employers and employed, as the almost exclusive form of economic life in Britain, has, at length, resulted in a general Trade Unionism of the employed workers.

This is not to suggest, however, that the position of British Trade Unionism is to-day a satisfactory one. The number of Trade Unionists is rising and at the time of writing (1937) has passed 5 million.[1] But this is not only but a small proportion of the total wage-workers, but is also substantially lower than the number of Trade Unionists attained to at one moment. (There were $8\frac{1}{2}$ million Trade Unionists in 1920.) Moreover, the position of British Trade Unionism is to-day unsatisfactory in some respects even as compared to its pre-war situation. The Unions are strongest in the great staple industries of cotton, coal and some aspects of engineering. But these are precisely the

[1] Of whom $4\frac{1}{4}$ million are affiliated to the Trade Union Congress.

trades, the relative importance of which has substantially declined in recent years.[1] Unemployment has been severe in almost all of them during the whole post-war period. The great, long established Trade Unions have on the whole maintained themselves to a remarkable degree in the face of these adverse circumstances. But, on the other hand, the British workers have been much less successful in organising themselves in the newer expanding, light, secondary industries. The opposition of the employers, to some extent reconciled to Trade Unionism in the older industries, to Trade Unionism in the newer industries has been intensive and tireless. The old battle for the elementary right of organisation is being re-fought in hundreds of British factories to-day. Nor, for reasons which it is a major purpose of this book to discuss, are the British workers any better equipped, in many respects, for the winning of this battle than they were thirty years ago.

But these considerations do not qualify the main, broad conclusion, which it is an object of this chapter to establish, namely, that when a capitalist system becomes fully established, the pressure towards Trade Union organisation amongst the wage-workers becomes strong and persistent. For after all, and in spite of everything, the number of Trade Unionists in Britain has never since the war sunk below 4,400,000 (in 1933) and has nearly always been above 5 million (with a maximum figure of $8\frac{1}{2}$ million) while it never rose to 4 millions before the war.[2] Moreover, 3,900,000 was a peak point reached in 1914 after an unprecedented growth of no less than a million members

[1] In 1924 the mines and quarries contributed $14\frac{1}{2}$ per cent of the total value of the output covered by the official census of production. At the next census in 1930 this proportion had fallen to 10 per cent. Between the two censuses the total number of workers in productive industry, in the narrow sense of the term, as opposed to distributive trades, had fallen by 2 per cent, in spite of a large increase in the total number of persons gainfully employed. But see G. D. H. Cole's *The Condition of Britain* for much further information on this point.

[2] See G. D. H. Cole's *The Condition of Britain*, p. 388-91 for these and much more detailed figures. Again these are estimates of the total number of Trade Unionists in Britain, not of the number affiliated to the Trade Union Congress. In 1933, for example, there were only 3,367,000 Trade Unionists affiliated to Congress.

in the immediately preceding four years. In 1910 the
total was 2,446,000; in 1905, 1,920,000; in 1900, 1,955,000;
in 1895, 1,494,000. At earlier periods in the last century
the numbers, though not accurately known, were incomparably smaller. The Webbs (*History of Trade Unionism*)
estimate that they did not exceed 100,000 in the eighteen-
forties and fifties and were still under 500,000 in the
eighteen-sixties. We may then conclude that, allowing
for fluctuations, the typical number of Trade Unionists in
Britain was until the last decade of the nineteenth century
under a million, was nearer 2 million than 3 million in
the pre-war period, and has fluctuated between $4\frac{1}{2}$ and
$8\frac{1}{2}$ million in the post-war period.

First, then, the creation of Trade Unions, and then of
Labour movements, is the inevitable reaction of the wage-
workers to the establishment of Capitalist relations of
production.

Second, Capitalist relations of production have been
established later, less completely, and more unevenly in
both Britain and America than is often supposed.

Third, this accounts, to a greater extent than is always
recognized, for the uneven, episodic, incomplete character
of the development of the British and American Labour
movements in the past.

Fourth the relatively recent establishment of capitalist
relations of production as the virtually exclusive economic
arrangement in Britain and, to a lesser extent, in America,
now faces the Labour movements of these countries with
the alternative of transforming their social environment or
of being destroyed by it.

Fifth, the figures of British Trade Union membership
over the past fifty years illustrate this view.

CHAPTER II

THE TRADE UNIONS AND POLITICS

THE MEN WHO, in the eighteen-fifties, laid the foundations of the Trade Unions from which the present organisations of the British workers are uninterruptedly descended were unconscious, or were hardly conscious, of the political implications of what they were doing. They would have denied that political consequences were bound to flow from the very act of creating successful and stable combinations of workers designed for bargaining with their employers.[1]

They would have denied the political implications of Trade Unionism somewhat vehemently. And their vehemence would have betrayed the fact that they were not really unaware that the organisation of Trade Unions is an act which may have, and ultimately must have, political consequences. Indeed they could scarcely have been unaware of this fact, for in the preceding twenty years an intensely political Trade Union and Labour movement—Chartism— had dominated the life of the British working class. But that movement had gone down to defeat, so that now wreckage alone remained.

The British workers had been decisively headed off from independent political action. British capitalism was

[1] The British Trade Unions of the eighteen-fifties were not of course new organisations altogether. In almost every case, other organisations, some, but not all, of which had participated in the Chartist movement, were reconstituted both in structure and in spirit. But it is usually agreed that the modern British Trade Union movement as we know it cannot trace its descent in a substantially unbroken line to a point before the eighteen-fifties. On the other hand, the influence of Chartism upon the Trade Unions began to decline rapidly as early as 1842. But the forties are best regarded as a sort of interregnum between the revolutionary, Chartist or Owenite Trade Unionism of the thirties and the emergence of the modern Trade Union movement in the fifties.

triumphant both politically and economically. Still, the inexorable pressure of capitalist relations of production was still acting upon the workers. It still drove them towards combination for mutual protection. Hence well before the last forces of Chartism had been driven from the field, a new Trade Unionism had come into being. But just because the British workers, after having had the historic honour to put forward the first major challenge to capitalism which any working class ever made, had suffered defeat, the Trade Unionism which emerged after that defeat was extremely cautious; was ultra modest in its demands and expectations; was determined to offer no challenge whatever to the capitalists as a class; was content if it might obtain a foothold for the mere fact of working-class combination within the capitalist system. The pattern of history had decreed that just as the British workers, in the Chartist epoch, had achieved a hitherto unrivalled consciousness of the aims, principles and methods of working-class political action, so in the next phase, their organisations should be conservative to the point of denying that the act of working-class combination need have any political implications whatever.

We may think of this period as the embryonic, preconscious phase in the life of British Trade Unionism. It is difficult to say how long a Trade Union movement might stay in this preparatory phase if no outside pressure drove it on to the adoption of some conscious attitude to politics. It is certain at any rate that Trade Unions never abandon their original non-political position at the behest of outside advisers. In every developing capitalist society Trade Unions are at a certain point driven into political life.[1] This occurs because at a certain point in their growth the Trade Unions become conscious of laws, administrative measures and Court decisions which stand in the way of their further development.

[1] In every capitalist democracy that is to say. In those capitalisms which developed within the framework of autocracies, such as the Tsarist, for example, such Trade Unions as manage to exist cannot openly, of course, enter political life since they are illegal.

In Britain this point was reached with the sudden growth of Trade Unionism which occurred (as we noticed above) between 1870 and 1876. During the sixties, the new, conservative type of Trade Unions were steadily growing in size, wealth and strength. Gradually they began, almost unconsciously to themselves, to re-enter the political arena. But they re-entered it by quite other methods than those used in the revolutionary politics of the Chartists. The leaders of the new type of Union (nicknamed the Junta) began to take up political activity, not in the form of mass agitation, but by putting discreet pressure upon accessible members of both the capitalist political parties. As the strength of their organisations grew their work began to bear some fruit, as in the case of the repeal of the worst features of the old Master and Servants Act, in 1867. (Thus removing the last, and not altogether unsubstantial, elements of serfdom from the British workers.)

The leaders of the new Unions (the membership of which consisted almost exclusively of highly skilled and relatively well-paid workers) began to concentrate their attention on this kind of political activity, and on Friendly Society functions, to the exclusion of attempts to better their members' conditions by strike action. Indeed this leadership came strongly to discourage industrial action, and to favour political lobbying, of a discreet sort, as the only wise form of working-class activity. Accordingly, what we should now call the left-wingers or militants of the movement came to stand for industrial action and against any mixing in politics. Thus within thirty years the relative positions of the left and right wings of the Unions had been exactly reversed. From 1830 to 1842 a left-wing leadership had participated[1] in an implicitly revolutionary form of political activity, while a right-wing minority wished the Trade Unions to confine themselves to industrial action. In the sixties a right-wing leadership led the movement into

[1] By no means all the Unions had participated in either the Owenite Grand Nationalist Consolidated organisation or in the Chartist movement. But the general spirit of Trade Unionism in the thirties and early forties was highly political.

parliamentary political activity while a militant minority considered that anything but industrial action was useless. We shall observe this alternation of rôles running through the whole history of the British working-class movement. It is only within the last decade that a realisation of the necessity of a combination of industrial and political action has been achieved; and even now that realisation is most imperfect.

In the eighteen-sixties political activity soon became a necessity for the Trade Unions. For they were subjected to a series of attacks, by means of Court decisions, proposed enactments, and investigatory Commissions, which, it soon became evident, were designed by the employers to remove, in fact if not in form, the legality which British Trade Unionism had enjoyed ever since 1824. Failing that, the employers strove to make it impossible for the Unions ever to become sufficiently large, wealthy and stable to constitute a challenge to the capitalists' right to fix wages and conditions of work as they thought fit. By 1870 the Unions had become of sufficient importance for their existing, ill-defined, anomalous position to have become impossible. The British governing class had to decide either to attempt to crush the Unions or to recognise and make the best of them. A long drawn out struggle developed.

The story is an extraordinary one. Measures were introduced and passed through Parliament which were ostensibly designed to regularise and recognise the Unions. But it was always found that they had been so drawn, or amended, or were so interpreted by the courts, that they in fact made effective Trade Union activity illegal. Up till the election of 1874 it seemed that the British governing class was in fact taking the road which led to an attempt to stamp out Trade Unionism. But that election marked a turning point. The majority of the Trade Unionists had been enfranchised by the Reform Bill of 1867. The entire strength of the movement, which, as we have seen, had in the preceding two years shot up to over a million, was now thrown into an effort to defeat the Liberal Government of Mr.

Gladstone, which, as the most direct representative of the industrial employers, was, naturally enough, the bitterest enemy of the Unions. The Tory candidates, on the other hand, pledged themselves, in many cases, to an effective recognition of the Unions. Thus they secured strong Trade Union support. In thirteen constituencies, however, the Trade Unions went so far as to run what were in effect Labour candidates of their own. [Two were elected, but only because in these particular constituencies the workers (miners) had captured the Liberal Party machine and secured the withdrawal of the Liberal candidates.]

It seemed for a moment that the British Trade Unions had taken not only the first step in their development, that of participating in politics by attempting to influence the rival capitalist parties, but had leapt on to the second stage (to be described below) of creating an independent political party of their own. But the very success of the Unions' political campaign prevented this. For it made the creation of an independent political party unnecessary to the achievement of a recognised legal status for the Unions—and this was the Unions' sole aim. The Liberals were routed (this was only partly due to Trade Union support of the Tories; but was much more due to it than is allowed for in the conventional history books) at the election of 1874 and a Tory administration returned to office. Moreover, the Tories, after some hesitation, actually fulfilled their pledges to the Unions. Cross, the Tory Home Secretary, put two Bills through Parliament in 1875 which effectively recognised not only the Unions as institutions, but gave them legal protection for carrying out their work, including the calling of strikes, with a certain measure of protection for peaceful picketing. This was one of the major (though still underestimated) turning-points in the social and economic policy of the British governing class. It was a cardinal instance of that flexibility and relative immunity from panic when faced with signs of working-class activity on which the British governing class so prides itself. This phlegm is, however, in fact almost wholly attributable to the extraordinary economic advantages and consequent power of manœuvre which the British capitalists have always hitherto possessed.

A majority, however, of the British industrialists of the seventies were gravely alarmed at the sudden growth of Trade Unionism. This was why they impelled the Liberal administration to attempt to stamp out Trade Union activity. They had deluded themselves into believing their own propaganda, to the effect that the existence of influential Trade Unions would make the carrying on of their enterprises unprofitable and so impossible. But a continuance of the Gladstonian administration's attempt to crush the Unions, while it might well have succeeded for a time, would certainly have produced, sooner or later, a revival of revolutionary working-class activity. It would have prevented the limited class of skilled workers from raising their standard of life so substantially above that of the unskilled as to cut them off from the rest of the working class. A suppression of Trade Unionism in the eighteen-seventies would have reproduced, perhaps in the early nineties, the conditions of the thirties, namely a homogeneous, outrageously oppressed, desperate, and politically united, British working class. If such had been the conditions of the British workers when Socialist thought reappeared in Britain, history would certainly have taken a different course.

The cooler minds of the British governing class seem to have sensed this danger. Moreover, they evidently took a realistic view of what the consequences of legalising the extremely conservative Unions of their day would be. The Tory leaders (probably because of their greater detachment from production itself—since they still represented to some extent the landlords rather than the industrial employers) seem to have realised that though the existence of influential Trade Unions, able to secure for some million skilled workers relatively good pay and conditions, would no doubt cost the employers a good deal of money, yet this money would be well spent if it secured the contentment and passivity of these skilled workers, who form the natural leaders of the working class.

The Tory politicians were completely justified by the event. No sooner had the Unions won their essential claim to legality than their outburst of political activity disappeared. The project of running independent working-class candidates against both the Liberals and Conservatives was dropped. The great Unions of the skilled workers became more cautious and conservatively minded even than they had been in the previous decade. It was seen that the idea that such organisations threatened the existence of British capitalism had been a laughable delusion of the less far-seeing employers. Moreover a slump, coming very opportunely for the employers, almost completely obliterated the gain in membership of the seventies, so that in 1880 the strength of the movement was back at much what it had been ten years earlier. And in its ideas the movement had definitely retrogressed. Legal recognition had been won, but at the cost of an acceptance of every idea of the British employing class, down to the most extravagant details of liberal, utilitarian, *laissez-faire* philosophy.

For the next ten years the British Trade Union movement stagnated. An extremely reactionary leadership dominated its every thought and action. The Unions did not indeed go out of politics in the sense of abandoning the attempt to influence the two capitalist parties on working-class questions, in the narrowest sense of that term. And they secured one useful concession, the Employers Liability Act of 1880. But all thought of passing on to the second stage of working-class political development, namely the creation of a working-class political party had disappeared.

Thus we may say that from their foundation in the fifties to about 1865 the British Trade Unions were in their embrionic, non-political stage of development. From about 1865 to 1895 the British Trade Unions were in the first stage of working-class political development. From time to time they took an active interest in politics and applied strong pressure upon one or other of the capitalist parties.

But the idea of independent working-class politics was absent.

The new stirring in the almost moribund British Trade Unionism of the early eighties began not in any direct attempt to induce the small circle of ultra-conservative leaders (such as Broadhurst and Mawdsley) who dominated the movement, to found a Labour party, but in attempts to re-animate the movement in its own industrial sphere. A new set of young Trade Union leaders, of whom John Burns and Tom Mann were typical representatives, appeared to challenge the older men. But whence, it may be asked, did these new leaders of the British workers appear? The answer is that Burns, Mann, Tillett, and the other remarkable men who then began to transform British Trade Unionism had been trained by the new school of Socialists which had just arisen.

In Chapter V we shall discuss the two distinct schools of Socialist thought which appeared in Britain in the eighteen-eighties. They were, respectively, the Fabians, who rapidly came under the intellectual leadership of Mr. Sidney Webb and Mr. Bernard Shaw, and the members of the Social Democratic Federation, who, to the best of their ability, followed the intellectual leadership of Marx and Engels. As we shall see, it was the Fabians who, with catastrophic results, in the end captured the mind of the British Labour movement. But it was the Marxians who first succeeded in changing the course of development of the movement itself. For the impact of their Socialism, as we noted in the last chapter, played a vital part in starting that renewed advance of British Labour which has continued, through whatever checks and interruptions, to this day.

A group of gifted, vigorous, virile young Trade Unionists came under the influence of the speakers and teachers of the Social Democratic Federation. They were converted to Socialism, but, with true working-class instinct, they knew that the first thing to be done was to organise the great mass of unskilled workers hitherto untouched even by

Trade Unionism. They were themselves for the most part skilled workers (like Mann and Burns); and hitherto the British skilled workers had felt almost no impulse towards the organisation of the unskilled. They had felt the need of organisation for their *trade*, not for their *class*. Their solidarity and loyalty went essentially to their trade, and not their class. Contact with the S.D.F. made a group of active British Trade Unionists class-conscious again for the first time since the days of the Chartists. They went out as missionaries to organise the unskilled. The times were ripe (the avenues of escape from work for wages were, as we have seen, closing one by one); they succeeded; and in so doing started the modern British Labour movement upon its long struggle.

It was by imbuing the key Trade Unionists of the period with class instead of trade consciousness that the early British Marxian Socialists made their supremely important contribution to the movement. Indeed the quality of their Socialist theory was low. And, as we shall see, their failure upon the theoretical side had the gravest consequences. They played, however, an essential part in the great rebirth of the British Labour movement. For without the Marxists "the new Unionism", as it was called, could hardly have appeared.

What "the new Unionists" attempted to do was to induce the movement to adopt a more militant industrial policy, to organise the unskilled workers, and to support a programme of what we should call extremely moderate social reforms—containing such measures as the eight-hour day and the municipal ownership of public utilities, for example.

Moreover, this programme of social reform was to be attained by the old method of putting pressure upon one or other of the existing political parties. The degree to which the older leaders had fallen under the sway of the most extreme ideas of the employing class may be gauged by the fact that, in the name of the principles of *laissez-faire* they violently opposed even the most moderate measures of social reform, since these measures involved an element of State intervention in economic life. A struggle ensued in which the established, official leadership displayed an extreme lack of scruple in its choice of methods. Congress decisions were simply ignored when the leaders did not agree with them; delegate meetings were rigged; heresy hunting was indulged in. The old leaders appeared to carry everything before them. As late as 1889, at Dundee, for example, the left-wingers (as we should call them) at the Trade Union Congress were duly "routed". The old leaders were endorsed by 177 votes to 11. But that same year a new wave of Trade Unionism struck the British working class. For the first time since the eighteen-thirties (for the revival of the seventies had largely left them out) the unskilled workers began to come into organisations and take strike action. The dramatic London dock strike—lead by the new men, Burns, Mann, Tillett, Thorne—ushered in a great upsurge of Trade Unionism. By the time of the 1890 Trade Union Congress, held at Liverpool, the new Unionism had won such triumphs that the views of its exponents could no longer be defeated in the Congress. The social reform, mildly collectivist policy of the new men was adopted in its entirety by the Congress, and Broadhurst, the main champion of *laissez-faire*, resigned rather than carry out the mandate of the Congress.

It is important to realise exactly what had, and what had not, been achieved by this revolution within British Trade Unionism. The movement had been converted from an acceptance of the ideas of the capitalist class in their most rigid and uncompromising form. Henceforward the British Trade Union movement would press for social reforms even if these entailed Governmental interference with freedom of contract. But the movement had certainly not accepted any programme for the replacement of capitalism by Socialism, nor had it felt any necessity to organise a political party of its own in order to implement its new programme of social reform. Hence the triumph of the new Unionism of the eighties left the British movement still in the first stage of political activity, attempting to achieve its objects by putting pressure on the capitalist parties.

The story of how, after another fourteen years of hesitation, the whole movement was converted to the necessity of creating a political party of its own is especially instructive. Once again it was not the persuasion of Socialist writers and thinkers—though this time the Socialists did play a part—which drove the movement on to its second stage of political development. The dynamic factor was the exigencies of a struggle for the existence of the Trade Union movement. And once again, this struggle was forced upon the movement by a new series of blows aimed by the governing class at the existence of the Unions.

The sudden growth of Trade Unionism which began in 1889 alarmed the British Employers even more than had the previous spurt of the seventies. And once again an attempt was made to make Trade Union activity impossible. It might have been thought that the Trade Unions Acts of 1870–75 stood firmly in the way of any such attempt. But the courts, which have been, on the whole, the most vicious of all the agencies which the employing class has used in its struggle with its employees, found a way, as soon as the interests of the employers demanded it, to make these Acts, in effect, null and void. Cross's Acts made it impossible to prosecute Trade Unions and Trade Unionists engaged in strike action under the Criminal Law. But the Civil Law remained at the disposal of the lawyers. During the last decade of the nineteenth century the British courts threw themselves into the job of making strike action impossible by suing Trade Unionists and their officials for the damage which the strike was causing the employers! If once the principle could be established that both Trade Union funds, and the personal property of Trade Unionists and their officials, were liable to confiscation whenever a strike was called, a complete suppression of Trade Unionism by due process of law had, it was clear to the delighted lawyers, been discovered.

At first the attack was not pressed so far. The Trade Unions were merely harried by prosecutions for damages whenever picketing, or strike action in breach of a previously negotiated collective agreement, was resorted to.[1] But just after the turn of the century, in 1901, the British lawyers took the gloves off and, in the Taff Vale decision, dealt a blow at the Unions which they believed would stop effective strike action for many a long day. For this famous judgment made the Unions liable in damages for all the loss which their activities might cause to the employers.[2]

It was, above all, this renewal of the old attack on the right of the Unions to exist and function which drove the British Trade Union movement to create a political party of its own. For the more we study the history of the foundation of the Labour Party, the more striking appears the relative failure of all the long-continued efforts of the Socialists of the day to induce the Unions to create an independent political party, until such a party became essential in order to defend the very existence of the Unions.

Yet, as the reader will not have failed to note, a paradox is implicit in this estimate. The Socialists did not succeed in persuading the Unions to create a political party, until the employers' attacks forced them to do so in sheer self-defence. But the Socialists had played a vital part in the growth of the Unions to the point at which the employers

[1] In the nineties the injunction, the favourite weapon of the American courts, was used on several occasions in Britain.

[2] "In 1900 a tumultuous and at first unauthorised strike had broken out amongst the employees of the Taff Vale Railway Company in South Wales, in the course of which there had been a certain amount of tumultuous picketing, and other acts of an unlawful character. In the teeth of the advice of the company's lawyers, Beasley, the general manager, insisted on the company suing for damages, not the workmen guilty of the unlawful acts, but the Amalgamated Society of Railway Servants itself; and on fighting the case through to the highest tribunal. After elaborate argument the Law Lords decided that the Trade Unions, though not admittedly a corporate body, could be sued in a corporate capacity for damages alleged to have been caused by the actions of its officers and that an injunction could be issued against it, restraining it and all its officers, not merely from criminal acts, but also from unlawfully, though without the slightest criminalty, causing loss to other persons." (*The History of Trade Unionism*, by Beatrice and Sidney Webb, p. 600.)

The strike took place in 1900, the decision was handed down by the House of Lords in 1901.

felt compelled to attack them, and so to drive them to build a political party of their own! Thus, in a sense, it was the initial impulse of, especially, the Marxians of the eighties which, through a complex system of social actions and reactions, resulted twenty-five years later in the creation of the Labour Party.

The efforts of the Socialists at direct suasion may be said to have begun in earnest in 1887, when Keir Hardie, representing the Ayrshire miners, demanded at the Trade Union Congress of that year, that the workers' organisations should cut themselves loose from the Tory and Liberal parties. He had not the slightest success. The Unions remained unmoved for another thirteen years. Hardie and other Socialist propagandists were reduced to the hopeless task of trying to create a working-class political party without the backing of the fundamental, essential organisations of the workers, the Trade Unions. Naturally all they could accomplish was to found societies of individual Socialists. These Socialist Societies, of which the Independent Labour Party became the largest, did most important propagandist work. But in British conditions they could never become, without the Trade Unions, that working-class political party, the foundation of which marks the achievement of the second stage in the evolution of a working-class movement.

It would not indeed be true to say that the British Socialists made no progress in persuading the Unions to found a party of their own until the Taff Vale onslaught was delivered. All through the nineties the Unions were subjected to a constant stream of propaganda in favour of independent political action and the creation of a Labour Party. And in 1900 the Trade Union Congress at last carried a motion which called for the convening of a special congress representing the Trade Unions, Co-operative Societies and Socialist Societies "in order to devise means of increasing the number of Labour members". But this, though a great step forward, was not the decisive victory which it seemed. "The Labour Representation Committee" which was

B1

thereupon set up failed to attract the support, by affiliation, of even half the Unions. Moreover, the predominant leaders of the Trade Union movement remained unconvinced. At the General Election of 1900 the Committee only managed to put fifteen candidates into the field—and not one of them was successful. The creation of a British Labour Party seemed almost as far off as ever.

But what Fabian, Marxist and I.L.P'er. had found impossible, the Law Lords accomplished. These legal Ruperts of reaction, by the very impetuosity of their assault, drove the British Trade Unionists to independent political action. In 1901 the Taff Vale judgment was delivered. In 1902 the number and strength of the Unions affiliated to the Labour Representation Committee doubled. By the election of 1906 the Committee was in a position to put fifty candidates in the field and to secure the return of twenty-nine of them. The Labour Party has been born. The British working-class movement had at last passed the second stage in its development.

At some moments during the next eight years (1906–14) it appeared, however, as if the experience of the eighteen-seventies was to be repeated. It appeared as if an outburst of political activity on the part of the British workers had been evoked by a governing-class attack on Trade Unionism, had quickly achieved its object in repelling that attack, and would now subside again almost as if it had never existed. For the Liberal Government which came into office in 1906 quickly passed a Bill which undid the Taff Vale judgment and once more made effective Trade Unionism possible. It is a measure of the degree to which the Labour Party had been created by the Unions as an *ad hoc* measure designed to effect one thing only, namely the reversal of the Taff Vale judgment, that once that single purpose had been achieved, the enthusiasm of the Unions for their new instrument began rapidly to cool. The Unions began to feel that a political party of their own was a most expensive possession, which they doubted if they could afford, and the utility of which was by no means apparent to them.

Moreover the members of the Parliamentary Labour Party (themselves for the most part leading Trade Union officials) made it only too apparent that, once they had achieved their purpose of re-legalising Trade Unionism, they did not quite know what to do next. In practice they formed a not readily distinguishable part of the great Liberal majority which was embarking on a programme of social reforms at least as comprehensive as anything conceived of as desirable by the leaders of the Trade Unions. Of any comprehensive Socialist philosophy, capable of inspiring the working-class movement, the pre-war Parliamentary Labour Party was destitute. In a word, the Parliamentary Labour Party did not possess a consciousness of principles or purposes sufficiently distinct from those of the Liberal Party to justify its separate existence. It is quite possible that if no further attack upon Trade Unionism itself had been made, the Unions would gradually have withdrawn from independent political activity again (would, in our nomenclature, have retired from stage two to stage one), and have left the Labour Party to wilt into obscurity.

This is indeed the considered opinion of the leading historians of the British working-class movement, who themselves participated closely in all these events. Mr. and Mrs. Webb write (*History of Trade Unionism*, p. 686) that in this period (1906–14):

"What saved the Labour Party from decline, and gave it indeed fresh impetus in the Trade Union movement, was the renewed legal assault on Trade Unionism itself, which in 1909, as we have described, culminated in the Osborne Judgment of the highest Appeal Court, by which the Trade Unions were prohibited from applying any of their funds to political activities and to the support of the Labour Party in particular. The refusal of the Liberal Government for four whole years to remedy this gross miscarriage of justice, though conscious that it was not permanently defensible; and the unconcealed desire of the Liberal Party politicians to put the Labour Party out of action as an independent political force, swung over to its side the great bulk of active Trade Unionists, including many, especially in Lancashire, who had hitherto counted to the Conservative Party."

Thus just as the assistance of the Law Lords had been required to drive the British Trade Union movement into independent political action, so these dignitaries proved the only people capable of keeping it there. Made instruments, all unknown to themselves, of the historical process, the Law Lords, in December 1909, handed down the Osborne judgment prohibiting any Trade Union from spending any of its funds upon political objects. Even though the Unions were at the moment tiring of independent political action, they were extremely angry at being prohibited from ever using any of their funds to promote legislation. Moreover, the judgment went much further than that. By a quite fantastic piece of legal subtlety, not to say chicanery, it made illegal, or cast grave doubts upon the legality of, every form of Trade Union activity other than collective bargaining. It became extremely doubtful whether the vast friendly society activities of the Unions were legal, while their whole educational work, their participation in municipal affairs and their association for common purposes in Trades Councils, and in the Trade Union Congress, became definitely illegal. (Though little attempt was made to enforce this part of the judgment.) Thus once again the British Trade Unions found themselves subject to frontal attack. The menace was sufficient to rally the movement to the support of the Labour Party. That party was again given something definite and distinctive to do. It could attempt to get a new Act passed annulling the Osborne judgment, and this it succeeded in doing, though not until 1913.

Consideration of the unsuccessful attempt of the Socialists to induce, and the successful attempt of the Law Lords to drive, the British Trade Unions into independent political action, naturally provokes the following reflection. What would have happened if the British employing class and their representatives had had the forbearance, the patience, the *sang-froid*, to allow the Unions to grow in numbers and strength without delivering counter-attacks upon them? In that event would an independent working-class political party ever have been established by the Unions? It almost seems as if the existence of the British Labour Party is a consequence of the blindness of the British ruling class; as if, at least until the war, it would have been possible for the British capitalists to have kept their monopoly of political representation in Parliament. It is difficult to see how this conclusion can be avoided.

There is, however, another side to the question of the advisability or not, from their own point of view, of the employers' successive attacks upon Trade Unionism between 1890 and 1914. These attacks produced the Labour Party, but they also succeeded in substantially checking the growth and power of the Unions. The effect of the Taff Vale decision and the Osborne judgment in stalling off the pressure of the Unions for higher wages and better conditions amongst railway workers was particularly great. Mr. and Mrs. Webb comment as follows:

". . . it must not be overlooked that the temporary crippling of Trade Unionism seemed to be of financial advantage to that generation of employers. It was, perhaps, not altogether an accident that the brunt of the attack had to be borne by the Amalgamated Society of Railway Servants, a Union then struggling for 'recognition' in such a position as to make effective its claims to better remuneration and shorter hours of labour for the whole body of railwaymen. It may fairly be reckoned that the railwaymen were, by means of the two great pieces of litigation to which their Union was subjected, held at bay for something like a decade, during which the improvement in their conditions, in spite of a slowly-increasing cost of living, was (mainly through the evasions of the railway companies by their silent 'regrading' of their staffs) extremely small. A rise of wages to the extent of only a penny per hour for the whole body of railwaymen would have cost the railway companies, in the aggregate, something like five or six million pounds a year. If any such advance was, by means of the Taff Vale Case and the Osborne judgment, staved off for ten years, the gain to the whole body of railway shareholders of that generation might be put as high as fifty or sixty millions sterling—a sum worth taking a little trouble about and spending a little money upon, in items not revealed in the published accounts. But the crippling effect of the litigation was not confined to the Amalgamated Society of Railway Servants, which spent, altogether, nearly £50,000 in law costs in defending the pass for the whole Trade Union movement. If, in the temporary set-back to trade in 1903–5, and in the revival that immediately followed it; or in the recurring set-back of 1908–9, and the great improvement of the ensuing years, the whole body of wage-earners in the kingdom lost only a penny per hour from their wages, or gained less than they might otherwise have done to the extent of no more than a penny per hour, their financial loss, in one year alone, would have amounted to something like a hundred million pounds. And whatever they forwent in this way, they lost not during one year only, but during at least several years, and many of them for a whole decade. There is no doubt that the capitalist employers, thinking only of their profits for the time being, regarded even a temporary crippling of the Trade Union movement as well worth all that it might cost them. The historian, thinking more of the secular effect upon social institutions, will not find the balance-sheet so easy to construct."

There is no doubt, then, that the employers had substantial reasons for their attack upon the Unions. It is equally true, however, that it was this attack which played the part of midwife to the till then embryonic Labour Party. If the Unions had been allowed to grow unmolested, the wages of millions of British workers would have been a good deal higher, and the profits of British employers a good deal lower, in the fifteen years before the war. At the same time I do not think that it can be argued that the Unions, if they had been left alone, could have pushed up wages to a point which would have made the profitable working of British industry impossible. In that sense the attack of the employers, with its, for them, gravely undesirable political consequences, was unnecessary; or rather it was premature. For, equally, I do not think that it can be denied that sooner or later the Unions, if not counter-attacked, would have pushed up wages to a point intolerable to the employers.

No doubt the employers saw this tendency and considered it better to strike before the Unions became too powerful. Thus we cannot in the last analysis regard the employers' attacks upon the existence of the Trade Unions as accidental or mistaken. It is, indeed, clear that just as the appearance of Trade Unions is a necessary consequence of establishing capitalist relations of production in any society, so the growth of the Unions will sooner or later bring them into conflict with the employers, and with the political and legal representatives of the employers. Out of this conflict, out of its attacks and counter-attacks, political activity on the part of the Unions inevitably arises. At first this activity takes the form of putting pressure upon the existing political parties of the capitalists; at length it takes the form of the creation of an independent political party controlled and financed by the Unions themselves.

CHAPTER III

THE TRADE UNIONS IN POLITICS

IT WOULD BE an exaggeration to say that the British
Labour Party was founded with the specific purpose of
reversing the Taff Vale decision, and was kept in existence,
when that had been achieved, in order to reverse the Osborne judgment. But it would be an exaggeration which
would reveal a seriously underestimated aspect of the
truth; it would be an exaggeration which would help us
to avoid many opposite errors when we come to consider
the question of the character of that new political party which
a working-class, acting through its Trade Unions, is always
driven sooner or later to create.

For the pre-war British Labour Party, when it was not
confronted with these two specific issues, showed unmistakable signs of not really knowing what to do with itself.
It failed almost completely to develop any distinctive programme of social reconstruction. It merely worked for the
same social reforms as the Liberal Party was itself en-
acting—but pleaded that they should go somewhat further.
Its difficulties were implicit in the manner of its birth. For
it had not been created as a result of the conversion of the
main body of British Trade Unionists by the Socialist
propagandists who were so active amongst them from 1886
onwards. The propaganda of the Socialists had played its
part;[1] but the Unions had in the end taken action only
when forced to do so by a threat to their own existence. Hence their action was a more or less blind and auto-

[1] As we have seen, it had been a decisive part, in the sense that the Socialist
impulse had been a vital factor in the growth of the Unions to the point
at which they had to have a political party of their own. But it was this indirect
work of the Socialists rather than their direct propaganda for a Labour Party
which had been important.

matic *re-action* to an initiative coming from the other side. It did not imply that the Unions had acquired any distinctive political attitude, still less that they had consciously adopted any philosophy of social reconstruction.

In a word, the pre-war British Labour Party was not a Socialist party. It was a party which admitted Socialists such as Ramsay MacDonald, Keir Hardie and Sidney Webb, to its ranks (we shall discuss the kind of Socialism possessed by these Socialists in the next chapter). But as a whole, as an organisation it was uncommitted, and was indeed indifferent or actually hostile to, any coherent Socialist programme of social reconstruction.

Thus the political party created by the British Trade Unions had at first no definite colour. Indeed, it is hardly too much to say that the one thing upon which all its members could agree was that the new party should exist. They expressly decided not to enquire into the ultimate purposes *for which* it should exist, lest they should discover disagreements so powerful as to dissolve the new organisation. For, curiously enough, although they could not define its purposes they all intuitively dreaded the prospect of such dissolution.

The debates in which the character of the new party was established are well described by Mr. Max Beer in Chapter XIII of his standard work, *British Socialism*. As he remarks, no sooner had the new party been formed than its members were impelled to enquire as to what was its nature. Most of them had just come from the Liberal Party. But clearly the new party could not be a Liberal party, for if it were it had no reason for separate existence. And there was no doubt that the new Labour Party did, somehow or other, and to the general surprise of its members, exist. Was it then a Socialist party? The small group of Socialists organised in the Social Democratic Federation asserted that it was, or, rather, that it ought to be. At the inaugural Conference of the Labour Party (or Labour Representation Committee, as it was significantly called) in 1900, and at the next Conference in 1901, the delegates of the Social Democratic Federation proposed resolutions which, if they had been passed, would have declared the party to be definitely Socialist. But these resolutions were decisively rejected and the S.D.F. disaffiliated itself from the Labour Party. (We discuss this major disaster to the development of the movement below.)

Accordingly it was decided that the new party was neither a Liberal nor a Socialist party. A process of elimination had begun which promised to end in the discovery of what the party was. At the same (1901) Conference two resolutions were moved which went far towards defining the position which the Labour Party was to maintain right up to 1914. The first was moved by one of the Socialist members, Keir Hardie. It read as follows:

"That this conference is in favour of establishing a distinct Labour Group in Parliament, who shall have their own Whips, and agree upon their policy, which must embrace a readiness to co-operate with any party which for the time being may be engaged in promoting legislation in the direct interest of labour, and be equally ready to associate themselves with any party in opposing measures having an opposite tendency."

It will be seen that this resolution did little more than reassert the bare idea of a separate party—and did so in the most narrow, most purely parliamentary, terms. It reveals nothing whatever of what the party is to attempt to achieve. The second resolution was moved by James Sexton. It read:

"That this conference declares that in view of the combinations of capital and the federation of employers it is necessary for the trade unions of the country to use their political power to defend their existence and secure their demands, and while it deprecates the introduction of mere party politics into the trade union movement, it urges upon trade unionists the necessity of combining on an independent platform for the following purposes: (1) The defence of the legal rights of combination. (2) The passing of such laws as will put an end to a system under which the producer of wealth has to bear an enormous burden in the shape of rents and profits which go to maintain large classes of non-producers."

The most noticeable thing about this second resolution is that it twice emphasises the real, specific, very limited purpose for which the new party had been founded; to wit, to use political power to defend the existence, and secure the demands, of the Trade Unions. It is only when we get to (2) that an anti-capitalist purpose is mentioned. But then suddenly we are told that the purpose of the new party is to end the burden of rents and profits. This demand is, indeed, sweeping enough; in one sense when you have said that you have said all. But put in that way it was a reversion to Chartism rather than a step towards Socialism. Its phraseology gave no hint of the vast work of social reconstruction which could alone make possible the ending of rents and profits. Two years later, at Newcastle in 1903, these ideas were given definite form. In a detailed discussion on a resolution reasserting the bare fact of the independent existence of the new party, the delegates to the Conference of the L.R.C. made it clear that they would neither recede from, nor advance beyond, this position. They were determined to create a new and genuinely independent political party designed to promote and defend their interests as Trade Unionists; but discuss, let alone define, what broader purposes such a party might have, they would not.

"Let them," said Curran (the prominent gas-workers leader and Member of Parliament), "strengthen their constitution in a way that would not tie down the Trade Unionist to Socialism, nor the Socialist to Trade Unionism, but both to Labour." Moreover this was not merely the opinion of the Trade Unionists. Keir Hardie, of the I.L.P., the leader of the Socialists (and he was perfectly right to do so considering the actual state of mind of most of the men whose adherence had to be won if a genuine Labour Party was to exist) took his stand squarely on the ground that the creation of an independent party, representing the organised workers, but with no defined social philosophy was the sole measure on which the movement could unite. Keir Hardie specifically recognised that as late as 1903, many even of these relatively advanced British Trade Unionists, who had come together with the express purpose of forming the new party, were Liberals or even Conservatives in their conscious political opinions (although this did not prevent them somehow feeling the need for a Labour Party). He said:

"They all, Liberal, Tory and Socialist alike, rejoiced at the magnificent conference got together in that hall. What was the principle that enabled them all to come together and discuss this matter? Independence. If they, the Socialists, had insisted that all should be Socialists, there would be no such gathering. Had the Liberals insisted that all should be Liberals, they would have had the like result. They had fixed upon a common denominator that, when acting in the House of Commons, they should be neither Socialists, Liberals, nor Tories, but a Labour Party. They were seeking by the resolution to prevent individuals from disrupting the movement. . . .

"Let them have done with Liberalism and Toryism and every other 'ism' that was not Labourism. . . ."

A revised constitution giving effect to these sentiments was adopted at the Newcastle Conference on a card vote by 659,000 to 154,000. This basis of undefined independence was not in fact altered until the war. It is true that all sorts of resolutions of a generally Socialist character were carried at particular annual conferences in the next eleven years. But political parties should be judged, and, what is more, are judged, both by their opponents and supporters, far more by what they show themselves to be by their actions, and the general character of the pronouncements of their leading figures, rather than by what at particular moments their annual conferences may say they are. Judged upon this realistic basis there is no doubt that the pre-war Labour Party on the one hand remained (though not without longing backward looks being cast by many of its leaders at the Liberal administration) a genuinely independent party, devoted to the promotion of the interests of organised labour; but that on the other hand it never acquired a coherent, distinctive, definable outlook, capable even of directing the attention of the British workers towards the immense task of reconstructing society.

Here we have an example of what the achievement by a Labour movement of the second stage in its development does, and does not, do. We have defined that second stage as the passing on from attempts to influence the existing capitalist political parties to the creation of a political party of its own. The achievement of this new stage is an event of enormous importance; but it only takes a Labour movement a certain distance. In particular it does not necessarily imply the acceptance by the Labour movement in question of a Socialist, or any other, political philosophy. In British and American conditions the acceptance of a distinct political philosophy itself constitutes a separate, third stage in the evolution of a Labour movement. And this third stage does not necessarily, or usually, coincide in time with the achievement of political independence. Moreover, from one aspect the achievement of this third stage constitutes a longer leap forward than does the passage from the first to the second stage. For the establishment of a Labour Party, so long as that party acquires no distinctive outlook, can be regarded merely as the pursuance of the old strictly Trade Unionist aims by a new method.

From this point of view the achievement of the stage of the creation of a Labour Party is of importance chiefly in that it inevitably drives the movement on towards political self-consciousness; for once the workers have achieved their own political organisation they are bound sooner or later to enquire: "For what purpose are we to use this new organisation?" In itself the second stage has more in common with the first than the third. Indeed the first and second stages can be grouped together. It is possible, and useful from one point of view, to describe a Labour movement which is in either of them as being in the phase of "Trade Union politics". In certain circumstances a definite theory that Labour movements ought to remain in this phase of development may arise. In the Russian Labour movement between 1890 and 1900, for example, this theory became very prevalent. It was called by Lenin Economism. In Tsarist conditions the type of development through the two stages of Trade Unionism which we have recounted in the case of the British movement, was of course quite impossible, for the Trade Unions were illegal. But, in spite of this, there developed a strong tendency among the men and women who were devoting themselves to the attempt to organise the Russian workers, to concentrate upon the direct, economic interests of the workers, by promoting demands for higher wages, better conditions, shorter hours and the like, to the absolute exclusion of more specifically political demands such as the demand for free speech, freedom of assembly and a democratic republic, for example. It is clear that this attitude of mind is the analogue, in conditions of autocracy, of the advocacy of exclusively Trade Union politics (no matter whether they are conducted by influencing the capitalist parties or by creating a specific Trade Union party) in capitalist democracies. For both tendencies arise from a failure to realise the inseparability of economic and political issues. They arise from a failure to see (to take the most elementary example possible) that to demand higher wages is to demand the liberty to demand higher wages. They arise from a failure to see (to take the most advanced example possible) that to demand (in the words of James Sexton's resolution, above) that the "burden in the shape of rents and profits which the producer has to bear" should be "put an end to" is to demand the complete reconstruction of society; is to demand that the whole vast structure of capitalism, with all its political institutions, including the existing form of the State itself, should be abolished, and a Socialist economic system, with all its equally extensive political corollaries, shall be established.

The limitation of political activity to the defence of Trade Unionism even if that activity is carried on by means of an independent political party, is, then, a form of collective myopia; it is a failure to see the inevitable consequences of things; a failure, in particular, to see that you cannot change economic conditions, beyond a very limited extent, without changing political conditions. But since Labour movements grow up in the economic sphere; since they grow up as Trade Unions; since the workers are impelled into organisation by their most immediate and simple economic needs, it is entirely inevitable that they and their movements should only gradually apprehend the political issues which must arise from pressing their economic demands. The conflict which immediately impresses itself upon the worker's mind is the conflict with his employer. He does not necessarily realise that sooner or later this conflict will involve his employer's State. Indeed he may not guess that the State is an agency of his employer's, which, unless he can put exceedingly strong pressure upon it, will certainly be used against him.

Thus the advance from exclusively Trade Union politics towards Socialist politics cannot happen all at once or easily. For Socialist politics involve a realisation of the whole vast task of social reconstruction which must be achieved if the instinctive demands of the Trade Unions are ever to be realised. The Trade Unions, by the very fact of their existence, as the bargaining representatives of the wage-workers, in perpetual opposition, either open or latent, with the employers, are impelled towards social reconstruction. But it is a major achievement to turn this instinctive impulsion into a conscious determination. Such an advance in political consciousness can only happen as the result of slowly accumulating experience. Moreover, most formidable influences are inevitably brought to bear on any Labour movement, influences designed for the express purpose of keeping it in the stage of Trade Union politics. For Labour movements do not develop in a social vacuum. Especially in capitalist democracies, they are subjected to the full force of the social philosophy of the class which dominates such societies. The process by which the capitalists—the owners of the means of production—established themselves in power inevitably involved the emergence of a comprehensive view of human society, suitable to society's new rulers. And since the rulers of society control almost every form of education, and of effective means of expression, their point of view will necessarily permeate the communities which they dominate through and through. The social philosophy of the capitalists will, naturally, be intensely inimical to working-class organisations becoming conscious that they cannot achieve their ends without reconstructing society from top to bottom. Such a philosophy will naturally explain what was bad in the past (since the past had to be overturned to make way for capitalism), and what is good in the present, since the present is capitalism. But it will include no account of what will be in the future—for that would not be capitalism.

Everything which members of a working-class movement have learnt at school, and every influence to which they are subjected in after life, will be designed to prevent them realising the vast social and political implications of their own demands; to persuading them that the existing order of society is not one of a number of possible arrangements, but is reality itself, which it is absurd even to try to alter. It is not, be it understood, that the teachers, preachers, authors, journalists and statesmen who form our minds deliberately and consciously set out to prevent the organised workers from passing beyond the stage of Trade Union politics. On the contrary, the spokesmen of the capitalists are, for the most part, themselves genuinely unable to conceive of anything other than capitalism. They are convinced that they are simply attempting to prevent the organised workers falling into errors. It is not that they sit down and think out how they may prevent the Trade Unionists from becoming Socialists (though at a later stage this does occur). It is that they spontaneously create a mental climate intensely inimical to a realisation of the Socialist objective of the Labour movement. Their formidable power lies not in deliberate anti-Socialist propaganda (I am thinking especially of capitalist societies in their prime, before self doubt has come to them) but in their capacity to prevent the very question of the possibility of there being any alternative to capitalist relations of production from ever being posed.

Thus Labour movements develop in conditions which are highly unfavourable to the possibility of an early or easy achievement of adequate political consciousness. The very establishment of Trade Unions, then their effective functioning, then their participation in politics, then the organisation of their own political party, are each and all bitterly resisted by the employers and their agents. But these are as nothing compared to the efforts which are made to prevent the organised workers from realising the nature and extent of the task of social reconstruction into which they have been impelled. A million subtle threads hold back the workers' minds from a realisation of what they are doing, *even while they are actually doing it.* A Labour movement, as, for example, the American movement may have been engaged for years in most formidable struggles with capitalism, without even its leading members having arrived at more than the dimmest and faintest realisation of what the conflict is all about.

So difficult is it for workers in capitalist societies to achieve a full consciousness of the nature of the struggle in which they find themselves engaged that a working-class movement, or a section of it, may become intensely militant, may develop to an extreme its combative aspects, and yet may not achieve any adequate comprehension of the nature and extent of the task of social reconstruction which faces it. We must not, then, suppose that the distinction between Trade Union politics on the one hand, and Socialism on the other, is equivalent to a distinction between the right and left wings of a working-class movement.

In a subsequent chapter we shall describe a tendency which appeared within the British, and to a much greater extent within the American and French, working-class movements in the years immediately before the war. We may call this tendency "Left Trade Union Politics". We shall see that a section of a Labour movement can become intensely militant and even revolutionary, without succeeding in transcending narrowly Trade Union politics. This is a conclusion of great importance in the study of the British and American Labour movements. For a failure to think things right out, and a consequent inability to foresee inevitable consequences and conflicts, is undoubtedly the severest limitation from which these movements have suffered. Sometimes, as in Britain about 1900, or in America to-day (1937) it has been above all the right wing of the movement which has failed to realise the inescapable political implications of the effort of organised workers to better their lot. But at other times, as in Britain in 1875 (see above), or again both in Britain and America in the period immediately before the war (see Chapter VII), it has been the left wing which has been "anti-political". A right wing which has been participating in parliamentary politics, and which has actually got to the point of creating ts own political party has sometimes been attacked by a sincere but ill-informed left wing, not, as it should have been, for the poor, weak, narrow, timid character of its political activities, but for going into politics at all! Immense confusion has arisen in working-class movements when their most advanced, courageous and militant members have taken their stand on this barren, anti-political ground. The strength and persistence of purely Trade Union politics; the difficulty which all sections of working-class movements, including the most militant, have had, and still have in achieving a realisation of the full implications of their own activities must, indeed, strike the student very forcibly.

Now a realisation of the full implications of its own activities, on the part of a Labour movement, is a realisation of Socialism. There is no theory, no body of generalisations, other than Socialism available for a working-class movement. Its choice is not between some other coherent view of its own activities and purposes, and the Socialist view. It has only the choice between a blind, purely empirical method of carrying on its struggle, and the Socialist method. For Socialism as a theory is, in the first analysis, a Social philosophy born out of the conflicts in which the wage-workers of every capitalist society find themselves engaged.[1] But how hard it has been for the British and American workers, living in communities drenched with the ideas of the world's two most powerful capitalisms, to build up their own social philosophy! The British Labour movement did not, as we have just seen, become even nominally Socialist until after the war. The American Labour movement has not yet taken the preliminary step of creating its own political party, though it may be on the verge of doing so. And the American Labour, or Farmer-Labour, Party, when it appears, will inevitably pass through a period in which, like the pre-war British Labour Party, it admits Socialists and Communists to its membership, but is not itself Socialist.

It is evident that to generalise its experiences; to become conscious of what it is doing and why, is one of the last and most difficult of the achievements of a Labour movement. Yet the range and adequacy of the ideas which inspire a Labour movement is a decisive factor in its success or failure. The social struggle cannot be won if it is fought blindly. Until the wage-workers manage, not only to organise themselves both industrially and politically, but also to free their eyes from the thick blindfolds of the ideas of those who own the means of production, they cannot hope to win.

[1] But as we shall see in the next chapter, the workers' conflicts are only one of the parents of Socialism; they are its mother. But it is begotten by Science.

CHAPTER IV

THE POWER OF IDEAS

How, then, can Labour movements become conscious of what they are about? Whence comes the Socialism which they always do sooner or later acquire?

It might be supposed that, since Socialist theory is a body of generalisations deduced from the wage-workers' efforts to improve their lot, it would emerge naturally and imperceptibly from those efforts themselves; that there would be no need for special attempts to imbue Labour movements with Socialist views. Whole schools of thought within the European Labour movements have taken this view. There is no doubt, however, that it is quite false. For it grossly over-simplifies the real situation of wage-workers in a capitalist society.

The wage-workers, I repeat, carry on their struggles in communities which are soaked in the quintessentially anti-Socialist ideas of the owners of the means of production. Hence the workers cannot come easily or automatically to Socialist views, as they would undoubtedly do if they were not continuously exposed to the formidable counter-suggestion of the ideas of the still dominant capitalists. In the real world a working-class movement can only come to a comprehension of Socialism by means of an active process of freeing itself from the domination of capitalist ideas. This is why the evolution of every Labour movement towards Socialism is certain to be complex and stormy.

The three stages of development distinguished above[1] often exist together in the same Labour movement at the same time. As we saw, groups of Socialists appeared in Britain

[1] Trade Unions influencing existing political parties; Trade Unions forming a political party of their own; that party becoming a Socialist Party.

in the eighteen-eighties, while the leaders, and for that matter the rank and file of the Trade Unions, were still wholly under the spell of the most rigidly capitalist ideas. Moreover, this was a full fifteen years before the British movement even founded its own special, but still non-Socialist, party. Who then are these Socialists who often appear long before a Labour movement itself has become even socialistically inclined? The answer to this question is a somewhat startling one. The first Socialists who appear in a capitalist society are very rarely wage-workers at all; they are nearly, though not quite always, members of the middle class.

At first sight this must seem a very surprising fact. In particular is it not, it may be asked, a complete refutation of the view that Socialism is the natural point of view of the working class? On examination, however, it will be found that this fact is a refutation, not of any views held by Socialists (or at any rate by Socialists with a knowledge of scientific Socialism) but merely of views which are commonly imputed to them. The explanation of why Socialism, as an idea, first appears in the brains of members of the middle class is because, as the German Socialist writer Kautsky points out in the following quotation, Socialism can only arise out of "scientific knowledge". A man can only become fully conscious of the need to transform society when he has become conscious of the character of existing society. But in order to comprehend existing society it is necessary to have achieved a mastery of the knowledge and culture of that society. And this is almost, though not quite, impossible for wage-workers in a capitalist environment.[1]

Kautsky discussed this question in a criticism of a new draft programme which the Austrian Socialist Party proposed to adopt.

---

[1] This is not to say that many wage-workers have not by heroic efforts broken into the monopoly of contemporary culture which the ruling class enjoys. But such successes must in the nature of things remain the feats of specially gifted individuals. The wage-working class, as a class, will always be excluded from cultural opportunity in capitalist societies.

"In the draft programme it is stated," he writes, "'the more capitalist development increases the numbers of the proletariat, the more the proletariat is compelled and becomes fit to fight against capitalism. The proletariat becomes conscious of the possibility of and necessity for socialism,' etc. In this connection socialist consciousness is represented as a necessary and direct result of the proletarian class struggle. But this is absolutely untrue. Of course, socialism, as a theory, has its roots in modern economic relationships just as the class struggle of the proletariat has, and just as the latter emerges from the struggle against the capitalist-created poverty and misery of the masses. But socialism and the class struggle arise side by side and not one out of the other; each arises under different conditions. Modern socialist consciousness can arise only on the basis of profound scientific knowledge. Indeed, modern economic science is as much a condition for socialist production as, say, modern technology, and the proletariat can create neither the one nor the other, no matter how much it may desire to do so; both arise out of the modern social process. The vehicles of science are not the proletariat, but the *bourgeois intelligentsia*: it was in the minds of some members of this stratum that modern socialism originated, and it was they who communicated it to the more intellectually developed proletarians who, in their turn, introduced it into the proletarian class struggle where conditions allow that to be done. Thus, socialist consciousness is something introduced into the proletarian class struggle from without (*von Aussen Hineingetragenes*), and not something that arose from within it spontaneously (*urwchüsig*). Accordingly, the old Hainfeld programme quite rightly stated that the task of Social-Democracy is to imbue the proletariat with the *consciousness* of its position and the consciousness of its tasks."[1]

In a word the idea that the workers will come to Socialism easily and automatically as a result of their efforts to better their conditions of life is an over-simplification of the Socialist view. Socialists believe that men's ideas are a reflection of their environment. But they are most careful to lay heavy stress upon the richness and complexity of the process by which the ideas of a given epoch or a given class come into being. Thus, for example, the idea of modern scientific Socialism could not have developed fully in any other period but the nineteenth century, when

[1] This passage is quoted by Lenin in *What is to be done*.

both the technical powers and the social forces necessary for its realisation had begun to appear. But to suppose that the connection is more direct than that; to deny that once the idea of Socialism has appeared it enters into a partially independent process of development of its own; that it depends for its progress upon all sorts of factors, including personal factors; that it has its triumphs and disasters—to deny this is to stunt the Socialist conception, to reduce Socialism to a crude, mechanical and demonstrably false theory of the interaction of ideas and events. There is nothing contrary, then, to what an instructed Socialist would expect in the undoubted fact that the idea of Socialism comes, primarily, from thinkers drawn from the middle class.[1]

Lenin combated nothing more strongly than the idea that it was the duty of Socialists to wait patiently until the Labour movements of their countries spontaneously came to a comprehension of Socialism. This was a view widely held in the Russian Social Democratic movement about 1900. Lenin tells those who hold that view that they will have to wait till doomsday if they expect the Labour movement to acquire for itself a Socialist consciousness. Moreover he tells them that their idea that it is somehow wrong to go to the organised workers and expound Socialism to them is not only bad Socialist theory; it is also a conscious or unconscious surrender to the never-ceasing attempts of the spokesmen of the capitalists to prevent the workers acquiring an understanding of what they are doing. If out of an alleged false modesty the Socialists (whether middle-class or not) refrain from imparting a Socialist outlook to the workers; if, in Lenin's phrase, they "bow" respectfully to the non-Socialist point of view of a Labour movement, still in the first or second stages of its development, the workers' minds will not be freed from outside influences. On the contrary, the effect will be to hand the workers' minds over to the apologists of capitalism, to be

[1] Indeed it would have been hardly likely that Marx, the founder of Socialist theory, would have denied that this was so, since he himself was the archetype of such thinkers.

stuffed with all the most noxious ideas of the workers' unrelenting opponents.

"All those," Lenin wrote, "who talk about 'exaggerating the importance of ideology', about exaggerating the rôle of the conscious elements, etc., imagine that the pure and simple labour movement can work out an independent ideology for itself, if only the workers 'take their fate out of the hands of the leaders'. But this is a profound mistake. . . .

"Since there can be no talk of an independent ideology being developed by the masses of the workers in the process of their movement *the only choice is :* either bourgeois or socialist ideology. There is no middle course (for humanity has not created a 'third' ideology, and, moreover, in a society torn by class antagonisms there can never be a non-class or above-class ideology). Hence to belittle socialist ideology *in any way*, to *deviate from it in the slightest degree* means strengthening bourgeois ideology. There is a lot of talk about spontaneity, but the *spontaneous* development of the labour movement leads to its becoming subordinated to bourgeois ideology. . . ."[1]

Having thus put beyond question his view of the intense importance of a Labour movement creating its own social theory, as the only alternative to being dominated by the social theories of the capitalists, Lenin adds a footnote on the secondary question of whether this new social theory is to come from middle-class or working-class minds.

"This does not mean, of course, that the workers have no part in creating such an ideology. But they take part not as workers, but as socialist theoreticians, like Proudhon and Weitling; in other words, they take part only to the extent that they are able, more or less, to acquire the knowledge of their age and advance that knowledge. And in order that working men *may be able to do this more often*, efforts must be made to raise the level of the consciousness of the workers generally; care must be taken that the workers do not confine themselves to the artificially restricted limits of '*literature for workers*' but that they study *general literature* to an increasing degree. It would be even more true to say 'are not confined' instead of 'do not confine themselves', because the workers themselves wish to read and do read all that is written for the intelligentsia and it is only a few (bad) intellectuals who believe that it is sufficient 'for the workers' to tell them a few things about factory conditions, and to repeat over and over again what has long been known.''[1]

In a word, the movement must get its social theory from those who have been able to devote themselves to the job of becoming fully equipped social theorists. If such qualified social theorists are of working-class origin so much the better, for then they will have a closer, more instinctive, knowledge of the needs of the working class. But it is mere sentimentality to ignore the immense difficulties which confront workers in a capitalist society in the task of becoming masters of the culture of their time. Hence a high proportion of the Labour movement's social theorists will in fact come from the middle class. Lenin, however, was writing nearly forty years ago, and writing of a working class which had been kept in almost complete illiteracy by the Tsarist autocracy. To-day, in Britain and America, we may reasonably expect that a far greater proportion of the movement's thinking will be done by workers themselves. Still, even in the West, and even to-day, the part played by men and women of middle-class origin in the theoretical work of the movement is necessarily large. Moreover, whatever class they may hail from, the men and women who do the thinking of the movement will inevitably be of a special type. They will be what are commonly called intellectuals, and they will have the faults and virtues of their kind.

The intellectuals of a Labour movement have often aroused strong suspicion and hostility in the minds of the organised workers; and often with good cause. But yet no Labour movement can dispense with the services of this type of brain-worker. If it attempts to do so all that will happen will be that it will inevitably and immediately fall under the mental domination of the intellectuals of the capitalist class. For it is quite impossible for the most practical of practical men to live and work in a mental vacuum—however much they would like to do so or however much they may fancy that they are doing so. T. A.

[1] Lenin, *Selected Works*, Vol. II, p. 62.

CD

Jackson, one of the comparatively small number of fully qualified social theorists—whether of working-class or of middle-class origin—which the British Labour movement has as yet produced, has wise and balanced words to say in this connection.

"... the theoretician and the intellectual has played such a big part, for good and for ill, in the development of the proletarian struggle. Since he is specially trained for the work of investigation and theoretical co-ordination, the intellectual from the middle or upper class, if he is conscientious as well as really competent, can give the proletariat invaluable aid. On the other hand, if he is in fact incompetent, or, being competent, has no conscience, and serves the proletariat merely as a hireling adventurer or soldier of fortune, always with his nose atilt sniffing for higher pay and bigger booty, he can do incalculable harm.

"A sense of this harm and a deep resentment thereat is widespread among the more militant proletariat. Its general diffusion has produced (in combination with historically apposite circumstances) the phenomena, firstly, of a widespread belief that no intellectual is to be trusted; and secondly, that of a practical endeavour, widespread and persisting over extensive sections and periods, to *do without all theory and theorists whatsoever*.

"From its very nature this endeavour to dispense with theory has the result of limiting those who attempt it to the narrowest and most parochial forms of empirical opportunism—which in turn has resulted in the rise to leadership in the Anglo-American Trade Union and Labour movements of some of the most shameless opportunists on principle (who trade demagogically on the fact that they were *once* 'working men like yourselves'), and a company of no-less-unashamed theorists who exploit these prejudices of the proletariat to the advantage of policies and programmes of petty-bourgeois and reformist eclecticism."[1]

But, it may be asked, if Socialism comes to the Labour movement, in Kautsky's phrase, "from the outside," is not this an admission of the truth of a familiar capitalist accusation? Do not the apologists of capitalism continually assert just this, that Socialism is something foisted upon the good, honest, if gullible, British and American workers by the diabolical machinations of "outside agitators"? A

[1] T. A. Jackson, *Dialectics*, Lawrence & Wishart.

moment's reflection will reveal the extreme bad faith of this allegation. The spokesmen of capitalism are not really intent on preserving the mental virginity of the working class. On the contrary, they never pause for a single second in their professional function of deluging the workers, by means of their newspapers, their cinemas, their schools, and their books, with a flood of capitalist ideas. Nor do they hesitate for one second in using the most degraded and degrading methods, if only they may achieve their grand purpose of preventing the workers from thinking straightforwardly and simply about their positions in capitalist society.

The provision of the amplest facilities for drinking and gambling are two time-honoured methods of preventing the workers, if possible, from thinking at all. But lest that ideal condition of things cannot always be attained to, infinite pains are taken to bemuse and confuse the minds of those workers who show signs of an ineradicable tendency to think for themselves. Endlessly the spokesmen of capital pump out their own confusing, because false, view of human relationships. They suit their methods to their audiences. But all the way from the majestic bemusements of a Bosanquet, lucubrating upon the State, to the crudest article in the *Daily Mail* or the *Saturday Evening Post*, capitalist propaganda constitutes one sustained attempt to prevent the wage-workers from realising what capitalist society is doing to them. (And it is all the more effective when its authors are themselves as genuinely confused as they make their readers.) This is the contemporary opium of the people. It lacks all the charm, mystery and beauty of the traditional variety. (And will be, and is being, therefore, far less effective in the long run.)

What, however, are we to say to these wholesale purveyors of mental confusion and degradation, when they accuse the socialists and communists of perverting the otherwise pure and guileless minds of the workers? We shall say that their especial fury with those whose function it is to enlighten that overwhelming majority of the population which consists in wage-workers, as to the cause, nature and objective of the struggle in which they find themselves engaged, is a supreme honour and reward. So long, but no longer, as we are assailed by the spokesmen of capital we shall know that we are doing our job aright. So long as they represent us as the perverters of innocent minds we shall know that we are serving the workers well; that we are performing the one task in the working-class movement for which we are suited; that we are illuminating the workers' struggles with that degree of consciousness without which it cannot be successful. But if this must be the reaction of socialist and communist propagandists, what, we may well ask, will the organised workers think of these self-appointed guardians of theirs, who treat them as innocent children, who must be carefully protected from wicked men who would corrupt their minds? The workers are grown men and women with excellent minds of their own; the conditions of their life and work may prevent many of them (though an increasing number now accomplish this very difficult feat) from specialising in the work of actually expounding social science. But they are fully qualified to judge as to who it is that is telling them the truth, and who is telling them lies. It is an intolerable insult to the able, mature workers of Britain and America that any self-appointed guardians should tell them what ideas they may or may not study.

Finally, we may be told that by agreeing that Socialist ideas come, for the most part, to Labour movements from the outside, we have admitted that it is the Socialists who cause all the trouble and disturbance of industrial disputes; that but for these malicious "trouble makers" the wage-worker and the capitalist would lie down together in perpetual amity. We have already shown that historical experience belies this favourite fancy. The truth is that the absence of Socialist teaching from a Labour movement does not in the least prevent the occurrence of labour disputes. On the contrary some of the most obdurate, most bitter and most violent industrial disputes occurred at

periods when the British and American Labour movements
were almost unaware of the very existence of Socialist
thought (e.g. The vicious disputes which led to the Sheffield
"outrages" of the sixties in Britain or the Homestead
strike in America in 1892.)

Indeed, we may say that experience shows that as the
organised strength and political consciousness of a Labour
movement grows, so the violence which accompanies
industrial disputes, other things being equal, tends to
diminish. Nor is this unexpected, for violence is a consequence of the despair and frustration of a working class.
Once the wage-workers become organised and conscious
of their own aims and how to achieve them, they will
certainly not resort to violence, unless violence is unleashed
against them. What Socialist teaching does is not to create
class conflict (class conflict is the fatal effect of capitalist
relations of production themselves); what Socialist teaching
does is to raise such conflict from the level of a blind, and
so violent, revolt of men made desperate by the conditions
imposed upon them, to that of a conscious effort to reconstruct human society.[1]

So far we have only considered the question of the
endowment of a Labour movement with a social theory
—which can be no other than Socialism. But Socialism
itself can be of several kinds and of very varying qualities.
The next question to take up, then, is that of the kind and
quality of the Socialism which a Labour movement may
acquire. This question is to-day of crucial importance for
both the British and American Labour movements. For the
Socialism which the British movement gradually acquired
during the first decade of the present century, and which

[1] The whole history of the American working-class movement is one long
demonstration of this contention. For the American movement has been at
once the most violent and the least Socialist working-class movement in the
world. Moreover, the most famous of the acts of violence which have chequered
American Labour history have come, not from left-wing organisations such
as the I.W.W., but from members of highly skilled Craft Unions, or of non-
political industrial Unions such as the miners, who were being driven to
desperation and despair by their defeats at the hands of the organised American
employers.

dominated it in the post-war period, was of a peculiar sort, very different from the main body of Socialist thought. In the title of the next chapter, which analyses this peculiar variety of Socialism, I have called it "British Socialism". I confess that my patriotism is outraged by the necessity to do so. For this peculiar type of Socialism is so intellectually inferior to the main body of Socialist thought that it is difficult for me to admit that this is British Socialism.[1]

For the honour of the British contribution, and it is a vast one, to the intellectual life of the world, it must be pointed out that the peculiar kind of Socialism which we are about to discuss dominated British social thinking only between 1880 and 1930. In the first half of the nineteenth century British thinkers began to lay down the foundations of Socialist thought. Robert Owen, Bronterre O'Brien, Hodgskin, Thompson, Harney, Ernest Jones all did pioneer work of the first importance. Without their work Marx and Engels could not have reared the vast structure of Socialist science. Again, about 1930 the hold of British Socialism was broken. Since then the first steps, at any rate, have been taken towards the re-creation of a school of British Socialist thought, freed from the outrageous parochialism of the previous period, and equipped with a knowledge of Socialist science as it has developed in the rest of the world. Still, when all that has been said it cannot be denied that for half a century there developed in Britain a peculiar, insular kind of Socialism, for which the natural and appropriate name is British Socialism.

The peculiar character of this kind of Socialism had immense and disastrous consequences for the British Labour movement. Moreover, although the influence of this kind of Socialism is now disappearing, its hold over the mind of the British Labour movement is still considerable. It is true that on the one hand the most alert section of

---

[1] I take the phrase, as a matter of fact, from a review in the *Daily Herald* (the official organ of the British Labour Party) of my book, *The Theory and Practice of Socialism*. The *Daily Herald* told its readers that the volume was mis-titled, since it described, amongst other things, the views of Marx and Engels. And "British Socialism" had never had anything to do with Marxism.

the movement has now passed over to scientific Socialism, and that, on the other, a part of its official leadership has (as I shall show) receded from British Socialism to the non-Socialist Trade Union politics defined in the preceding chapter. There still exists, however, a predominant middle section of the British Labour movement which clings to what remains of British Socialism. Hence we cannot, even now, regard the influence of this school of thought as extinct.

CHAPTER V

BRITISH SOCIALISM

SOCIALISM IN ITS modern form appeared in Britain in 1880. At that time, it will be remembered, the British Labour movement was more wholly under the domination of capitalist ideas than it had ever been before or has ever been since. The leaders, and for that matter the rank and file, of the major Trade Unions accepted *laissez-faire* Liberalism in its most extreme form.

The British workers had been systematically indoctrinated with the views of their employers. The "Societies for the Promulgation of Useful Knowledge" (useful indeed, but to whom?), the "Mechanics' Institutes" and similar bodies had spread amongst the more reflective British workers an almost religious belief in the infallibility and perfection of the existing economic system. Trade Union Congress after Trade Union Congress turned down resolutions asking for the most modest measures of social reform on the grounds that they involved Governmental interference with industry. The leaders of the movement held economic views of a conservatism which would to-day be thought extreme amongst the professors of economic theory at the London School of Economics, or on the bench of the Supreme Court of the United States. The typical leader of the A.F. of L. before 1929 held fundamentally the same type of opinions (and Mr. Green holds such views even to-day). But the American Labour leaders were, and are, more empirical. They have a minimum of social philosophy of any sort. The nineteenth century British Trade Union leaders exhibited the monstrous spectacle of workers who had swallowed the entire social philosophy appropriate to their employers and, like well taught school-boys, could repeat it by rote.

It was in this atmosphere that the pioneers of modern Socialism in Britain had to begin their work. From the first they were divided into two groups. The Social Democratic Federation was founded by Hyndman in 1881. Hyndman took his Socialism—originally without acknowledgement—from the work of Marx and Engels. Two years later the Fabian Society was founded and soon attracted to it the two men who were to lay the foundations of British Socialism, Mr. Sidney Webb and Mr. Bernard Shaw. The essential comment to be made on these two bodies is that while the Social Democratic Federation failed to do the right thing, the Fabian Society succeeded in doing the wrong thing.

The British Labour movement was never converted to Marxism, but it was in the end converted to the form of Socialism preached by the Fabians. The causes of this momentous fact are complex, and we shall attempt to unravel them piece by piece. But the importance of the fact itself cannot be overestimated. It has profoundly affected the whole thinking, character and destiny of the British working-class movement.

In 1883 there existed, let it not be forgotten, a fully developed Socialist ideology,[1] awaiting the consideration of the British working class. Marx and Engels had practically completed their vast work. It was almost entirely unknown to the British Labour movement, but in default of the emergence of any other form of Socialism, it could hardly have failed to capture, bit by bit, the minds of the decisive members of the movement during the next thirty years.

The Marxists were first in the field. We have already noted that it was they who gave an invaluable initial impulse to "the new Unionism" of 1889 onwards. How was it, then, that the British Marxists failed in their greatest task, that of imbuing the mind of the movement with scientific Socialism? It was not that the early British

---

[1] It would be pedantic to avoid any longer the use of this convenient, if ugly, word, ideology. It means "system of ideas", "point of view", "attitude of mind", "body of social theory", "social philosophy".

Marxists lacked ardour, vigour and pertinacity in spreading their views. On the contrary, nothing could have been better, in many respects, and taking the resources at their disposal into account, than the agitation which they maintained for nearly forty years (1881–1914) throughout the cities of Britain. That agitation laid the foundation of Socialist opinion in this country. There are still thousands of British workers who got their Socialism, directly or indirectly, from the original group of British Marxists. The Social Democratic Federation was an intensely active propagandist body. Though it always remained small, its membership fluctuated to an extreme extent so that quite a considerable number of British workers went through its training. The Socialist League, which was an offshoot of the original Marxists, in spite of the confusion and anarchical ideas of most of its members, possessed in William Morris a Socialist author of the very highest gifts. The *Clarion*, both as a newspaper and as an organisation, served to relay a Socialism which, though it was extremely adulterated, had come originally from the Marxist source.

This whole volume of propaganda, which spread out from the original Marxists, performed an absolutely indispensable work, from the example of which we have very much to learn to-day (When, for instance, are we going to produce as popular a brief exposition of Socialism as Blatchford's *Merrie England*, of which two million copies were sold, without reproducing its errors and inadequacies?) Why was it then that in the end it was not the views, the whole point of view, of the Marxists which prevailed? Why was it that, in spite of their incomparable propaganda activity, the Marxists had the mind of the movement taken from them and put under the fatal guidance of the declared and envenomed enemies of Marxism? The fundamental answer to this question lies in the strength which the external environment lent to the Fabians, and to the anti-Marxist Socialists generally. The Fabians were incomparably nearer to the existing capitalist outlook, and, as we shall see, adapted themselves especially to the new Imperialist phase of that outlook. The very fact that the Fabians set before themselves the eradication of Marxism from the British Labour movement as one of their principal tasks, naturally won them invaluable middle, and even ruling, class support.

The other reason for the defeat of the Marxists lay in the extremely defective character of their own grasp upon the essentials of scientific Socialism. They did not fail because, as is so often imputed to Marxists, they talked over the heads of the workers. On the contrary, many of them were extremely capable popularisers. They failed for precisely the contrary reason. They failed because they were not themselves really interested enough in social theory to undertake the work of introducing Marxism, *as a science*, to the British Labour movement. It is tragic that they did not add to their splendid work of *agitation*, which did indeed influence strongly the unskilled, and still for the most part unorganised, workers, an equal work of *propaganda* which could have captured the minds of the reflective, and often studious, organised workers, and of the intellectuals.

If the Social Democratic Federation had had sufficient faith in the power of its own doctrines to have undertaken even the translation into English and publication of all the essential works of Marx and Engels, how great the effect, in the long run, might have been! Above all, had the Federation possessed thinkers capable of themselves wielding adequately the sword of Marxist analysis, and applying its cutting edge to contemporary British conditions, the Labour movement would have had some alternative to Fabian Socialism presented to it. But, with fatal British contempt for thought and theory, the spokesmen of the Federation spent themselves in an agitation which could not succeed for lack of any real basis of understanding in either the agitator or his audience.

Finally the Federation committed the horrible error of cutting itself off from the British Labour movement just two years after that movement had taken the immense step forward of creating a political party of its own. In the early eighties the Federation had started out not merely indifferent, but actually hostile, to Trade Unionism. But this attitude was greatly modified in the early nineties and S.D.F. delegates took an active part in the work which resulted in the formation of the Labour Representation Committee. But then, in the second year of the Committee's existence, and because James MacDonald and Harry Quelch had as yet, after only two attempts, failed to get S.D.F. resolutions passed through the Labour Representation Committee, the S.D.F., at its 1901 Conference, disaffiliated itself from the future Labour Party and withdrew its two delegates.

It was against a Marxism thus enfeebled by the errors of its leading exponents that the Fabians pitted themselves. Their official historian records their victory over it as their first great achievement. Mr. Edward Pease in a well-known sentence in his summary of the work of the Society, wrote:

"Its first achievement, as already mentioned, was to break the spell of Marxism in England. . . . The Fabian Society freed English Socialism from this intellectual bondage, and freed it sooner and more completely than 'Revisionists' have succeeded in doing anywhere else."[1]

The principal historian of British Socialism, Mr. Max Beer, also saw Fabianism, as the conqueror of, and successor to, Marxism. Mr. Max Beer has a remarkable passage in which he compares the work of Owen, Marx and Webb. His conclusion is that each thinker was right for his own time. Owen had to be a Utopian because the working class in his day was helpless. Marx had to be a revolutionary because in his day capitalist society was undemocratic, even in Britain, and so the workers could not possibly achieve their object except by revolutionary means. ("Marx's theories are the adequate expression of their period; they epitomise the conditions created by a fiercely competitive

[1] *The History of the Fabian Society*, published 1916.

economic life, a non-democratic constitution, and a society split up into antagonistic warring classes.") But, Beer continued, "between 1865 and 1885, . . . the British constitution was turned into a democracy". Mr. Sidney Webb noticed this fact, and adapted Socialism to democracy.

". . . it appeared to Webb that it was no longer admissible to allow a socialist theory which was grounded on past conditions to continue unchallenged and unrevised. A democratic State which was prepared to take upon itself social reform duties, a working class with economic influence and power, a nation with a growing social conscience, could not be treated from the standpoint of revolution and class struggle. The fundamental socialist concepts needed a new basis and new methods more in harmony with new conditions. Socialism had to be adapted to democracy. This adaptation has been performed by Sidney Webb. It represents the transition from Marxism to Fabianism, or from social revolutionary doctrine to social practice."[1]

Here we have one of the keys to the understanding of Fabianism. Fabianism is the rejection of what had been, hitherto, the main tenets of Socialism, namely the theory of the class struggle and the labour theory of value, *as inapplicable to a capitalist society which had adopted a democratic constitution*. Fabian theory stands or falls by the proposition that the granting of the vote, and other democratic rights, to the wage-workers of a capitalist society fundamentally alters the nature of that society. It rests, in particular, on the view that democratic institutions change the nature of the State, converting it from being a coercive instrument of the governing, capitalist class into a neutral, independent mechanism, equally accessible to, and usable by, all.

Before going on to enquire whether, in the light of historical experience, Fabianism has proved to be true or false, it is important to notice that the Fabians rejected the whole existing body of Socialist theory without making an analytical study of it. The original Fabians, when

[1] *The History of British Socialism*, Vol. II.

they came to make their first pronouncements, did not tell the world why they rejected the views of Marx and Engels. They simply ignored these views. They did not attempt to overcome Marxism by mastering it and then superseding it. They blandly left on one side, as unworthy of their attention, the whole vast structure of thought which Marx and Engels had created.[1]

Mr. Pease tells us it is true that discussions at the Hampstead Historic "had much to do with settling the Fabian attitude towards Marxian economics and historical theory". But the Fabian leaders never honoured the world by giving it their grounds for the rejection of Marxism, or indeed producing any evidence that they really knew what Marxism was.

Mr. Bernard Shaw, however, contributed an Appendix to Mr. Pease's book in which he informs his readers that he adhered to Marx's economic theories until one day he happened to encounter Mr. Philip Wicksteed who had no difficulty in convincing him of the superiority of the Jevonian theory of value. (The original variant of all marginal utility economics.)

"Accordingly," Shaw wrote, "the abstract economics of the Fabian Essays are, as regards value, the economics of Jevons. . . . This really exhausts the history of the Fabian Society as far as abstract economic theory is concerned."

Apparently it all happened just like that!

But Fabianism could not remain a mere tacit rejection of Marxism. A positive side to Fabian Socialism had to be developed. As Mr. Pease writes: "Something had to be put in the place of Marx. If German Socialism would not

---

[1] "We were however aware of Marx, and I find that my copy of the French edition of *Das Kapital* is dated 8th October, 1883; but I do not think that any of the original Fabians had read the book or had assimilated its ideas at the time the Society was founded."—Pease.

On the other hand Mr. Bernard Shaw in the Fabian tract Number 41, tells us of the Fabians of the 'eighties, that "We had to study where we could and how we could. I need not repeat the story of the Hampstead Historic Club, founded by a handful of us to read Marx and Proudhon, and afterwards turned into a systematic history class in which each student took his turn at being professor".

suit, English Socialism had to be formulated to put in its place." What then was this new English, or British, Socialism which two men, Webb and Shaw, for they were in fact the formative intellects of the Fabian Society, evolved to take the place of the Marxism which they so summarily rejected?

The whole character of Fabian thought was conditioned by a rejection of the existing Socialist view of economic science and an "acceptance of economic science as taught by the accredited British professors" (Pease). It is probable that Webb or Shaw, when they founded their views on an acceptance of marginal utility theory, did not at all realise that in doing so they were determining the character of their whole social theory also. Indeed the Fabians, for all their interest in theoretical questions, did not attach nearly sufficient importance to what they called "abstract economics" to realise what would be the consequences of their acceptance of Jevons' theory of value, and the whole structure of marginal utility economics, which is built upon one or other version of that theory. They did not by any means fully realise that this decision would predominantly determine the quality of the Socialism to which they converted the British Labour movement. Webb and Shaw would, I think, have said—indeed would probably still say—that their rejection of the labour theory of value and the economic concepts which go with it, in practice made little difference to their views. They would say that while they rejected Marx's labour theory of value as "out of date" they accepted his conclusion, namely that the means of production ought to be socialised.

But, it may be asked, how did the Fabians, since they accepted marginal utility economics, come to this conclusion? For marginal utility economics, if they are given any meaning outside of an extremely restricted and artificial conceptual world of their own, provide a complete justification for the capitalist system. The essence of economic science "as taught by the accredited British professors" was that the existing economic system, if undisturbed, must infallibly produce the very maximum possible amount of wealth, or human satisfaction, at the very minimum cost in human effort and sacrifice. For, the professors taught, if only the law of demand and supply was left to regulate the production and distribution of commodities, men would turn their limited supply of labour, and other resources of production, to producing what they most wanted, and would do so in the least toilsome and unpleasant way. All that was needed to produce the best of all possible worlds was to sweep away the remaining hindrances to the play of demand and supply upon a perfectly free market, and, above all, to prevent the appearance of any new restrictions or hindrances. How then, if they accepted, as they did, this whole body of doctrine, could the Fabians advocate the abolition of this already almost perfect economic system?

There is no satisfactory answer to this question. The only valid reasons for rejecting the capitalist system involve the rejection also of marginal utility economics and the acceptance of economics based upon the labour theory of value. For this kind of economic thought, albeit that it is without benefit of "the accredited British professors", can alone account for the facts of the capitalist world; can alone explain to us why the miner remains upon the subsistence level however hard he works and however frugally he spends, while the millionaire becomes a multi-millionaire however little he works and however much he spends. The labour theory of value can alone elucidate the great central fact of the exploitation of the wage-workers by the owners of the means of production, and account for the existence of the vast unearned incomes of every capitalist society. The economics of "the accredited British professors" simply ignored the existence of these incomes and the exploitation upon which they are built, or justified them by suggesting that their recipients deserved them as a reward for the abstinence or "waitings" (as Marshall put it) involved in refraining from spending their capital all at once.

In short, according to the economic thought which the Fabians dutifully accepted, capitalism as such, if uninterfered with by any kind of monopoly, created no unearned incomes. In the words of an "accredited", though in this case American, professor (J. B. Clark) there was "a natural law" which caused "free competition (to tend) to give to labour what labour creates, to capital what capital creates and to entrepreneurs what the co-ordinating function creates". If you accepted all this, what possible reasons remained to you for objecting to capitalism?

Webb and Shaw, however, constructed for the Fabians a kind of basis for their rejection of capitalism by an extension of the Ricardian theory of rent. In a word, they chose to regard all, or almost all, of the unearned income derived from the ownership of the means of production as a form of rent derived from a monopoly of the ownership of land. In this way they attempted to reconcile their acceptance of marginal utility economics with their feeling that the vast unearned incomes of the capitalists, which they saw all about them, were in some sense wrong, and ought to be abolished.

Mr. Sidney Webb's introduction to the 1920 Reprint of Fabian Essays contains an interesting confirmation of the view that the Fabians' economics governed the whole of the rest of their thinking. In reconsidering the Essays "in the light of thirty years of subsequent experience" Webb writes:

"It is perhaps significant that the part of the book that comes most triumphantly through the ordeal of such an examination is, throughout, the economic analysis. I think it is not merely the partiality of friendship that finds in the first essay a survey of the economic evolution of society which, for terse comprehensiveness and brilliant generalisation, has not since been excelled in any language. But throughout the whole book what is distinctively economic is, in my judgment, as incisive and accurate to-day as it was when it was written. Tested by a whole generation of further experience and criticism, I conclude that, in 1889, we knew our Political Economy, and that our Political Economy was sound."

Thus the Fabian colours were renailed to the mast of marginal utility even after the storm of general crisis had descended upon capitalism. The first Fabian Essay, which Webb so much admires, is Shaw's famous exposition of the conversion of Adam into Adam Smith. It describes the gradual colonisation of a new territory, the first settlers taking all the best land, and the later settlers having the choice of taking inferior land or of paying the earlier settlers a rent, or unearned income, equal to the difference between the productivity of the best and worst land cultivated. But this is, at best, a mere special case of capitalist exploitation in general. For capitalist exploitation is founded, not specially on the monopolisation of the land, but upon the progressive monopolisation of all the means of production. Accordingly the obvious practical deduction to be made from Shaw's quite inadequate analysis is not the abolition of capitalism and the establishment of planned production for use, but the Henry Georgian proposal of land nationalisation, or the taxation of land values to extinction. And in fact if one reads Shaw's much less well-known second Fabian Essay on "The Transition to Social Democracy" one discovers that this is the immediate programme which he advocates.

But the reader will again ask: In any event the Fabians did eventually come to the conclusion that the means of production ought to be socialised; so what difference did it, or does it, make that they thought so for reasons which you think inadequate? It made this vital difference. Their acceptance of marginal utility economics necessarily caused the Fabians to believe that there was nothing inherently wrong, *in the sense of unworkable*, with capitalism. They did not think, to be precise, that there was anything in the nature of the system which would cause it to produce more and more violent symptoms of social dislocation, such as slumps and wars. Thus, for the Fabians, Socialism was undoubtedly a desirable thing, but it was not in the least a necessary thing. If Socialism did not come, well then that was regrettable, but capitalist civilisation would simply continue indefinitely much as it was about 1900. The Fabians' arguments for Socialism were, paradoxically enough for men who believed that they were pre-eminently social scientists, humanitarian, moral and aesthetic, rather than scientific or economic. Shaw, for instance, wanted Socialism because capitalism outraged his strongly developed moral sensibilities. But none of the Fabians wanted Socialism because they had realised that the alternative to it was not the calm continuance of capitalism but the collapse of human civilization.

It must not be thought that I am claiming intellectual superiority over the original Fabians when I state without qualification that their basic premise, the rejection of Marxian, and their acceptance of marginal utility economics, was a fatal error. It may well be that none of us, fifty years ago, would have avoided that error; but it is equally true that to-day there is no remaining excuse for persisting in it. For the development of capitalism over the past fifty years has conclusively proved which view is correct. We now know that the labour theory of value, and the other concepts of Marxian economics which are associated with it, give the only description of the work-ings of capitalism which can account for that system's history during the last half century. We now know as a fact of all too immediate experience that the alternative to Socialism is an ever accentuated series of booms and slumps and an ever greater contrast between the size of the incomes received by earners and owners respectively, leading to an ever more distorted operation of the system. We now know that this in turn leads to an intensified disproportion in the economic development of different capitalist nations and, as a consequence, to an unending series of world-wide wars between the major capitalist empires. And we know that this development, if it is not interrupted, will certainly destroy organised human society.

It is, above all, this knowledge of the catastrophic con-sequences of leaving capitalism in existence, of the sheer

unworkability of the system, which impels us to work for
Socialism. And this all-important realisation the Fabians
never achieved. They knew that Socialism was desirable. But
they did not understand, and indeed strongly denied, that
it had to be achieved within a certain limited space of time
if capitalism was to be prevented from destroying us all.

It required genius to *foresee* that the very nature of a
system of the private ownership of the means of production
would in the end produce social catastrophe. No one is
entitled to blame the Fabians for failing in 1885 to foresee
the blood-stained world of the nineteen-thirties. But equally
no one is to-day entitled deliberately to blind themselves
to conclusions which are now beyond dispute.

The Fabians made a disastrous error in their estimate
of the nature and consequences of capitalism. This error
resulted in the major events of their time always taking
them completely by surprise. This is, above all, true of the
two wars which occurred in what we may call the Fabian
period. No historian could be more frank than is Mr. Pease
in his account of their reaction to the South African War.
He describes how in the later nineties the Fabian Society
was going through "a period of quiescence"; it had founded
the London School of Economics and had distributed book
boxes to working-class organisations; it continued to deliver
lectures, and had defined its electoral policy. Then "war
was declared by President Kruger for the South African
Republic on October 11th, 1899. Up to this point the
whole of the Society, with very few exceptions, had scouted
the idea of war".

On the question of what attitude, if any, the Fabians
should take up in regard to the war the Society was at first
divided. But its central leadership, headed by Webb and
Shaw, soon defined its attitude, and after some difficulty
carried almost the whole membership with it. That attitude
is summed up in a remarkable sentence taken from the
statement of the Executive Committee. The war was an
issue, the Fabian leaders declared, "which Socialism

cannot solve and does not touch". There is little need to characterise the Fabian attitude towards either war or Imperialism any further. In fact, however, this purely negative attitude, for which Webb was probably chiefly responsible, was immediately developed by Shaw into the definitely pro-Imperialist position which he has held ever since. While the South African War was still being fought out Shaw composed a pamphlet called *Fabianism and the Empire*. In it, after much equivocation (since it was designed for the time honoured purpose of keeping the party together), Shaw comes down explicitly on the side of the right of any Imperialist State to conquer any territory which it may consider backward, in the name of "efficiency". His practical conclusion was that the British Consular Service should be enormously strengthened so as to meet the growing threat of German competition to British export trade.[1]

The outbreak of the World War found the Fabians still of the opinion that this was a question which "Socialism cannot solve and does not touch". "The Society," said Pease, writing in 1915, "has made no pronouncement and adopted no policy." In these words the Fabians formally declared their perfect bankruptcy upon what is by far the greatest issue of our age. Moreover, they exhibited a quite startling complacency in doing so. The idea of even questioning a social theory which had proved wholly unable to forewarn its adherents that capitalism was leading to Imperialism and that Imperialism was leading the world to war does not appear to have occurred to one of them. Pease, their historian, for example, writing in the middle of the war, correctly claims that the Fabians had had a profound influence upon the German Social Democrats. Principally through their conversion of Bernstein when he was in England they were instrumental in fostering the "Revisionist" movement (the movement for revising Marxism, that is

---

[1] Mr. Shaw has even accentuated his pro-Imperialist views in the post-war period, becoming in the nineteen-thirties the apologist of the Italian seizure of Abyssinia.

to say, and in all essentials revising it out of existence) "which", Pease wrote, "has attracted all the younger men, and before the war had virtually, if not actually, obtained control over the Social Democratic Party". It was only too true. But the amazing thing is that it never occurred to Pease, though he wrote in the middle of the war, that this castration of German Marxism, for which he actually claimed the credit, had been a decisive factor in destroying the German Social Democratic Party's will and capacity to prevent or resist the war! Even when the storm had broken upon them the Fabians remained stone blind to its causes. They could still actually boast that they had been responsible for destroying the will and purpose of the organised German working-class movement, which might have been the one effective obstacle to the outbreak of the Imperialist war!

The explanation of the Fabians' astonishing attitude towards the supreme issue of our epoch, the issue of inter-Imperialist war, is, logically, to be found in their failure to achieve an understanding of the nature of capitalism. In spite of their interest in research and theory, they never achieved a comprehensive view of the society which surrounded them. They never saw the inter-connections of things. They never understood the elementary fact that capitalism causes war. They never noticed, or at any rate never considered, the consequences of the profound change in the nature of capitalism which was taking place precisely during the first twenty years of the existence of their society. They failed to observe the birth of Imperialism.

This was all the more remarkable in that the Fabians would not have had to turn to Marxist sources in order to acquire a knowledge of the cause, at any rate, of Imperialism. There was published in 1902, from the pen of an English liberal, a book which definitely established the economic causes of Imperialism and so of modern war. Mr. J. A. Hobson in his then famous, but now neglected, study, *Imperialism*, clearly described why and how capitalism had turned into Imperialism and was now rapidly causing war.

Hobson was under no apologetic illusion that the great empires had in the last twenty years annexed to themselves a vast part of the globe, and were coming nearer and nearer to fighting each other for the right to annex the rest, out of a love of "efficiency".

"It is not too much to say that the modern foreign policy of Great Britain is primarily a struggle for profitable markets of investment. To a larger extent every year Great Britain is becoming a nation living upon tribute from abroad, and the classes who enjoy this tribute have an ever-increasing incentive to employ the public policy, the public purse, and the public force to extend the field of their private investments, and to safeguard and improve their existing investments. This is, perhaps, the most important fact in modern politics, and the obscurity in which it is wrapped constitutes the gravest danger to our State.

"What is true of Great Britain is true likewise of France, Germany, the United States, and of all countries in which modern capitalism has placed large surplus savings in the hands of a plutocracy. . . . Thus we reach the conclusion that Imperialism is the endeavour of the great controllers of industry to broaden the channel for the flow of their surplus wealth by seeking foreign markets and foreign investments to take off the goods and capital they cannot sell or use at home."[1]

Mr. Hobson's book marks the highest point of development ever reached by liberal thought in Britain. Nor can the reader of to-day fail to be struck with the incomparably wider, more adequate, and more profound comprehension of the real world about him which Mr. Hobson shows as compared with the contemporary Fabian Socialists. While they were concentrating wholly on municipal reform, Poor Law questions, Parish Councils and the like (on questions, that is to say, to which it was perfectly right to devote close attention, but which it was disastrous to suppose existed in a political vacuum), the world was thundering down the path to its doom in inter-Imperialist war. The Fabians failed to notice this fact, and they refused to listen, not only to the Marxists, but to their friend and

[1] *Imperialism* by J. A. Hobson.

compatriot, Mr. Hobson, when he explained exactly what was happening.[1]

Such blindness to the predominant facts of their epoch could not be, and was not, due to mere intellectual error. The truth is that the Fabians overlooked Imperialism precisely because they themselves were one of the products of Imperialism. The whole anti-Marxist school of British Socialism, of which the Fabians were the intellectual leaders, was, at bottom, but a reflection of the temporary (and how dearly bought!) easing in the position of British capitalism, which had been effected by the wave of Imperialist expansion between 1880 and 1914. British capitalism seemed, to myopic observers, to have solved the difficulties which so evidently beset it in the eighties. It had secured new markets, new fields of investment, new super profits. It was now once again in a position to make concessions to some of the British workers, concessions which could be used as the basis for diverting them from real Socialism.

When either the Marxists, or even when Mr. Hobson, told the Fabians that this pseudo-solution had only been achieved at the cost of making world war into a certainty, they would not and could not listen. For their whole position would have been destroyed by an admission of this fact.

The deliberate blindness to the real forces working within capitalist society which the Fabians had accordingly to impose upon themselves is the explanation of the narrow, arid, half-comical element which everyone has noticed in

[1] The weak side of Mr. Hobson's book is its failure to suggest any adequate way of arresting the drive towards inter-Imperialist war which he diagnoses so well. His only remedies are measures of social reform which will tend to redistribute income, increase mass purchasing power at home, and so decrease the drive for foreign markets and fields of investment. But social reform can be but a palliative, and a feeble palliative at that, for the formidable drive towards Imperialist expansion into which, as he himself describes, the very nature of a system of the private ownership of the means of production projects the competing empires. Mr. Hobson's decisive chapter "The Economic Taproot of Imperialism", in which he gives the admirable analysis of Imperialism quoted above, staggers the contemporary reader. For it fails so strangely to advocate the one possible remedy for the social disease which has been so well diagnosed, namely the public ownership of the means of production. So near did British liberal thought, at its culminating point, approach to the Marxist analysis; and so far away did it remain from realising the remedy.

Fabian Socialism. The Fabians have always been jeered at for concentrating on the affairs of the parish pump; for reducing the gospel of international Socialism to the proposal to municipalise gas and waterworks. At first sight such criticism seems quite ill-founded. The Fabians were always able to retort most effectively that it was precisely because they concentrated upon certain definite, limited objectives that they got things done. But the jeers were at bottom well founded. Socialism became, in Fabian hands, an affair of gas and water because the Fabians deliberately shut their eyes to the blood and iron of the Imperialist world all around them. A Socialism which boasted that "it could not solve and did not touch" Imperialism and war, the life and death issue of the twentieth century, had forfeited the right to men's serious attention. The mass of the population was justified in regarding it, as they did, as at bottom a trivial, artificial thing, which had no message for them. And yet this was the kind of Socialism which was increasingly in the pre-war period, and almost completely in the post-war period, to dominate the mind of the British Labour movement.

CHAPTER VI

BRITISH SOCIALISM (*Cont.*)

THE SECOND MAJOR effect of the Fabians' acceptance of "economics as taught by the accredited British professors" was to cause them to reject the view that wage-earners and employers must come into more and more serious conflict within any capitalist society. Just as they saw no reason why the general establishment of capitalist relations of production should lead, through Imperialism, to war, so they saw no reason why these relations should drive the two classes of employers and employed into ever-sharpening conflict with each other.

Believing that there was nothing inherently self-contradictory in the nature of capitalism, they supposed that the interests of the wage-workers and the capitalists, while, no doubt, they could not be completely harmonised so long as the means of production remained in private hands, would yet tend to come closer together rather than to go further apart; that in particular the workers' standard of living would steadily improve and the level of unemployment fall.[1] The Fabians drew an important practical conclusion from this view. They preached Socialism, not to the workers as their one way of escape from intolerable conditions of life, but to all classes of society impartially, as something inherently good and desirable for everybody. At first the

---

[1] Thus Mr. Pease, writing about six years before unemployment became the incurable, dominating feature of British capitalism, remarks:

"The world is at present so avid of wealth, so eager for more things to use or consume, that however quickly iron and copper replace flesh and blood, the demand for men keeps pace with it. Anyway, unemployment in the twentieth century has so far been less prevalent than it was in the nineteenth, and nobody now suggests, as did Mrs. Besant in 1889, that the increasing army of the unemployed, provided with work by the State, would ultimately oust the employees of private capitalism."

Fabians carried this non-class view of Socialism very far indeed. Thus Mr. Pease, writing of the first two tracts published by the society, states that

"it may further be noticed that we were as yet unconscious of the claims and aims of the working people. Our Manifesto covered a wide field, but it nowhere touches Co-operation or Trade Unionism, wages or hours of labour".

Fabian Essays, the very basis of Fabian Socialism, show no awareness of the fact that the Trade Unions and, to a lesser extent, the Co-operative Societies, *were* the Labour movement of that period. One of the essayists, Bland, foresees clearly the unity of the Liberal and Conservative parties faced by a Socialist party. But he has no realisation that that party must be founded on the Trade Unions. Again Pease writes, still more significantly:

"The autumn of 1889 is memorable for the great strike of the London Dockers, which broke out on August 14th, was led by John Burns, and was settled mainly by Cardinal Manning on September 14th. The Fabian Society held no meeting between July 19th and September 20th, and there is nothing in the minutes or the Annual Report to show that the Society as such took any part in the historic conflict."

Once again we get the impression of great events thundering by the Fabians without having the slightest effect upon them. Is it not tragic and extraordinary that a society which was as hopelessly aloof from the Labour movement as this should yet have succeeded in supplanting the influence of the early British Marxists who had played so great a part in the rebirth of the movement?

The extreme aloofness of the Fabians from the Labour movement was, of course, modified in the second decade of the Society's existence. It was not that the Fabians revised their view of the classless nature of Socialism. But they did become convinced, by practical experience, that the Labour movement was the one organised body which could ever become converted to Socialism. Hence, though they did not by any means give up their attempts to permeate the capitalist parties (and especially the Liberal Party) they did, from about 1890 onwards, devote an increasing effort, first to induce the Labour movement to create a political party of its own, and then to impregnate this party with Fabian Socialism.

The Fabians accomplished the greater part of their work of indoctrinating the ever-growing British Labour movement indirectly. They accomplished it through the medium of an intermediate body which, as it were, relayed a somewhat modified and diluted version of Fabianism to the Labour movement. This transmitting body was the Independent Labour Party, which was founded in 1893. The I.L.P. originally hoped to become itself the political party of the working class. But since it failed to attract the affiliation of the Trade Unions it soon discovered that it had become merely another Socialist society. But it was a Socialist society differing from the S.D.F., in that it rejected Marxism, and from the Fabian Society, in that it did intend to make a direct appeal to the mass of the British workers. It is not always realised or remembered how consciously and specifically the Fabians recognised the I.L.P. as the ideal medium for diffusing their version of Socialism in the Labour movement. Up till 1893 the Fabian Society had been slowly building up a nation-wide organisation. In that year seventy-four Fabian branches existed. But by 1900, although the influence of Fabianism had grown greatly, only four local and four university branches remained. For the local Fabian societies

"were succeeded by and merged into branches of the Independent Labour Party, which adopted everything Fabian except its peculiar political tactics. A few years later the Labour Party followed, more than Fabian in its toleration in the matter of opinions, and virtually, though not formally, Fabian in its political policy" (Pease).

The I.L.P., Pease continues, "set to work to organise Socialism on Fabian lines, adopting practically everything of our policy". Surviving members of the early years of the I.L.P. would, I think, protest strongly against this view. And indeed the I.L.P. appeared to possess an ideology quite distinct from Fabianism. For example, where the Fabians were dry, precise and factual, the I.L.P. was nothing if not emotional. Or again, while the Fabians took, on the whole, a pro-Imperialist line, the I.L.P. was strongly pacifist. But these were essentially temperamental differences representing as much as anything else the difference between the temperaments of Webb and Keir Hardie. There is no doubt that the Fabians were justified in their calm assumption that the I.L.P. had "set out to organise Socialism on Fabian lines". Once Keir Hardie and his associates had rejected Marxism, this, whether the I.L.P.'ers knew it or not, was inevitable. For the I.L.P. had no independent social theory of its own and had no leading figure capable of creating one. Hence it was bound to accept one or other of the theories available at the time. It was bound to come under the intellectual domination either of the Marxists or the Fabians.

In this earlier and smaller instance of the I.L.P., just as later in the case of the Labour Party itself, the fact that the Fabians had worked out a coherent, even if profoundly erroneous, body of social principles, gave them immense influence on the British movement. The leaders of the I.L.P. and the leading Trade Unionists, might, and often did, strongly repudiate the Fabians and all their works. But, since they had no body of social theory of their own, and as their movement could not in the long run exist without some kind of Socialism, the more they repudiated them, the more they fell under the intellectual domination of the very Fabians whom they were denouncing. The immense power of the political ideology with which a developing Labour movement first comes into contact was revealing itself

It was in this same year (1893) that the Fabians first formally appealed to the British Labour movement to form a political party of its own. (Up till then most Fabians had regarded their main task as being the permeation of the Liberal Party, and as late as 1888 Webb had been drafting a new programme for that party, a programme which was in part actually adopted as the well-known Newcastle programme.) "A Plan of Campaign for Labour" was drafted by Webb and Shaw, and issued as a pamphlet which enjoyed a wide circulation in working-class circles. This document recognised the indispensable rôle of the Trade Unions in the formation of a Labour Party and advocated, in general, the steps by which, as described in the last chapter, the Labour Party actually was formed some seven years later.

As we saw, the Fabians partly directly, but mainly indirectly, through the I.L.P., played a part in the setting up of the Labour Representation Committee in 1900. But it was not they, but the employers of Great Britain, through the Taff Vale decision, who made this attempt successful. Indeed, the Fabians, after the founding of the Labour Party, relapsed again, to a considerable extent, into their original view that Socialism would come, not so much by the efforts of the working class, even if these efforts were confined to the most constitutional channels imaginable, as by the conversion to Socialism of all classes. Pease gives the following characteristic account of the lukewarm attitude of the Fabians to the young Labour Party.

"For several years after this the Fabian Society did not greatly concern itself with the Labour Party. I attended the Annual Conferences and took a regular part in the work of the Executive Committee, but my colleagues of the Fabian Society as a whole showed little interest in the new body. In a sense, it was not in our line. Its object was to promote Labour Representation in Parliament, and the Fabian Society had never run, and had never intended to run, candidates for Parliament or for any local authority. We had made appeals for election funds on a good many occasions and had succeeded once or twice in collecting substantial sums, but this was a very different matter from accepting responsibility for a candidate and his election expenses. Therefore, for a good while, we remained in a position of benevolent passivity."

Equally characteristic of the Fabian attitude is the fact that although the Society had become, after 1900, a body affiliated to the Labour Party, several of its members continued to be members of the Parliamentary Liberal Party. On balance it may be said that, although the Fabians took an active part in the formation of its own political party by the British Labour movement, and although they achieved an intellectual domination over that party when it had been formed, they never abandoned their original view that the political struggle of the workers against their employers was not the essential means by which Socialism could be achieved. The Fabians, indeed, were always and inevitably tending to go still further than this, and to feel that the workers' struggle was a rude and disastrous interruption to their own work of winning over the capitalists themselves. They were continually tempted to feel that the workers' struggle should, therefore, be damped down as much as possible lest, by alarming the capitalists, it should postpone the social reforms which they had, they imagined, almost persuaded this or that capitalist politician to introduce. How far their rejection of the workers' struggle always went is shown in the concluding pages of Pease's book.

"I think it may be said that the dominant opinion in the Society—at any rate it is my opinion—is that great social changes can only come by consent. The capitalist system cannot be overthrown by a revolution *or by a parliamentary majority.* [My italics, E. J. S.] Wage slavery will disappear, as serfdom has disappeared, not indeed imperceptibly, for the world is now self-conscious, not even so gradually, for the pace of progress is faster than it was in the Middle Ages, but by a change of heart of the community, by a general recognition, already half realised, that whatever makes for the more equitable distribution of wealth is good."

An entirely constitutional imposition of Socialism by a majority of the House of Commons on unwilling but unrebellious capitalists is, the reader will notice, rejected quite as strongly as is revolution. It is important to realise that in this view the Fabians were but carrying their rejection of the workers' struggle against their employers as the vehicle of Socialism, to its logical conclusion. If the workers are not to take human society forward to Socialism by their struggle, however conducted, then indeed Socialism can only come by general consent, including the consent of the capitalists themselves. The repudiation of the class struggle must involve, as the Fabians saw, the repudiation not merely of revolutionary action in any circumstances, but also, and even, the attempt of the wage-earners to use their constitutional right under a democracy to pass a series of laws which will amount to the expropriation of the capitalists.

For these, after all, are only two different forms of working-class struggle. The organisation of a great political party, capable of gaining the majority of the votes cast at an election, involves the mobilisation of the wage-workers as a class. The carrying through of a great series of Socialist measures will certainly involve the overcoming of manifold forms of resistance, ranging all the way from counter-electioneering, through administrative and economic sabotage, to possible armed revolt on the part of the employing class and its agents. There is, as the Fabians were clear-headed enough to realise, no possible dividing line between these different forms of working-class struggle. If the working-class struggle is accepted as the road to Socialism then all we can say is that, naturally, the workers will far prefer to carry it on by peaceful, constitutional means. The workers will naturally much prefer to come to power peacefully and as a result of winning a majority of the votes at a general election. The workers will prefer that the capitalists should accept the verdict of the ballot and allow their factories, mines and fields to become public property by due process of law.

But the workers' wishes are, unfortunately, by no means the decisive consideration in this matter. In the social struggle the choice of weapons can never be in the hands of the workers. It is always possible for the capitalists, at any stage in the struggle, to throw over democratic, constitutional methods; to substitute the bullet for the ballot. And the grimmest fact of the contemporary world is that hitherto, in every single case in which their possessions have been even threatened, they have done so. When they do so the workers have no choice whatever but to follow them into the new sphere of struggle. For you cannot answer bullets with ballots, vote down a poison gas attack, nor protect your home from raiding bombers by passing resolutions. Thus, if the working-class struggle is accepted as the indispensable vehicle of Socialism, it is impossible to rule out any of the forms which that struggle may take. But similarly, if the workers' struggle is rejected, all thought of achieving Socialism by a parliamentary majority must be abandoned; for the election of a parliamentary majority is itself an important part of the workers' struggle. Those who reject the workers' struggle must reject even its most constitutional forms. For no one can pick and choose amongst the weapons with which his opponent may make his fight. And if the workers' struggle is rejected then any hope of Socialism rests on converting the capitalists. You must expect the capitalists themselves to lead the community forward out of capitalism.

It is of the highest importance that we should realise that this is the real issue. For it is constantly pretended that the issue is one of evolution or revolution, peaceful methods or force and violence. This is a wholly false issue. The workers can never finally choose what methods they will use in their struggle, though they will, of course, stick to peaceful, constitutional methods so long as even the barest possibility of their use is left to them. The real issue is inescapably this: Do you accept the political and industrial struggle of the organised Labour movement as the only possible force which can lead the community out of capitalism into Socialism? Or do you hope, with the Fabians, to persuade the capitalists themselves into abolishing capitalism?

The Fabians, so far as I am aware, never put forward any plan for gaining the consent of the capitalists to their own extinction, except their characteristic policy of permeation. Now permeation can, and did, have some success in persuading capitalist governments, *if they are faced with increasing working-class pressure*, to put through certain

Dᴅ

measures of social reform. But it can never under any circumstances convert them to Socialism. And, to do the Fabians justice, their ultimate object has always been to achieve Socialism, that is to transfer the means of production from private to public hands.[1] For example, Mr. Pease, defending his Society against the imputation that it had a tenderness for the capitalist entrepreneur as against the rentier and landlord, writes:

"Him we propose to deal with by the favourite Fabian method of municipalisation and nationalisation. We take over his 'enterprise', his gasworks and waterworks, his docks and trams, his railways and mines. We secure for the State the profits of management and the future unearned increment, and we compensate him for his capital with interest-bearing securities. We force him in fact to become the idle recipient of unearned income, and then we turn round and upbraid him and tax him heavily precisely because his income is unearned! If there is any special tenderness in this treatment, I should prefer harshness. To me it seems to resemble the policy of the wolf towards the lamb."

It was to this ultimately thoroughgoing policy that the Fabians hoped to convert the capitalists and their agents! No wonder that at the end of his book Mr. Pease has to write:

". . . it must be confessed that we have made but little progress along the main road of Socialism. Private ownership of capital and land flourishes almost as vigorously as it did thirty years ago."

A rejection of the attempt to achieve Socialism by endowing the wage-workers' struggle to improve their lot with self-consciousness, is the decisive characteristic of Fabian Socialists. I have here represented that rejection as a consequence of the Fabians' acceptance of economic science "as taught by the accredited British professors". And so logically, and as a matter of chronology, it was. But we must not suppose that Mr. Shaw's chance encounter with Mr. Philip Wicksteed, and consequent rejection of the labour theory of value, was responsible for the whole

[1] Though they conceived of this transfer in an extraordinarily narrow way. (See p. 100 below.)

future character of Fabian thinking, and so for the tenuous quality of British Socialism! It is by no means likely that had Mr. Shaw not encountered Mr. Wicksteed he would have remained a Marxist, and converted his fellow Fabians to Marxism. It is far more probable that from a subjective, instead of a logical, point of view, the fundamental Fabian characteristic was their rejection of the workers' struggle; it is far more probable that they adopted economic views to fit this instinctive emotional attitude.[1]

So far we have discussed the consequences of the Fabians' rejection of the economics founded on the labour theory of value. The first consequence was their failure to notice the transformation of capitalism into capitalist imperialism, and so to foresee the inevitability of recurrent world wars so long as capitalism remained in existence. The second was their belief that the interests of the owning and working classes would tend to converge instead, as they have undoubtedly done, to diverge, and their consequent rejection of the workers' struggle for better conditions of life as the indispensable vehicle of Socialism. But there was a third consequence, namely their total failure to understand the nature of the State.

As, for the Fabians, there was nothing in the nature of capitalism which was bound to create ever-growing class antagonisms, and ever-recurrent wars, the real prospect, they taught the British workers, was one of steadily improving economic conditions, broadening democracy, more stable peace and increasing social reform. All that was needed was that all enlightened men and women, acting partly, no doubt, but by no means exclusively, through the Labour movement, should combine to secure the transference of the major industries to the State.

But what did the Fabians mean by the State? They meant, roughly speaking, the Government—the existing, British

---

[1] This I take it is Engel's implication when he writes of the Fabians' early propaganda:

"But as soon as they come to their specific tactic, to hush up the class struggle, it gets rotten. Hence also their fanatical hatred of Marx and all of us—because of the class struggle."

Liberal Government from 1906 onwards, for example. They meant in practice, the State just as it was, just as the workers knew it and experienced it. By Socialism the Fabians meant that some British Government, either under Mr. Asquith, or Mr. Lloyd George or, may be, some day Mr. Arthur Henderson, should nationalise the main British industries, such as railways, coal, cotton, steel and the like. They meant that and nothing more.

Is it any wonder that so soon as they became aware of it, this view of Socialism began to repel the British workers? For the workers knew from experience that the existing State—the Government—was no friend of theirs. It intervened constantly in strikes and lock-outs, and it always intervened on the employer's side. The proposal that *this* State, between which and the great employers the workers could see precious little difference, should take over industry, excited no enthusiasm. What those British workers who were becoming conscious of the position of their class in society wanted, was to take over industry themselves. Of course, if the State was *their* State, then it might be convenient to run certain of the biggest industries through the agency of the State. But that was a very different proposition to the mere transference of this or that industry from the employers to the employers' State.

These doubts inevitably raised the question: To whom does the State belong? But such an enquiry as this was not dreamt of in Fabian philosophy. From the point of view of the Fabian, classless conception of society, such a question could have no meaning. The State was just the State. If a definition of the State was required, it might perhaps be called "a great League of consumers". The effect of this Fabian assumption that the State was a sort of neutral, impartial agency, hanging above the community, suspended in a sort of social vacuum—this typically Civil Servant's view of the State—was to narrow down and tone down the concept of Socialism to something which could not excite much enthusiasm on the part of the workers.

This blankly uncomprehending view of the State was of a piece with the rest of Fabian Socialism. It was, of course, a direct consequence of the Fabians' refusal to face the fact that class conflict is the decisive social phenomenon in any capitalist society. Just as they would not allow themselves to see that, permeate never so sweetly, they could not prevent the capitalists, in the last resort, from opposing Socialism with all their might; just as they refused fully to recognise that, however impervious to ideas the Labour movement might seem, yet it must in the end struggle against capitalism; so also they would not recognise that every State is an apparatus of administration and coercion, *belonging to a particular class*. They would not see that each class forges a State apparatus of a particular kind, suitable to its particular purposes; that no new class coming into power can use the old State apparatus for its new and very different purposes, without transforming it from top to bottom. For the State is not simply the State; still less is it "a great League of consumers". The State is always a State of a particular kind, and it always belongs to a particular class. The British State belonged, in the Fabian period, and belongs to-day, to the British capitalists. Hence the transference of the title deeds of some industry to this State was just as uninteresting and uninspiring a proposal as the advanced British workers felt it to be. As we shall see, the identification of Socialism with this arid proposal did in fact turn a vital section of the organised workers away from Socialism.

The work of the Fabians has been both under- and over-appreciated. Its importance has been under-appreciated, its quality grossly over-appreciated. It is still not fully realised that British Socialism, which monopolised, till very recently, the thinking of the British Labour movement, is Fabian Socialism. In essence it is a diluted, adulterated version of the thinking of two men, Webb and Shaw. This was more clearly recognised before the war than it is now. Mr. G. D. H. Cole, for example, writing at a time when he was sharply critical of the Fabians, declared:

" . . . we have been saved from important divergences within the Labour movement not because our intellectuals have had no influence, but because a single and very practically-minded body of them long ago carried the day. Mr. and Mrs. Sidney Webb, were able so completely, through the Independent Labour Party, to impose their conception of society on the Labour movement that it seemed unnecessary for any one to do any further thinking."[1]

Fabian thinking conquered the British Labour movement by default. A theory which, if we compare it to Marxism, shows itself to be, not merely false, but almost absurdly inadequate; as pitifully unable to cover the complex stormy, dynamic social phenomena of the twentieth century, was allowed to become the theory of the British working-class movement; and not merely of the British working-class movement. As was suggested above, the Fabians are justified in their claim that they profoundly affected and modified the Socialism of the European and, to some extent, of the American movement. Revisionism, though no doubt it was essentially the child of the social conditions prevailing in the richer Imperialist empires (as was Fabianism itself) was enormously aided by Fabian teaching. Thus we might almost apply Swinburne's melodramatic line to the Fabian, and declare that "the world has gone grey with thy breath".

No one who has once become aware of the quality of thought of such Socialists as Marx, Engels and Lenin, can fail to feel the immense difference in intellectual stature between these men and even the best of the Fabians. There was something unmistakably inhibited, stunted and arid about Fabian thinking. No one could really suppose that theirs was a doctrine capable of leading human society forward to the next stage in the development of man. In the event, Fabianism led the British workers' movement into a morass of defeat and disillusionment.

[1] *The World of Labour*, published 1913. I have spoken throughout of Mr. Sidney Webb. But it should be recognised that the firm of Webb is a partnership in which it is impossible to disentangle the contribution of husband and wife. Mr. Cole seems to me to ignore the smaller but important influence of Shaw.

CHAPTER VII

THE WORKERS' REACTION TO BRITISH SOCIALISM

"State Socialism, in part a bureaucratic and Prussianising movement and in part a reaction against the distribution of wealth in Capitalist society, continued to develop, at least in its Prussian aspects. But, from the working-class point of view, State Socialism was intellectually bankrupt."[1]

THIS IS HOW the most prominent of the younger generation of the thinkers of the British Labour movement, writing in 1917, described the position of Fabianism in the immediately pre-war years.

Cole was here voicing the views of some of the most vigorous and advanced sections of the British movement. It is evident that the Fabian conception of Socialism had produced a strong protest. That reaction was indeed of a world-wide character and absorbed the energies and talents of some of the ablest and most vigorous working-class leaders of the period. For just as Fabianism was, as we saw, an extreme British variety of a world movement to tone down Socialism, so the reaction against this revised and diluted kind of Socialism was also world-wide.

This reaction had its principal centres in France and in America. In France, during the nineteen-hundreds, the Labour movement was rapidly splitting into an extremely conservative section occupied exclusively with Parliamentarianism, and a militant, syndicalist section which rejected all participation in parliamentary politics. In America, where the movement was then, as it still is, in the first stage of development, having not yet founded its own political party, the same left-wing, anti-parliamentary and,

[1] G. D. H. Cole, *Self-Government in Industry.*

finally, anti-political tendency appeared, above all in the form of the Industrial Workers of the World. These French and American militant, syndicalist, anti-political tendencies influenced the British movement. But in any event the same situation which had produced them had arisen, by about 1910, in Britain also.

It was not until 1902 that the British movement finally made up its mind to create a political party of its own. During the next eight years this party was gradually being permeated with the ideas of British Socialism. Yet by 1910 much of what was most vigorous and healthy in the movement was repudiating both Socialism and politics, and was turning back to direct action and the strike as the only effective weapon in the hands of the workers! The truth was that the leaders of the Parliamentary Labour Party and their Fabian mentors had, respectively, made politics and Socialism stink in the nostrils of many of the best members of the movement. For the leaders of the pre-war Parliamentary Labour Party had interpreted independent working-class politics as the creation of a particularly subservient section of the Liberal Government's majority; while of Socialism the Fabians had made gas and water.

Another of those remarkable reversals in the attitude of the Left and Right of the movement to political action which we noted above had occurred. Originally it is always the Right of a Labour movement which is averse to politics, and especially to independent working-class politics. The next step is for the Left to pull and push the movement into, first, politics and then independent politics. But then the Right discovers that in politics, and above all parliamentary politics, it is in its very element. The official leaders become converted, not merely to the movement going into politics, but to the view that political action is the only function of a Labour movement! Strikes they now denounce as out-of-date, barbarous, useless, as indeed an unpardonable hindrance to their statesmanlike activities in promoting the interests of the workers by speeches in

Parliament. But how does the Left react to all this? Time after time (as in the seventies with George Potter, the militant of his day, and above all in 1910–14) the Left reacts by becoming anti-political again, denouncing all Labour participation in politics and demanding that the movement shall go back to industrial action as its sole form of activity!

This tragic oscillation of opinion will clearly not take a Labour movement very far. It is clear that what is needed is a Left, militant section of the movement which when it sees what the Parliamentarians are doing will explain to the workers that what is wrong is not the unassailable principle of working-class participation in politics, but the working-class politicians! What was needed in the pre-war years in Britain, for example, was a Left clear-headed enough, confident enough in its own principles, to say to the movement: "Yes, this thing here which we have created is a caricature of an independent working-class political party. But this does not mean that an independent working-class political party, one of the functions of which will be to fight our battles in Parliament, is not an indispensable weapon in our armoury. What it means is that we must take immensely more trouble to select, to train, and then to control, the men and women whom we send to Parliament to represent us. Above all, we must put behind us, as belonging to the childhood of the movement, the idea that on the one hand strikes and on the other the attempt to elect Labour majorities to Parliament are alternative, mutually exclusive forms of activity. Of course the truth is that they are merely two edges of the working-class sword. They must be used simultaneously and in co-ordination. Moreover, we shall by no means always be able to choose which edge we shall use at any given time. Our opponents will often force us to fight now on this front, now on that; now on both fronts simultaneously. But above all let us realise that, however many weapons we may choose, or be forced, to use, it is all part of the same struggle; that we can only win that very difficult, and indeed des-

D1

perate, struggle if we learn how to use every one of our weapons, and use them far more skilfully, determinedly and efficiently than we are doing at present."

In the pre-war period no voice was raised to preach so simple and commonsensical a view as that. The battle between the now right-wing advocates of the exclusive use of political action, and the now left-wing advocates of the exclusive use of industrial action, became extremely violent. The two wings of the movement almost completely lost touch with each other. Between 1910 and 1914 the Parliamentary Labour Party[1] stagnated and even declined. But the Trade Union movement entered, as we have seen, into one of the greatest periods of growth and activity which it has ever experienced. This was the great period of "Labour unrest" as it was called by alarmed observers. Strike after strike, in coal, in railways, in transport, each larger than anything which had been seen before in Britain, shook the country. The effect of this great Trade Union offensive was to stop the decline of real wages which had been going on since 1900, and for some workers to effect real improvements.

It is almost incredible that all this intense industrial activity, much of which was extremely successful, and which certainly raised the self-confidence of the British workers to a high point, did not react favourably on the fortunes of the Labour Party. That it did not can be explained by the fact that the leaders of the Labour Party were for the most part deprecating the wave of industrial militancy, and that the industrial militants reacted, not by a determination to change the character of the Labour Party, but by an undiscriminating hostility to it. We have to turn back to the literature of the time in order to realise the bitterness and contempt with which the men engaged

[1] Note the name. The Labour members of Parliament were not (and are not) called *the Labour Party in Parliament*. They were not (and are not), that is to say, a certain number of members of the party who had been selected for the special job of working in Parliament. They were on the contrary the *Parliamentary Labour Party*—the Labour Party having become parliamentary; the Labour Party which had left the outside world behind it and had entered the great Westminster chamber for the euthanasia of inconvenient agitators.

in the industrial offensive regarded the pre-war Parliamentary Labour Party. We may quote from G. D. H. Cole's first important work, *The World of Labour* (1913), remembering always that Cole stood on the right of the left wing; that while strongly stressing industrial as against political action, he was not a syndicalist. (The comments on the Parliamentary Labour Party of the militant members of the movement who were leading and inspiring the Trade Union offensive were unprinted, and were mostly, no doubt, unprintable.) Here, for example, is a brief description of the Labour Party and its leaders as it appeared to Cole on the eve of the war.

"To attack the Parliamentary Labour Party nowadays may look rather like flogging a dead horse. If a General Election came to-morrow, there is not the least doubt that 'Labour' would lose many seats, and that those it retained would belong to it by Liberal favour and sufferance. The party consists of about thirty Liberals, often of the mildest type, and six or seven Socialists. It is led by a man who quite honestly believes in independent Labour representation, but believes also in the Liberal alliance. It consists largely of men who do not believe in independent Labour representation at all, and of a small section that does not believe in the Liberal alliance. That is to say, it is under a strong personality who is both a Liberal and a Socialist—of sorts; but it consists of Liberals and Socialists, and not of hybrids. The philosophic outlook which has enabled Mr. Ramsay MacDonald to span the impassable gulf is not intelligible to the simpler souls he has to lead. They do not detect the finer Hegelianism in a party that is both 'independent' and 'not independent'; they can only scratch their heads in bewilderment when they are asked to be Liberals most of the time, and then suddenly told, on a spectacular occasion, that they have to demonstrate to the world their absolute independence of the Liberal party. Mr. MacDonald threads his way cunningly; but his party is not sophisticated enough to follow him, and it looks as if the united Labour Party were about to 'pass into otherness', and become many, if we may speak of Mr. MacDonald's poor little party in his own Hegelian language."

We see how light, in Cole's view, was the blush of Socialism which the Fabians, either directly or through the

I.L.P., had been able by 1914 to impart to the cheek of British Labour. Moreover, in his view, most of the Parliamentary leaders had not even been converted, at heart, to the principle of an independent political party organised by the Trade Unions. The pre-war Labour Party, as we suggested above, was born at Taff Vale and reared on the Osborne judgment. If and when these supports disappeared it was likely to die.

But the tragedy was that neither Mr. Cole, nor the vigorous group of young Socialist theorists which he led, nor the militant Trade Unionists who were taking the Trade Union movement from strength to strength, felt any urgent need to revive the Labour Party, by turning it into a real weapon of the working class. They had been so sickened of Labour politics and Fabian Socialism that to a lesser or greater extent they all wanted to throw the political weapon away altogether and to concentrate upon direct industrial action. Mr. Cole and his fellow Guild Socialists never went so far as to exclude political action altogether. But this was the policy (to a lesser or greater degree) of those militant British Trade Unionists who had become imbued with syndicalist theory, imported, largely from America, into Scotland and South Wales. In 1912 the most active and alert members of the South Wales Miners' Federation set out their views in a pamphlet which soon became famous under the title of *The Miners' Next Step*. The two crucial proposals made in the programme set forth by the Welsh miners were Nos. XIII and XIV. They read as follows:

"XIII.—That a continual agitation be carried on in favour of increasing the minimum wage, and shortening the hours of work, until we have extracted the whole of our employers' profits.

"XIV.—That our objective be, to build up an organisation that will ultimately take over the mining industry, and carry it on in the interests of the workers."

The authors of the pamphlet comment on these proposals as follows:

"The Elimination of the Employer.

"This can only be obtained gradually and in one way. We cannot get rid of employers and slave-driving in the mining industry, until all other industries have organised for, and progressed towards, the same objective. Their rate of progress conditions ours, all we can do is to set an example and the pace.

"Nationalization of Mines.

"Does not lead in this direction, but simply makes a National Trust, with all the force of the Government behind it, whose one concern will be to see that the industry is run in such a way as to pay the interest on the bonds, with which the Coal-owners are paid out, and to extract as much more profit as possible, in order to relieve the taxation of other landlords and capitalists.

"Our only concern is to see to it that those who create the value receive it. And if by the force of a more perfect organization and more militant policy, we reduce profits, we shall at the same time tend to eliminate the shareholders who own the coalfield. As they feel the increasing pressure we shall be bringing on their profits, they will loudly cry for Nationalization. We shall and must strenuously oppose this in our own interests, and in the interests of our objective. . . .

"Our objective begins to take shape before your eyes. Every industry thoroughly organised, in the first place, to fight, to gain control of, and then to administer, that industry. The co-ordination of all industries on a Central Production Board, who, with a statistical department to ascertain the needs of the people, will issue its demands on the different departments of industry, leaving to the men themselves to determine under what conditions, and how, the work should be done. This would mean real democracy in real life, making for real man-hood and womanhood. Any other form of democracy is a delusion and a snare.

"Every fight for, and victory won by the men, will inevitably assist them in arriving at a clearer conception of the responsi-bilities and duties before them. It will also assist them to see that so long as shareholders are permitted to continue their ownership, or the State administers on behalf of the share-holders, slavery and oppression are bound to be the rule in industry."

The reader will see that this programme almost amounted to the view that the miners, and the other workers, could win a complete victory, and totally abolish capitalism, by the exclusive use of one weapon, the strike. The miners, for example, were simply to go on striking until they had secured such high wages as to make the operation of the pits unprofitable to the coal-owners. Once that had been accomplished, the owners would be only too thankful to abandon their unprofitable property. The miners would take over, and from thenceforth operate the pits for their own benefit. The State was almost ignored. The contest was simply one between the miners and the mine-owners. The miners considered indeed that the State might intervene. But they thought that it would intervene in a very peculiar way. They thought that as their squeeze on the owners became more and more formidable, the State, begged and prayed to do so by the owners themselves, might attempt to nationalise the mines. The miners must strenuously oppose any such move, which would merely enable the owners to sidestep, as it were, the miners' attack on their profits.

After the experience of the past twenty-five years it is very easy to point out where the South Wales miners went wrong. They were quite right in thinking that the State might intervene in their struggle with the owners; indeed they grossly underestimated the prospect of very early intervention on the part of any capitalist State in such a situation. But the State would not intervene by nationalising the mines in order to save the owners from the miners' attack. On the contrary, the State would be used, and used to the limit, to smash that attack long before it had got to the point of making the operation of the mines unprofitable. *For the State belonged to the mine-owners, and their friends, in just as real a sense as did the mines.* The State was the mine-owners' State, and so long as it remained so, there was not the faintest possibility of it allowing the mines to pass out of the hands of the owners and into the hands of the miners. In a word, the only way by which the miners can get hold of the mines, or the workers generally can get hold of the means of production, is for them first to get hold of the State. Until and unless this fact is faced there can be no reality in any programme or policy for the working-class movement.

But equally, once the State itself has passed under the control of the workers; or rather once the workers have abolished the employers' State and built up a State of their own, the whole objection to State ownership of suitable industries becomes invalid. It would not necessarily benefit the workers at all for the capitalists' State to take over this or that industry. But this is no objection to a workers' State owning and, if convenient, actually operating the major industries of the country. For such a State will operate them on behalf of the workers instead of the capitalists.[1]

The question of the nature of the State; this was the question which no one engaged in the controversies of the pre-war movement would face. For no one had any clear conception of what the State was or to whom it belonged. The Fabians, as we have seen, had a most favourable view of the State. Their conception of Socialism amounted to little more than the proposal that the State—the existing State just as it was—should become the owner and operator of the major industries of the country. Such a conception of Socialism was bound to outrage every healthy working-class instinct. From the extreme revolutionary anarcho-syndicalists to the sober Guild Socialists the counter-cry arose that the State was a monster from which at all costs men must be saved; that this proposal to hand over everything to the State would not only fail to solve the social problem but would make matters a thousand times worse.

---

[1] Here I have only pointed out the Syndicalist error in *The Miners' Next Step*; for it is from our errors that we can learn most. But this treatment is quite unfair to the brilliant group of young South Wales miners who wrote *The Miners' Next Step*. The pamphlet, with its far-reaching proposals for the reorganisation of the South Wales Miners' Federation, and, by example, the whole Trade Union movement, on much more democratic lines, was of the greatest value. Its publication was a landmark in British Trade Union history. It will be a welcome sign of returning health and vitality when groups of young Trade Unionists come together in different parts of the country and publish work of a similar value for the solution of the present-day problems of the movement.

Hence arose the great controversy of the pre-war years: Was the State good or bad? Were reformers to advocate that its powers should be enormously increased by the absorption by it of industry? Or were they, on the contrary, to advocate that the State should be abolished overnight, as did the anarchists and syndicalists? Or, choosing a middle path, should they propose that the State be "balanced" by a Guild Congress with equal sovereign powers, as did the Guild Socialists? Pro-State or anti-State? These were the terms in which the controversy was fought out, or at any rate talked out. Shaw and Belloc had a coruscating debate about it. Cole insulted and deserted the Fabian Society over it. Mr. and Mrs. Webb were judicial about it. *The New Age* was founded, brilliantly to champion the anti-State view, in its moderate Guild Socialist form. In the valleys of South Wales and on the Clyde there grew up a vigorous school of militant, anti-State Trade Unionists, who had reacted to Fabianism and the pseudo-politics of the right-wing Trade Unionists by creating what we have called "Left Trade Union Politics". There arose, that is to say, and not only in Britain, a school of working-class opinion which, in spite of its extreme militancy, was still at bottom bounded by a Trade Union conception of politics; which had not become genuinely Socialist. It had not become Socialist because the only Socialism which had been made available to it was the gelded Socialism of the Fabian Society, the American Socialist Party, the German revisionists, or the still more debased Socialism of the right wing of the French Socialists—the "ministerial Socialism" as Lenin used to call it of such men as Millerand and Briand.

A distinguishing common characteristic of these bastard kinds of Socialism was their complete failure to understand the nature of the State; to understand that the contemporary State was the Capitalists' State. No wonder this kind of Socialism positively repelled the most advanced workers. Inevitably such an uncritical idealisation of the State bred the opposite attitude in the working class. It bred an attitude of syndicalist or anarchist refusal to face the fact that the workers would need *their* State. For in all this huge controversy, which used up an appallingly high proportion of the energies of the Labour movements of Western Europe and America, no one asked the simple little question: "To whom does the State belong?"

Yet this was the only question which permitted of a rational answer. Once it was asked and answered it became apparent that the question of whether the State was good or bad was a barren one. The existing State, the capitalist State, was almost wholly bad. Extensions of its powers were extremely dangerous to the workers. Above all, there could be no question of the workers achieving their essential purpose of acquiring the means of production while this State, created and maintained by the capitalists as their watchdog, was in existence. So far the left-wing anti-politicals were right. But, equally, it became apparent that an attitude of uncompromising hostility to the existing State did not in the least mean that the workers would not need a State of their own, to be *their* watchdog, when they were establishing an economic system to suit themselves. On the contrary, it was but common sense to agree with the Fabians that *a* State would play a very great part in the reorganisation of industry after the expropriation of the capitalists. But it would be a very different kind of State from the existing one. For it would be wielded by a different class.

For a State is not "a great league of consumers". It is a weapon. And a weapon is neither good nor bad. A revolver in the hands of a bandit, terrorising the inhabitants of a captured village, is bad. A revolver in the hands of one of the villagers expelling the bandit is good. But the villagers will not have much chance of safety if instead of uniting to get the revolver out of the hands of the bandit and into their own they sit down to an acrimonious discussion amongst themselves as to the innate, ethical nature of revolvers and, consequently, as to whether or not it would be a good thing if the power of revolvers were to be increased.

Mr. Cole in the two principal books which he wrote during this period, *The World of Labour* and *Self Government in Industry*, discusses all these questions very fully. But again the question he always canvasses (see, for example, pp. 410–15 of *The World of Labour*) is whether the State is so bad that it must be "abandoned", or whether it can be "reformed". The idea that the thing to do was to "abandon", or rather abolish, *their* State and then build up *our* State, simply does not arise. And this is all the more remarkable when we reflect that Marx and Engels' view of the State, as the instrument of the class governing society at any given time, had been current in the world for fifty years. Yet none of the pre-war disputants so much as referred to it. It was not that they examined and rejected it. They simply ignored this whole vast body of political thought (which after all was the official [if neglected] doctrine of all the Labour movements of Continental Europe) as if it had never existed. They started thinking out their own theory of the State from the beginning.

This feature of the thinking, meagre enough in itself, of the Anglo-Saxon Labour movements is particularly depressing. Our movements have been led and inspired by a series of auto-didacts; by men, that is to say, of outstanding gifts and idealism; but by men who failed to make themselves masters of the work and experience of the previous thinkers and leaders of the working class. Hence from the Chartists in Britain, and the Knights of Labour in America, until to-day, discoveries are made, experience is gained, only to be lost again. Then new leaders and thinkers appear who with great difficulty, and at a heavy cost, rediscover the old principles.

The failure of all the schools of Socialist thought in the pre-war period to understand the nature of the State was at bottom a failure to see how deep class divisions went. And this failure extended not only to the Fabians, but to many, at any rate, of their opponents. In spite of the militant language of the Guild Socialists they, almost as much as the Fabians, slurred over the question of the necessity of struggle to overcome the resistance of the capitalists before there could be any possibility of taking over the means of production and building up a new economic system. Guild Socialists failed to realise that before the workers could reconstruct anything they had to get the power, *the power of the State*, into their hands. If to-day we re-read their elaborate proposals for the future conduct of Socialised industry; for the creation of some fifteen self-governing National Guilds, to which the State was to lease out the main productive enterprises of the country; or their proposal for a Guilds Congress, which was to be a sovereign body parallel to Parliament, we obtain the most painful impression of unreality.

To-day no one can help seeing that the Guild Socialists never really came to grips with the problems either of the Socialist reorganisation of industry or of the political characteristics of a Socialist society. To a large extent history had not provided the necessary materials for the solution of these problems. But there was the illuminating example of the Paris Commune. The Commune, it is true, did not touch the question of industrial organisation, but it threw light on the political problem. Marx and Engels had studied it intensively, but these studies lay as neglected by all the schools of British Socialist thinkers as did the rest of Marxism. Instead of themselves working upon the records of the Commune, or upon Marx and Engel's studies, the Guild Socialists simply drew upon their imaginations, and soon lost themselves in a barren world of fantasy. However ingenious were their schemes, they had no adequate point of contact with reality. It may even be that in some countries, in some phases of Socialist development, forms of economic organisation not unlike their proposals will actually come into existence. But these problems can hardly, in reality instead of in fantasy, be even approached, much less solved, until the workers have power. And then, it is certain that they must, in the main, be solved by experience, by trial and error, as the sovereign workers of the Soviet Union, having got power, have been engaged in solving them, these twenty years past. On these questions of the forms of Socialist reconstruction, the really scientific Socialist must be in the main an empiricist, insisting only that all the forms tried shall be genuinely Socialist; that they shall exclude, that is to say, the exploitation of man by man, the living off the labour of others.

It was in regard to these questions that Lenin used to use his favourite quotation from Napoleon: "On s'engage et puis on voit"—One joins battle and then one sees. This was Napoleon's simple recipe for victory—not to have rigid battle plans, which were certain to be upset by the incalculable and unforeseeable chances of the field; to plan simply to beat the enemy; and for that purpose to be ready to change your direction of advance, your methods, your tactics, your whole battle order, again and again and at a moment's notice. The same principles apply to the struggle of classes. Engage the enemy, and see. For the forms of Socialist reconstruction will not, and cannot, be thought out ahead in the form of neat blue-prints for Utopia. They can only emerge from the hot crucible of struggle itself, rough edged, unshapely at first, but real, and capable of endless further adjustment to the needs of man. To lay down any but the broadest and simplest principles for the future tasks of Socialist reconstruction is, to quote Lenin again, to join the ranks of those "who preferred to dream about a better future rather than *explain* the abominable present".

CHAPTER VIII

THE THREE INEVITABILITIES

THE WAR WIPED away the controversies within
the Labour movement which have been described in the
last chapter. It transformed the British Labour Party from
a small and ill-assorted group of Members of Parliament,
whose future seemed dubious, into, first, the official Opposition and then the Government.

In particular, the war almost obliterated the controversy
between the Fabians and the Guild Socialists on the subject
of workers' control versus nationalisation. This question
fell into the background as soon as the Labour movement
became a major force in public life. For then, whether the
thinkers of the movement liked it or not, and whether they
were fully conscious of it or not, the neglected question of
political power forced itself, to some extent at any rate,
on their unwilling attention. It became apparent that it
was absurdly premature to divide the movement over a
question of the form which Socialist reconstruction should
take. It became impossible wholly to deny that the thing
which really mattered was the question of how the movement was to fight to gain its next objective, or often, to
maintain its very existence, amidst the ferocious turmoil
of the post-war world.

Before the end of the war, in 1917, the British Labour
Party was reorganised so as to admit individual members;
local Labour parties were formed all over the country,
and the party was given a new programme. This programme,
entitled *Labour and the New Social Order*, marked the final
conquest of the mind of the organised workers of Britain
by Fabian or British Socialism, as we have defined that
ideology. Mr. Webb (who drafted the programme) recog-

nised this very clearly. In a preface to a new edition of Fabian Essays, published in 1920, he wrote that

"those who read *Labour and the New Social Order*—the detailed, constructive programme which the Labour Party adopted for the general election of 1918—will see how completely and definitely 'socialist' (Mr. Webb's inverted commas) this party has become; and how exactly it corresponds with what the last two essays of the present volume had, in 1889, in contemplation".

It was all too true. The next eleven years were to demonstrate what were the consequences, in the post-war world, of the domination of the mind of a Labour movement by Fabian or British Socialism. Still, it must be recognised that in becoming impregnated with this kind of Socialism the British Labour movement took, in a sense, a step forward. For, let it be reiterated, the pre-war movement was not Socialist at all, though it included Socialists and often advocated particular Socialistic proposals. On the whole, then, we may say that the post-war British Labour movement was definitely Socialist; but that its Socialism was of the peculiar Fabian or British variety.

No doubt the distinction is somewhat arbitrary, for there remained right through the 'twenties important non-Socialist elements in the movement—both in the Trade Union and Labour Party leadership. Moreover, the Fabianism of those members and leaders of the movement who did, on the whole, become Socialists was of a very diluted and indiscriminate kind. Thus at first sight an observer might have supposed that there was nothing distinctively Fabian about the thinking of the post-war British Labour movement. But this view is, I think, erroneous. Vague, illusive, ill-defined as were the political opinions of British Labour leaders during this period, these opinions almost all came, in the last analysis, though most of them indirectly, from Fabian sources. Hence it is of the first importance to ascertain exactly what Fabianism meant in practice when it was applied to the situation of post-war Britain.

Fabianism, itself, was re-stated by its principal spokesmen, Mr. and Mrs. Webb, in two books published soon after the war, and in the aforementioned party programme, *Labour and the New Social Order*. The first of these books, published in 1920, was called *A Constitution for the Socialist Commonwealth of Great Britain*; the second, *The Decay of Capitalist Civilisation* (1923). Most readers have found the former to be one of the least, and the latter one of the most, satisfactory of their authors' many works. But there is no need for me to describe them, since they do little more than summarise, if in some respects they develop, the distinctive ideology of Fabianism as it had grown up in the previous three decades, and as we have attempted to define it in preceding chapters.[1]

If we re-read the annual addresses delivered to the Trade Union Congresses and Labour Party Conferences by their chairmen and presidents we shall find that year by year the movement became more dominated by Fabian or British Socialism. In 1919, Mr. McGurk, the Labour Party chairman, was hardly a Socialist at all. He was still in the second stage of Trade Unionism, having accepted the principle of an independent Labour Party, but seeing no need to equip such a party with a point of view of its own. He hoped that "aggressive militarism had been brought to its final downfall", and found it "most encouraging that the people dislike war". Of any consciousness that there was a causal connection between capitalist Imperialism and war there is in this 1919 speech no sign. Mr. McGurk saw in the peace negotiations then being conducted

[1] A third book which played a significant part in forming the point of view, not so much of the Labour movement itself, as of the young men and women (of whom I was one) who were coming into it from the middle class at the time, was Tawney's *Acquisitive Society* (1924). Those who re-read it to-day will not be able to avoid a measure of disillusionment. The moving and sometimes pungent style is still there; the high idealism is undimmed. But they will find, to their chagrin, that this was none the less, for all practical purposes, a Fabian or British Socialist book (with a certain admixture of Guild Socialism). For a comprehension of historical forces they will look in vain. What they will find instead is that the struggle of the wage-workers is regarded, not as the dynamic which can lift society to Socialism, but as a dreadful punishment with which we shall all be visited if we do not listen to Mr. Tawney's appeal.

in Paris the struggle of President Wilson and Mr. Lloyd George for a good peace against the forces of darkness as represented by the French. He remarked with satisfaction that Mr. Lloyd George had drawn support for his beneficent activities from British Labour.

Mr. Stuart Bunning at the 1919 Trade Union Congress spoke of industrial matters in a similar spirit. But from then onwards the inaugural speeches and reports of both meetings gradually become those of a non-Marxist, but Socialist, Labour movement. In 1923 it so happened that Mr. Webb himself was the year's president of the Labour Party. He delivered an address which was incomparably more lucid and comprehensive than those of his predecessors and successors. But it was so just because it stated adequately the ideology to which they all, to a greater or lesser degree, subscribed. It will be convenient to analyse the essential conceptions of this speech. For three main ideas underlay both Mr. Webb's speech and the whole far less precisely formulated thinking and speaking of the British Labour movement at this time. All three find some expression in the justly famous phrase "the inevitability of gradualness" which Mr. Webb then coined.

The first and most important of the three assumptions which underlay the ideology of the British Labour movement throughout the 'twenties was that the general course of social development was still upward, as it had been during the past century. This idea was never, or very seldom, explicitly formulated. Indeed it was occasionally denied. For example, in the aforementioned work, *The Decay of Capitalist Civilisation*, Mr. and Mrs. Webb at least half accept the concept of a declining capitalism which must be abolished before it wrecks human civilisation. They agree that there is "a dictatorship of capital" and they foresee (with real perspicacity) that capitalism and political democracy will prove mutually incompatible. Again *Labour and the New Social Order* opens by suggesting that European civilisation as it existed before the war actually has collapsed, and proclaims that Labour will not seek to rebuild it.[1]

But such passages remained occasional affirmations. They did not condition the general thinking, still less the actions, of the movement. The movement's thought and action remained firmly based upon the hypothesis that the existing economic system would remain as a stable foundation for all its work. The men who moulded the mind of the movement always accepted the assumption that capitalism was something which would, indeed, be gradually modified by the will of the Labour movement. But they never even considered the possibility of capitalism rapidly changing, and for the worse, on its own account. They saw the political struggle as one in which the initiative must necessarily and always be on their side. Hence the general atmosphere of unanalytical optimism which pervaded them. Mr. Webb, for example, in his 1923 speech, half playfully calculated that a Labour majority might well come in 1926, since if you plotted, and then protracted, the curve of increase of the Labour vote since the foundation of the party, the line on the graph which marked 50 per cent of the electorate would be crossed about that date.

This was one inevitability. It was, in a sense, a double inevitability. It was inevitable that the capitalist system should go on developing and expanding as it had done throughout the nineteenth century. Thus it would provide a stable and effective basis for securing a long series of reforms and concessions to the working class. Secondly, it was inevitable that on this basis the Labour movement would just grow and grow until it dominated the political

---

[1] "Count Okama, one of the oldest, most experienced and ablest of the statesmen of Japan, watching the present conflict from the other side of the globe, declares it to be nothing less than the death of European civilisation. Just as in the past the civilisations of Babylon, Egypt, Greece and Carthage and the great Roman Empire have been successively destroyed, so, in the judgment of this detached observer, the civilisation of all Europe is even now receiving its deathblow. We of the Labour Party can so far agree in this estimate as to recognise in the present world catastrophe, if not the death, in Europe, of civilisation itself, at any rate the culmination and collapse of a distinctive industrial civilisation, which the workers will not seek to reconstruct." (*Labour and the New Social Order*, p. 3.)

scene. Then, of course, it would proceed, slowly but surely, to socialise industry. The idea that something might be happening to capitalism which would impel the capitalists to interrupt the course of this double inevitability never occurred to anyone. Hence the first aspect of the concept of inevitability is itself both economic and political. It is inevitable that capitalism will stay *put*, while the Labour movement is approaching the point at which it can begin the process of socialisation. And it is inevitable that the Labour movement will uninterruptedly gather support.[1]

In the nineteen-twenties almost all of the leaders and the members of the British Labour movement held this view unquestioningly. To-day the simplest of us can see how ill-founded it was. We can all see that as the inherent position of capitalism grew weaker, and the strength of the Labour movement more formidable, a period of combined economic and social crisis was bound to occur. To suppose that the ruling class would calmly allow their political power to fall into the hands of a movement which must ultimately dispossess them was extremely naïve. Why did the men and women of the British Labour movement who were, many of them, very shrewd in other respects, make this astonishing error? Writing as one who at the time I entered the British Labour movement (1924) fully accepted this point of view (I never even met a Marxist in five or six years of daily work in the I.L.P. Central Office, in a constituency in Birmingham and later at the head office of the Miners' Federation of Great Britain), I have no doubt that it was because we had none of us assimilated the concept that the development of capitalism was now downward. Consequently, we never saw that it was this decline of capitalism, and not any sudden conversion of ourselves and the workers to a sense of the immorality of the capitalist system, which was at bottom the cause of the upward development of the Labour movement.

[1] "So far," said the report of the Executive to the 1923 Conference, "we have not experienced a set-back."

We still refused to recognise the economic causation of political events. We thought of the growth of the Labour movement as a quasi-moral revolt against capitalism—as caused by the success of Socialist propagandists in "opening the eyes of the workers". We never really grasped the fact that it was the world-wide crisis of capitalism which had opened the eyes (in so far as they were open) of the Socialist propagandists themselves. For if we had really understood that a crisis in capitalism was the great conditioning fact behind the rise of our movement, we could not have envisaged the future in the above astonishingly one-sided way. We must have realised that not only the workers, but the capitalists also, would react to the growing difficulties of their system; that just as the workers would react by joining the Labour movement and becoming Socialists, so the capitalists would react by attempting to solve their difficulties at the expense of the workers.

If we had any real sense of economic causation, we could not have failed to realise that there was nothing in the least inevitable about a slow, steady, stately, undisturbed advance of Labour, which the capitalists would contemplate in passive awe, until it had swallowed them up. We should have known that, on the contrary, of all the innumerable things that could happen this, at any rate, could not. We should have seen that whatever unpredictable form it took, the future must be one of conflict.[1] For not only was the working class being set in motion by the pressure which capitalism in decay put upon them, but the capitalist class was also on the move. We should have seen that the capitalists were at least as alive to the situation as the workers and were determined to impose their remedies for the crisis. And their remedies could consist in nothing

[1] How remote were the thinkers of the movement from the realities of the epoch which the world had entered is illustrated by these words from the Webbs' *A Constitution for the Socialist Commonwealth of Great Britain.* "We may possibly be confronted with an interval of costly social friction and degrading strife." And this was written in 1920! It was a little as if the guides of a Polar expedition, which had just been caught in a furious blizzard, had remarked that it might possibly get a little chilly before they reached their destination.

but attacks upon the liberties and standard of life of the rest of the population.

Men who had realised that their own advance was but one consequence of the pressure put upon society by the break-up of its economic foundations; men who had realised that the other consequence was bound to be intense activity on the part of the capitalists to restore the stability of their system; must have foreseen that the real prospect was one of inescapable conflict between the two classes. Equipped with such a realisation, the guides of the move-ment would have realised that the situation could not in any case remain as it was. The only question was this: Should the ever more menacing social problem be solved by the workers at the expense of the capitalists, by means of the socialisation of the means of production? Or should the capitalists attempt to solve it by making capitalist production temporarily profitable again at the expense of the workers, by means of wage cuts and the destruction of social services, breaking, in the process, the power of the Trade Unions and working-class political organisations? From the very day of the armistice this was the alternative which confronted the British people. If the British Labour movement had realised that this was so, the history of the last twenty years would have been very different. For a realisation that the above gigantic social alternative was the only inevitable thing about the prospect must have entirely altered not only the policy but also the very character of the movement. A comprehension of the exis-tence of this alternative would have enabled the movement to realise that a failure by Labour to impose its solution of the crisis implied the rise of those forces of unbridled capitalist reaction which we have learnt to call Fascism. And if British Labour had ever learnt that lesson, the present situation of both Britain and the world would be very different.

So much for the first inevitability. But when Mr. Webb spoke of the inevitability of gradualness he was not only addressing the capitalists and informing them that the advance of Labour was inevitable. He was also, and especially, addressing the workers and telling them that this advance must inevitably be gradual. He was voicing the favourite Fabian doctrine that whatever "scatter-brained revolutionaries" might choose to advocate, the advent of Socialism must, in the very nature of things, be a gradual process. Both Shaw and Webb have written repeatedly on this theme. They would be only too glad, they have told us, to achieve Socialism suddenly and even catastrophically; it is not that the thing is undesirable, it is that it is inherently impossible. There simply do not exist social institutions, administrative possibilities, actual staffs, capable of operating socialised means of production. Therefore, whether we like it or not, and quite apart from any other consideration, the process of constructing a Socialist economic system must be a gradual one. Mr. and Mrs. Webb have summed up this view in a character-istically persuasive passage in *A Constitution for the Socialist Commonwealth of Great Britain* (319–20):

"All this knowledge leaves the British manual-working class sceptical about the possibility of any sudden and simultaneous social transformation, especially when the revolution is un-accompanied by any deliberately thought out and generally accepted alternative scheme of organisation. It is not a matter of a merely 'political' revolution, in which a sudden wave of irresistible popular feeling might upset the Government, upset the Law Courts, upset Parliament itself, and instal in the seats of authority, national and municipal, with complete power to do what they thought fit, the leaders of the most insurrectionary 'Industrial Unionism'. There have been such revolutionary upheavals of 'illegal' and unconstitutional 'Direct Action' in this country as elsewhere, not without a certain measure of success, for their own purposes and in their own way, and it is not to be supposed that there will never be any others. But the drawback of every such sudden and simultaneous upheaval is that even its success leaves the job still to be done. Whoever gets into power, and whatever the instrument and circumstances of the revolution, the transformation of the social and industrial machinery of a whole nation takes time. It cannot be improvised.

It is in the very nature of things that the transformation can be effected only piece by piece. If it is not done on a systematically thought out plan it will presently be found, whatever orders and commands have been promulgated, that it has not been done at all."

This whole theory is based on a confusion between the building up of a Socialist economic system, which, it is perfectly true, must be a gradual and indeed experimental process, and the acquisition by the working class of the power to build such a system. For both historical and contemporary experience teaches us that power cannot be achieved gradually over a whole historical period, but must be achieved in a relatively short and decisive period.

Many members of the movement in the twenties did realise that it was necessary to achieve political power in order to begin building Socialism. But they conceived of the process of getting power and building a Socialist society as occurring gradually and simultaneously. The workers, they envisaged, would, partly by their pressure on capitalist governments and partly by establishing Labour Governments, put such pressure upon capitalism that a large measure of actual Socialist construction would be achieved long before full political power had come into the workers' hands. And they pointed to the fact that various measures of socialisation, local and national, had already taken place. What is wrong with this comfortable and plausible view? We now know that unfortunately things do not turn out in this pleasant way. When working-class pressure, and its own difficulties, begin to act powerfully upon capitalism, the reaction of the capitalists is not to make further concessions, by extending this or that social service or nationalising this or that industry. Their reaction is, on the contrary, to counter-attack. They seek to solve the difficulties of the system not by socialising parts of it, nor by granting this or that extension of the social services, but on the contrary by freeing private enterprise of all possible restraints and burdens and so making its operation, for a time, profitable again. And they can only do this by driving back the Labour movement, and in the end destroying it.

To sum up, the Fabian conception of the building of a Socialist society as a continuous process going on all through the parallel process of the transference of political power (of the power of the State as we called it in Chapter VII) to the workers, is founded, like all Fabian doctrine, on an enormous underestimate of the depth and gravity of the class division of society and of the conflicts which this division engenders.[1] It is, repeated experience has now demonstrated, impossible for the working and capitalist classes to share the power of the State over a whole prolonged period of social evolution. Far from the advent of any such a period being inevitable, it is impossible. Class antagonisms are far too fierce for such diarchies, or conditions of divided power, to be possible for more than brief periods, and then always precariously. It is an illusion, in particular, to suppose that the capitalist class will passively allow the political power of the workers to grow and grow, while the Labour movement pursues a steady policy of socialisation and other encroachments upon capitalism.

It is not merely that the capitalist leaders, being perfectly well able to see what is happening, use all their resources to trip and trap the growing Labour movement. The most important part of the capitalists' resistance to encroachments on their power and wealth is economic and is, partly at any rate, spontaneous. As and when a Labour movement grows influential in a modern community; as and when such a movement forms a Government and begins to attempt to solve the crisis of modern society by its characteristic methods, first of concessions of all kinds to the workers, and then by measures of socialisation; in

[1] The report of the Executive Committee to the Labour Party Conference of 1924 remarked with satisfaction that "the viler slanders" of Labour on the part of the capitalist Press have now "vanished". This report was published a few weeks before the launching of the Zinovieff Letter. To take a military analogy, the Labour General Staff announced that the use of poison gas had disappeared from modern warfare, just a few weeks before they were hurled from commanding positions by one of the greatest and most effective political gas attacks of all time.

general as and when a Labour movement begins to attempt to solve the crisis at the expense of the capitalist class, the capitalists inevitably begin a policy of economic sabotage. To put the matter briefly, the entrepreneurs refuse to "entrepren".

This is what the capitalists call "a loss of confidence". And in a sense this loss of confidence is perfectly genuine. Goodness knows, the obstacles to the healthy functioning of capitalist enterprise which that system's own inherent contradictions have now piled up are formidable enough, without there being any question of burdens and encroachments imposed by the Labour movement. Slumps often happen under the most orthodox capitalist administrations. When you add to these inherent difficulties the burdens which any Labour Government, if it is to do anything towards carrying out even a minimal programme, is bound to lay upon capitalism, plus the hatred[1] for such a Government which the capitalists must feel, it is clear that the capitalist leaders will have little difficulty in engineering a slump as their most effective method of interrupting the stately march to Socialism which Mr. Webb and his friends so confidently foresaw in 1923. In the period of the second Labour Government (1929–1931) for example, the great slump would have taken place whatever government had been in power. All that was needed to stop, for a decade, the advance of the British Labour movement was to throw the full onus of getting out of the slump in the capitalist way (i.e. at the expense of the workers) upon a Labour Government which did not even dare to dream of attempting to get out of it in a working-class way (i.e. at the expense of the capitalists).

In such circumstances it is, as 1931 proved, child's play deeply to discredit a Labour movement. The only policy which can save a Labour movement from destruction in such a situation is to make a resolute bid for enough power

---

[1] Unless indeed a Labour Government surrenders absolutely to the capitalists' demands, when their hatred is turned into a bottomless contempt.

to make possible the carrying through of a far-reaching programme for solving the crisis at the expense of the capitalists. For the alternative is not merely to abandon the attempt to execute any part of the old programme of gradual social reforms and socialisation; the alternative is actually to reverse that programme and to embark upon the capitalist method of solving the crisis by imposing cuts upon the workers.

This question is discussed in detail in the last part of this book. It is only necessary here to realise that a Labour movement which fails to foresee that Governments which it forms, or in which it participates, will, at any time after they take office, and certainly within, say, four years, be faced with a struggle with a ruling class which has no intention of acquiescing in an electoral defeat, is living in a fool's paradise. And such a struggle will rapidly and inescapably pose the question of power. In such a struggle this simple question must be answered: Which class has the power of the State in its hands, the capitalists or the workers?

All this was hidden from us in the twenties. Yet a controversy which occupied an enormous amount of the mental energy of the movement at that time would have been rendered almost meaningless by any comprehension of the way in which the social struggle was bound to develop. This was the great Compensation versus Confiscation debate, which agitated Summer Schools conferences and private discussions throughout the British Labour movement in this period. The Fabian view on the matter had long been formulated and, as usual, it became the official policy of the movement, which it still is. The Fabians were in favour of compensating the capitalists to the full market value of any property in the means of production taken from them. But, the Fabians continued, the money needed for this transaction must be raised by the taxation of the rich. Thus the capitalists would in fact merely compensate each other. The means of production would in the end

E_D

be taken from the capitalists: but the process would be taken in two steps. First the capitalists would be bought out with State bonds, thus becoming functionless *rentiers*. By this step the *control* of industry would pass to the community. But *ownership*, in the sense of the right to receive their accustomed share of the product, would remain in the hands of the capitalists, now become *rentiers*. But then the State would proceed to tax the interest payable on these Government bonds to extinction, thus finally transferring ownership as well as control of the means of production to the community. This view was summed up by Mr. and Mrs. Webb at the very beginning of the postwar period in *A Constitution for the Socialist Commonwealth of Great Britain*:

". . . those British Socialists who have experience of administration, do not contemplate a method of expropriation essentially different from that which prevails to-day whenever a Local Authority takes over a local gas or water company, or acquires property for widening a street. Each owner should receive in compensation a fair market value of that of which he is compulsorily dispossessed, as between a willing seller and a willing buyer. Whether he is paid such a sum in cash, or in Government securities at their own market value, or by an equivalent annuity for a term of years, or for life, is of no pecuniary importance. The community will, of course, be saddled with the interest and sinking fund, or the annuity; and will thus, on the face of it, be no wealthier than before; just as the expropriated person will be no poorer, and the aggregate tribute levied by ownership no less than before. The object of 'socialisation' is 'socialisation',—that is to say, the transformation of profit-making enterprise into public service; not the enrichment of the community by confiscation. But as the Socialist Commonwealth will certainly adopt the economists' emphatic canon of taxation, and levy its revenue on the citizens in proportion to their relative 'Ability to pay', the burden of compensation for expropriation will fall, in effect, almost entirely on the property owners as a class. They will, in short, in order to prevent the hardship which summary confiscation would cause to particular individuals among them, be allowed (like the holders of licences to sell alcoholic drink under the Licensing Act of 1902) gradually to extinguish each other's private ownership over a term of years, by the silent operation of the Death Duties and the graduated Income Tax and Super-Tax. No expropriation without full compensation; no payment of the annuities, or of the interest and sinking fund thereby incurred, otherwise than from the taxes on property ownership!"

Now there is nothing wrong with this Fabian logic. But once again the issue of power is simply left out of account. It will be noticed that Mr. and Mrs. Webb in the above passage describe a transaction by means of which the capitalists are to be finally expropriated by the "community". But unfortunately in present-day society no such entity as the community exists. There is no magisterial power from on high labelled the Community, which will come down and, firmly if kindly, expropriate the capitalists for us. The only people who can possibly do that are the workers and their allies. And before they can do any expropriating, either by direct confiscation, or indirectly by compensation and then the application of expropriatory taxation upon the former capitalists, they must win power.

It may be suggested that a promise on behalf of the Labour movement that it will compensate rather than confiscate will make the winning of power far easier, by greatly diminishing capitalist opposition. But this is much less true than might be supposed. The capitalists may not trouble to work out in detail what will be the final effect on them of a Labour movement's programme of compensation paid out of the taxation of the rich. But they are perfectly aware that their power will be taken away from them if they lose control of the means of production, and that if they lose their power their incomes will not long remain. Hence in practice their resistance to socialisation is not much diminished even by the most rigid promises of compensation. They interpret such promises rather as a sign of weakness and lack of self-confidence in a Labour movement, and are greatly encouraged thereby. Moreover, they are right in such interpretation. For the Fabians' compensation policy is, like the rest of Fabian doctrine, in one aspect an attempt to circumvent the necessity for a many-sided struggle for power. But that struggle cannot be circumvented. The workers with their allies, and by means of their political and industrial organisations, must get power before they can either compensate or confiscate.

This is not to say that after the achievement of a substantially dominating position in the community by a working-class movement and its allies, then a policy of compensation to owners of particular industries, taken over in advance of others, such compensation to be paid for out of taxation on the remaining owners of the means of production, should not be adopted on particular occasions by particular governments. But once again this is a question of the forms of Socialist construction. Its discussion to-day, before the power to construct anything has been won, is largely academic, and often actually misleading. For the truth is that thousands of quite unforeseeable circumstances will condition any Labour or progressive Government's actions, both in securing power, and in beginning to solve the problems of modern society at the expense of the interests of the capitalists. The problems of social reconstruction must for the most part be faced and solved when power has been won. They cannot be solved in imagination beforehand.

So much for the second inevitability. But there was a third inevitability. When Webb spoke of gradualness being inevitable, he meant above all, I believe, that progress towards Socialism could only be very gradual, not only because of the inherent difficulties of Socialist construction, but also because the power of the working class in relation to the power of the capitalists was, after all, very small, and must long remain so.

This was, and is, the cardinal belief both of the Fabians themselves and of those leaders and thinkers of the British Labour movement whose minds they have moulded. They had, and have, a profound lack of faith in the actual or potential power of the working class. This was why, in the last analysis, they recommended the extraordinary course of attempting to persuade the capitalists themselves to introduce Socialism. For underneath all the Fabian assumptions, both explicit and implicit, that there was no question of class power; that what mattered was something called the "community", which must be persuaded of the desirability of Socialism, lay a profound, if only semi-conscious, belief in the absolute power in contemporary society of the capitalist class. This belief, taken in conjunction with the adoption of a gradualist programme, inevitably causes a Labour movement to attempt the conciliation of the capitalists at all costs. Hence the programme and point of view with which the Fabians equipped the British Labour movement were above all designed to minimise, at any cost, capitalist opposition to Socialism. For the gradualist programme involves at a hundred points the acquiescence of a still almost omnipotent capitalist class.[1] Hence, above all, perhaps, the Fabians' tireless stress on extreme gradualness; on the securing of majorities in Parliament, and on local authorities as the sole method of the working-class movement; hence their absolute refusal to admit that a divergence of interest between the two social classes was the decisive fact of modern society; hence their refusal to recognise that the workers must acquire power before they could move towards any substantial degree of Socialism; hence their claim that schemes of rationalisation or consolidation, such, for example, as the setting up of the London Passenger Transport Board, are steps towards Socialism; hence, in particular, all their moral exhortations to the capitalists as to the wickedness of living by owning.

The Fabians often supposed that their appeals to the capitalists to cease, gradually and quietly, but in the end completely, to be capitalists, were having a great effect. Their books were often well received in the great newspapers. They enjoyed contact with many quite influential figures in the capitalist world, whom they believed that

[1] And as we shall see Mr. Attlee still affirms his faith in the "acquiescence" (Mr. Attlee's word) of the capitalists in the full consequences of a Labour electoral victory. (See p. 353.)

they were greatly influencing. They found, in short, that a section of the British capitalist class appeared to be quite ready to listen to them. The British capitalists did listen. The situation was that of the Russian folk story which Lenin quotes in one of his pamphlets (See *Selected Works*, Vol. VI, p. 52). The cook came into the kitchen and saw Vaska the cat on the table, eating the chicken which the cook had just plucked for dinner. So the cook began a long lecture to Vaska on the wickedness of stealing. Vaska, the story concludes, "listened but went on eating". It was only in this sense that the great, fat, sleek cat of British capitalism listened to the homilies of the Fabians and the other spokesmen of the British Labour movement. The capitalists listened but went on steadily appropriating the values created by the workers—for it was of their very nature to do so. Nor, since they utterly disbelieved in the power of the working class to chase Vaska off the table, could the Fabians and their pupils do anything but go on repeating their lecture.

The next chapter describes the catastrophic effects which its leaders' disbelief in the power of the working class had upon the movement in the period of the capitalist counter-offensive which began in the nineteen-thirties. In the twenties when capitalism was everywhere on the defensive, and was often hard pressed, this lack of faith hamstrung the movement at every turn, and time after time prevented it from reaping the fruits of magnificent, and in themselves successful, struggles. For if the only road to Socialism lay through the conciliation and persuasion of the capitalists, then it was above all necessary to prevent the workers, by "ill-timed strikes", or in any other way, from offending them. A Fabian-taught leadership could do no other than try to damp down in every possible way the outbreaks of that struggle of classes which it was their life's purpose to discount. They felt that an outbreak of some industrial dispute was continually occurring just as they were on the point of getting some piece of Socialistic legislation carried through. They became more and more hostile to the idea that the working class could ever accomplish anything by its own efforts.

Here it is necessary to differentiate between the Fabians themselves, such as Mr. and Mrs. Webb, and the main mass of the Labour members of Parliament and other secondary leaders of the movement, on the one hand, and a tiny group of men at the very top of the movement, on the other. The former body of opinion did on the whole sincerely believe in the possibility of achieving Socialism by means of the gradually increasing influence of the Labour movement combined with the acquiescence, if not the co-operation, of the capitalists. But this was never the view of the principal leaders of the movement. Mr. Ramsay MacDonald, Mr. Thomas and Mr. Snowden were much too worldly-wise to believe any such thing. These experienced politicians never took seriously the theory of Socialism by permission of the capitalists. But then they did not take Socialism seriously at all. Whatever they may have thought in their youth they had long given up any desire actually to achieve the transference of the means of production from one class to another. They had long ceased to believe that anything of the sort could ever happen. On the other hand, they more than shared the view that the power of the working class must necessarily be very small. (For example, Mr. MacDonald at the 1924 Labour Party Conference called the formation of the first Labour Government "an insane miracle". His speech showed that in his heart he had never dreamt that the Labour Party would ever grow large enough even to form a Minority Government.)

On the other hand, the men at the top knew that it was necessary for them to conform to the prevailing Socialist sentiments of the movement. Hence it suited them down to the ground that the thinkers and spokesmen of the movement sincerely believed in a kind of Socialism which was clearly quite illusory *and which necessitated the damping down of all vigorous activity directed towards the achievement*

of working-class power. The topmost group of leaders was
perfectly screened by the sincerity of the men just below
them, who really did believe in the Socialism by persuasion
theory, and who were genuinely outraged when their
sincerity was questioned from the Left. Much of the peculiar
strength of the British Socialist ideology which dominated
the movement in the twenties, was due to this curious
division of function within the leadership.

This almost universal disbelief of the leaders in the power
of their movement was all the more remarkable when we
recollect that the one indisputable success which the British
Labour movement won during this whole period was
achieved by direct working-class power, without any attempt
to conciliate the ruling class. This was the imposition in
1920 of peace with the Soviet Union upon an extremely
reluctant ruling class. The Coalition Government then in
office was determined to destroy the first example of working-
class power that had ever endured for more than a few
weeks.[1] The British Government failed in this important
enterprise and it failed because the British Labour movement prevented it. This unique and enormous success was
achieved by the formation of Councils of Action all over
the country directed by a Central Council of Action.
These Councils were formed officially on the initiative of
the Parliamentary Committee of the T.U.C., the Labour
Party Executive and the Parliamentary Labour Party (the
bodies which now make up the National Council of Labour).
The story of how it was done is too well known to need
repetition. (See, for instance, Hutt's *The Post-War History
of the British Working Class.*) What concerns us here is that
it was accomplished when, as Mr. Clynes (of all people)

---

[1] A. J. Cook once told me that in the course of some discussions during
an attempt to settle the coal lock-out of 1926, he asked Mr. Winston Churchill,
who was conducting the negotiations on the Government side, why he had
aided the White Russian Armies so determinedly in 1919, '20 and '21.
Churchill replied, Cook reported, somewhat as follows: "Wasn't it better to
try to kill the chicken then, rather than have to chase the b—— hen round
all the farmyards of Europe as we're doing now?" But the hen has now
become an unchaseable eagle, as Mr. Churchill is most uncomfortably aware.

said at the time, "no Parliamentary or political measures could be effective in themselves to save the country from being committed to war against its will".

As we look back on the twenties, this event, far more than the election of two Labour Governments, more than the betrayed valour of the General Strike, more even than the triumphant railway strike of 1919, or the great, if temporary, success of Red Friday in 1925, stands out as the one major accomplishment of the British Labour movement in the post-war world. This time the British working class really did force its rulers to abandon a project of major importance, a project upon the carrying out of which the ultimate safety of British capitalism depended (as Mr. Churchill and his colleagues correctly considered, see Note above). In 1920 the British working-class movement, by preserving the Soviet Union from attack, changed the history of the world. But this striking example of the reality of working-class power; this example of the ability of the movement, if and when it was united, to challenge the will of the ruling class on a major issue, was to remain wholly unheeded throughout the twenties—just as it is unheeded to-day. It was, and is, a cardinal principle of those who then led, and of those who now lead, the movement that nothing can be accomplished, or must be attempted, along these lines. For the movement was (and to a large extent is still) dominated by the ideology of British Socialism, and the triple inevitabilities which we have sought to analyse in this chapter.

This then is what we thought in the twenties; and we were wrong. We thought that capitalism would prosper, or at least remain stable, so that it would be possible for the workers to win, and for the capitalists to give, a long, cumulative list of concessions. We confused the winning of power with the building of Socialism, and almost ignored the former while planning and scheming about the latter long before any of the conditions for the solution of its problems had arisen. Finally, we had no faith in the power

E1

of the working class to impose its will upon society, and a great faith in the unchallengeable power of the capitalists. It was this ideology (which was itself the application to post-war conditions of Fabian or British Socialism) which prevented the British Labour movement from achieving historic successes in the nineteen-twenties.

For the leadership of the movement then possessed almost everything necessary to success—except a mind and a will. During the twenties the structure of the industrial organisations of the British workers was greatly simplified and improved. A good deal of Union amalgamation took place —though very much is still to do. The General Council of the Trade Union Congress became a guiding organ, which has since proved its capacity to lead the Unions and to give them a common outlook. The country was almost perfectly covered with a net-work of local Labour parties. The Co-operative movement expanded enormously. The industrial and political sides of the movement were drawn much closer together. The old prejudice, which has been described above, that political and industrial action were somehow incompatible, was to some extent overcome. Above all, the movement definitely passed out of the second stage in the development of a Labour movement, namely political Trade Unionism which has founded its own party, into the third stage of a movement possessing a political party which has become Socialist. But it was not enough. For that Socialism was of a bastard kind.

The general situation of the British Labour movement could scarcely have been more favourable. European capitalism, shattered almost to pieces by the war, was desperately striving to keep itself in existence. British capitalism, though in a far less desperate condition, was pinned to the defensive for the whole period. A movement which had known what it wanted and had meant to have it could have gone far towards the reconstruction of British society, though not indeed without severe political and economic struggles. For the post-war period was the golden opportunity, which may or may not return, for the achievement of substantial social advance with the minimum of social dislocation. But in order to achieve anything you must want to get the power to achieve it. You must want power resolutely and even passionately. And the British Labour leaders neither wanted nor expected power. On the contrary, when an important measure of power, which might have been utilised to get much more, was thrust into the hands of Mr. MacDonald in 1924, he called it "an insane miracle".

The failure of the British Labour movement to have achieved a comprehension of scientific Socialism by the nineteen-twenties was a historical calamity. It was part of a far wider calamity, in that the same causes which prevented the British Labour movement from securing substantial successes prevented the Labour movements of Central Europe from reconstructing human society in their countries. In the major states of Europe, in Italy, in Austria, in Germany, the same ideology (though in the alternative form of revisionist Marxism) dominated the leaders of the organised workers. And in each country the foremost characteristic of the leaders was their lack of faith in the ability of the workers to take and hold power.

In Eastern Europe, in Russia, such leaders, it is often forgotten, existed also. In Russia also they for a time dominated the Labour movement and spread their characteristic views of the impossibility of workers' power. On June 17th, 1917, for example, a representative figure of this leadership, Tseretelli, explained to the first All-Russian Congress of Soviets the position of himself and those who thought with him. A month before, during the crisis of May 3rd–4th "power", he said, "fell into our hands like a ripe fruit". But he and his colleagues, Tseretelli continued, had not held the power that had been thrust upon them. They had handed it back to the Russian middle classes, and they would do the same again. Indeed, he continued, there was not a single party in Russia willing to take power; there was not a single party that would be prepared to say: "Give us the power." But at this moment Tseretelli was interrupted; a delegate called out: "I say there is!" It was Lenin.

There was no such voice in Britain in the nineteen-twenties. When British capitalism was on the defensive and the strength of the working class was rapidly advancing, the workers found no leaders ready to say, as Lenin went on to say at this meeting of the All-Russian Congress of Soviets: "No party can refuse to do that, and our party does not refuse it. It is prepared at any minute to take over the entire power." How dear the absence of this will to power in its leaders has cost the British Labour movement during the nineteen-twenties is a matter of history. A whole decade of working-class strength was dissipated. And at the end came the industrial *débâcle* of 1926 and the political *débâcle* of 1931.

With the nineteen-thirties not only Britain but the whole of Europe entered a new period in which capitalism was no longer on the defensive, but was violently counter-attacking. Now it was the workers who had to man their defences. For in the hour of capitalist weakness their own leaders had neither dared nor desired to press home the attack. In the next chapters we shall describe the effect of the ideology of British Socialism upon the fortunes of a Labour movement fighting a defensive struggle against Fascism and War.

CHAPTER IX

THE END OF BRITISH SOCIALISM

"So I say," Mr. MacDonald, then Prime Minister and leader of the Labour Party, told the 1930 Labour Party Conference, "the work we are doing to-day will enable people to look back a few years from now and say: 'The harvest that we are now reaping comes from seed that the Labour Government in 1929–30 sowed so abundantly in the fields of its day.'"[1]

We do look back, and we agree that we have reaped the harvest sown by the second Labour Government; and a bitter harvest it has been. For six years after the fall of that Government the British Labour movement lay almost prostrate.

The present position of the British Labour movement is due to a series of events of which the record and collapse of the 1929–31 Labour Government was only a central episode. That series of events began with the calling off of the General Strike of 1926, went on in the Mond-Turner Conference of 1928–29, was unbroken by the appearance and disappearance of the Labour Government, and took in 1933 a new definition in a series of decisions on the proper method of combating Fascism, which were arrived at by the new leadership of the movement. These events have not been a series of unconnected and incomprehensible disasters. They have been the expression in British public life of something which happened between 1926 and 1933 all over Europe, indeed to some extent all over the world. During those years the great post-war wave of the working-class offensive against capitalism became exhausted, and the capitalists passed to the counter-attack. The working-

[1] *Report of the* 1930 *Labour Party Conference*, p. 192

class offensive had failed because its potentially irresistible forces had been frittered away in meaningless compromises; or rather in compromises which meant only one thing, namely, the consolidation of the shaken power of the capitalist class. Everywhere European Labour had been led by men like Tseretelli who, when the power of the State fell into their hands "like ripe fruit", handed it back in embarrassment to their traditional rulers.

In Britain power never left the hands of the capitalists. But in 1919 those hands visibly trembled. And here too the leaders of the working class drew back precisely because they saw that they were coming nearer and nearer to decisive success. This was probably a governing consideration, for example, in the mind of Robert Smillie, the leader of the British miners in the spring of 1919, when a decision to strike would almost certainly have resulted in extremely important gains to the Labour movement, such as the nationalisation of the mines on terms favourable to the miners. Mr. Smillie, as everyone knows, but as most people have forgotten, was induced to accept the written pledge of the Government that it would accept and put into operation the report of the Sankey Commission, whatever that report might be.[1] The Sankey Commission reported in favour of nationalisation, and the Government refused to carry out its report.

This was the type of all the transactions which took place between both the British and the European working classes and their respective rulers in the hour of the workers'

---

[1] The Government's pledge was as follows:

> "11 Downing Street,
> "Whitehall, S.W.
> "21st March, 1919.

"DEAR SIR,

"Speaking in the House of Commons last night I made a statement in regard to the Government's policy in connection with the Report of the Coal Industry Commission. I have pleasure in confirming, as I understand you wish me to do, my statement that the Government are prepared to carry out in the spirit and in the letter the recommendation of Sir John Sankey's Report.

> "Yours faithfully,
> "A. BONAR LAW."

strength. Everywhere the workers' leaders abstained from using the workers' strength, in return for promises which, the moment the danger point was passed, the ruling capitalists wholly repudiated. How are we to account for this extraordinary fact? Amongst the British workers particularly there was undoubtedly an element of simple-minded trust in the fairness of the capitalists. There was not then, and is not even now, a realisation amongst the British workers that, when substantial class interests are at stake, the question of keeping or breaking a promise will never receive the slightest consideration from a ruling class. But I do not think that the British leaders were primarily influenced by any hope that the various promises which they were given would have real fruits. Mr. Smillie said afterwards that he called off the miners from strike action in the spring of 1919 chiefly because of threats to use military force on the part of the Government: "If there is a strike they will use soldiers. My people will be shot down. Anything rather than that!" No doubt such threats were used (they were very likely empty threats, as the troops were unreliable in 1919). And no doubt they had an effect.

But it is said that at a final and decisive private interview between the Prime Minister (Mr. Lloyd George) and the men's leaders a different argument was used. Mr. Lloyd George, to the astonishment of the Labour leaders present, admitted the extreme weakness of the Government's position and the extreme strength of the workers'. "You have only," he is said to have told them, "to go ahead in order to force the Government's hand. But if you do so I and my colleagues are fully determined to resign. *We shall leave the responsibility for governing the country on you.* Good afternoon, gentlemen." It is reported that in face of this threat to impose power upon them the Labour leaders drew back appalled.

Whether or not this exact interview took place is uncertain. But what is certain is that it was this prospect—*the prospect of success*—which above all terrified the British and the

European Labour leaders in the immediately post-war years. As far back as 1905 Lenin had put to the leaders of the Russian Labour movement the piercing question: "Dare we win?"[1] For he found that a section of his party was already coming to the conclusion that "just at the moment" victory would be "inadvisable". All through the nineteen-twenties the leaders of British Labour did not dare to win. The leaders of European Labour, even when they had won, hastened to disembarrass themselves of victory. How else then could such a period end than in the exhaustion of the workers' offensive, and the passing of the initiative to the capitalists?

In Britain, at any rate, the movement's period of greatest opportunity was wasted above all because neither the leaders nor the rank and file had any adequate social theory to put in the place of capitalist ideology. The ideology of British Socialism, with its false inevitabilities, could not have been more perfectly designed to prevent the leaders of the working class from taking hold of the victories which lay within their grasp in the nineteen-twenties. Nothing was then lacking to the organised British workers except knowledge, and the will, faith, self-confidence and power which knowledge alone can give. For it is not so much conscience as ignorance that makes cowards of us. If we have only the haziest idea of what we are fighting for and why we have to fight, we are not likely to fight very well. Only men who have a firm grasp of a social science which shows them what is their place in the gigantic birth struggles of the new society; which enables them to understand both the necessity of struggle and the certainty of victory, can or will lead a working class along the long, rocky, and steep road to Socialism.

In the nineteen-twenties the workers' leaders flinched from struggle. But struggle was not to be avoided. Their

---

[1] "Two Tactics of Social-Democracy," *Selected Works*, Vol. III, p. 117. Curiously enough he was quoting Kautsky, who had put this question in his controversy with Bernstein in the nineties. In the nineties, on paper, and with no immediate possibility of victory before him, Kautsky answered Yes. In nineteen-nineteen, with victory actually in his hands, Kautsky, in deeds as well as words, answered No.

refusal to engage the enemy when the preponderance of strength was on their side has merely meant that the enemy has engaged them, now that the preponderance of strength has been reversed. Again it has been in Europe that this reversal of fortunes has been most pronounced. In Germany and Austria the pendulum has swung from the complete power of the workers in 1919 to the complete power of the capitalists in 1937.[1] In Britain the swing has been much more narrow. The Labour movement was never in power and to-day it is not destroyed. But the same swing has occurred. After being, from the end of the war to 1926–33 (the years between 1926 and 1933 were a sort of broad watershed), on the offensive, British Labour has been on the defensive for the past four years. In Britain also the power of capital (although absolutely it has continued to decline) has increased relatively to the power of the workers. This is the catastrophic harvest of British Socialism, and of the Labour Governments which were its most typical expression. The net result of twelve years of the domination of the movement by the representatives of this ideology has been to turn a triumphant forward march into a desperate defensive struggle.

The object of this book is not to repine over this reversal of fortune. "The political importance of sighing is nil," said Lenin.[2] The sole object of analysing the present predicament of the movement is to devise the proper measures to get out of it. Nor is there any need to repine if a Labour movement is thrown upon the defensive. For in modern political struggles, as in modern warfare, the defensive has many important advantages. A successful defence, by shattering the oncoming waves of the enemy, is the sure key to renewed advance. A successful defence may often,

[1] It is often to-day forgotten that for several months after the Armistice the German working class actually had the power of the State in their hands. We have, however, Kautsky's own admission that this was so. In his book, *The Proletarian Revolution*, he wrote:

"In November, 1918, the revolution was the work of proletarian elements alone. The proletariat was so all-powerful a position that the bourgeois elements, to begin with, did not dare to attempt any resistance."

[2] *Selected Works*, Vol. IV, p. 47.

and will to-day, prove the decisive engagement of the campaign, after which the road to complete victory is straight and open. But in order to make use of the advantages of the defensive we must clearly realise what kind of struggle we are waging; we must clearly realise that we *are* on the defensive, what we are defending, and why.

What then is the present position of the British Labour movement? So far we have only considered the reasons which drove it on to the defensive. But why, it may be asked, if Labour no longer challenges their position, do the capitalists need to counter-attack? They counter-attack because the state of capitalism has become so bad that it cannot tolerate the existence of even those gains which the working class has made in the last half century. The capitalists can tolerate indefinitely neither the standard of life, appreciably above subsistence, which particular sections of the British workers have won, nor the workers' liberty to organise politically, industrially and co-operatively for the further improvement of that standard. Our rulers instinctively feel, even if they do not think out the matter fully, that capitalism is now too unstable a system for it to be possible to tolerate indefinitely the existence of considerable organised forces which are even potentially hostile to it. For however much a Trade Union and Labour movement, under a particular leadership, may appear to be reconciled to capitalism, the capitalists are always aware that it may at any time be driven to threaten some basic support of their system.

It was a bitter irony of history that at the very moment when British Socialism had scored what seemed to be its greatest success, when 294 Labour members had been elected to Parliament and had formed the second Labour Government, capitalism all over the world suddenly revealed its extreme instability. The 1929 crisis blew to bits British Socialism's first inevitability, that of a long period of stable economic and social development during which the Labour movement could gradually modify the capitalist system. Within a year of the formation of the

1929 Labour Government it had become clear that a very condition for the existence of capitalism in the nineteen-thirties would be a sustained attack upon the standards and rights of the rest of the population. By the end of 1930, at the latest, it had become clear that a profound economic crisis existed which could only be solved either by imposing severe sacrifices upon the workers, or by trenching deeply on long-established expectations and property claims of the capitalists.

Now the possibility of the Labour movement making a resolute bid for the power necessary to solve the crisis at the expense of the capitalists, with the severe struggle that this would have involved, was ruled out of account, not only by Mr. MacDonald, but by every one of his colleagues also. Accordingly, only one question remained: Who should impose upon the workers the cuts necessary to the restoration (if possible) of the normal functioning of capitalism? Was it to be their own leaders, or a replaced capitalist government? Would the Labour leaders begin imposing the cuts themselves, or would they prefer to lay down the considerable measure of power which they had in their hands and hand the job over to the ordinary capitalist politicians? In the event the Labour ministers began the process; but, as it soon became obvious that they could not carry it through, they were bundled out of office and a powerful coalition of the consolidated forces of British capital was installed.

To-day we can see that the process of attempting to solve the crisis at the expense of the workers is a world-wide and ever-continuing one. It may be temporarily interrupted in the more secure capitalisms, such as Britain and America, during the upward phases of the trade cycle. But, on the whole, world capitalism, and especially, of course, the crippled, distorted capitalisms of Europe, can now only live by depressing the standards, rights and liberties of the wage-earners. *And this is precisely why the carrying through to success of a defence of those standards, rights and liberties has become the essential task of the Labour movements.* The private ownership of the means of production has now become, in the long run, incompatible with the most elementary interests of the mass of the population. Capitalism is everywhere becoming incompatible with political democracy (as not only the Marxists but Mr. and Mrs. Webb themselves foresaw that it would); with the maintenance of any standard of life above bare subsistence amongst the wage-workers; and finally with peace. Hence a successful defence of peace, democracy and the national standard of life will make the continued existence of capitalism impossible.

This is the primary political proposition of our day. He who has not grasped it has understood nothing of the present tasks and possibilities before the Labour movements of the world. To return to the military analogy, it is as if peace, democracy and the national standard of life were three vital bridgeheads which in Western Europe and America are held by the working class and its allies. If the capitalist forces capture these bridgeheads, as in Central Europe they have done, they open a way to a continuance, albeit for a brief period, and at the expense of devastating the world with Fascism and war, of the private ownership of the means of production. If, on the other hand, they fail to capture these three bridgeheads, then they are penned into a narrow territory on which they cannot live. Naturally the aim of every single member of the working-class movements who understands the situation is to mass the very maximum force possible for the defence of these vital points. For peace, democracy and the national standard of life are not only infinitely worth defending on their own account, but their successful defence is also a decisive factor in the struggle to abolish the private ownership of the means of production. In Britain and America, it is clearly possible to mass enormous forces for the defence of these three elementary interests of at least 90 per cent of the population. Many millions of the citizens of Britain and America, who have not discovered that it is, in the last analysis, the private ownership of the means of production which is causing the attack upon peace, democracy and the national standard of life, will none-the-less defend these things for their own sakes, and against whoever attacks them.

The concluding chapters of this book discuss in detail what should be the relationship between the conscious Socialists and the less fully conscious forces in the common defence of peace, democracy and the national standard of life. Here it is only necessary to emphasise, and then re-emphasise, that the massing of every available asset and ally for the defence to the last of these three strong points against the Capitalist-Fascist attack is the one thing needful for the Labour movements of the West to-day.

But this was not the policy of the leadership of the British Labour movement between 1933 and 1937. Our leaders found an alternative policy to follow in the new situations, and one which, it must be admitted, was a logical successor to the policy of the movement in the nineteen-twenties. This alternative policy was based, whether consciously or unconsciously, on the following argument. It was agreed that capitalism would no longer tolerate the existence of democratic institutions in general, or of the Labour movement in particular, so easily as before. In fact it could not be denied that Central European capitalism could not tolerate these institutions at all and had turned to Fascism as a means of destroying the power, become intolerable to it, of the wage-workers to interfere, by attempting to protect their interests, with the working for profit of privately owned means of production.

Now, if in this situation you have no faith in the capacity of the working-class movement actually to end the private ownership of the means of production, it is quite true that there is only one hope of preserving that movement, and with it, some elements of political democracy. And that is so to guide the Labour movement as to prevent it from interfering appreciably with the workings of capitalism; to make it accommodate itself on every essential point, to the needs of capitalism, even if those needs involve the gradual debasement of the national standard of life, the emasculation of democracy, and the toleration of war. For then, it is hoped, the capitalists will never need to turn to Fascism as the agent of the destruction of any organised opposition to their will. In a word, if a Labour movement adopts a consistent policy of accommodation, on essentials, to the present needs of capitalism, it will prevent the appearance of Fascism, by making it unnecessary.

It is the argument of the remainder of this chapter that this is the policy which was adopted, or perhaps rather drifted into, by the National Council of Labour. In one sense this policy was the application of British or Fabian Socialism to the situation of capitalist counter-attack. Just as during the twenties, when the workers were advancing, the adherents of British Socialism sought to get Socialism by persuading the capitalists of its desirability, so in the thirties they hoped to preserve peace, democracy and the national standard of life by persuading the capitalists that all these things were perfectly harmless to the continued existence of capitalism. In each case the overmastering impulse was to avoid a conflict at all costs. But unfortunately the second endeavour was as hopeless as the first. Peace, democracy and a national standard of life above the subsistence level are not, and cannot be made, harmless to present-day capitalism. On the contrary, they are deadly poison to it; if we try to make them compatible with capitalism, we destroy them and the Labour movement which sustains them. For present-day capitalism demands a subsistence standard of life for the wage-workers, an autocracy by which it can crush any attempt to improve this standard, and recurrent world wars for the partition and re-partition of the world, as indispensable conditions of its existence.

The policy adopted after 1931 by the leaders of the Labour movement became, however, something more than an application of its old ideology to new conditions. It became, in effect, and whether this was denied or not, and whether the denials were sincere or not, an abandonment of any kind of Socialism. It became a retreat from the third to the second stage in the development of a Labour movement. The British movement, in a word, was being led back to Trade Union politics—to the conception that it was quite sufficient for the Trade Unions to maintain a political party of their own without that party having any distinctive political philosophy. The logic of the attempt to make the Labour movement so harmless that the capitalists would never need to crush it, led back further still. It led towards the first stage of the development of a Labour movement, to the disbandment of the present Labour Party and the support of now this and now that capitalist party by the Trade Unions.

The leadership of the British Labour movement did not adopt the policy of accommodation, on all essential points, to the needs of a declining capitalism all at once, or without several intermediate stages. The attempt to accommodate the policy of the British Labour movement to capitalism began over ten years ago and it began in the industrial field. If we wish to date its starting-point precisely, we may take the presidential address of the Trade Union Congress of 1927, delivered by Mr. George Hicks. Mr. Hicks, who up till the time of the General Strike of the previous year, had been the outstanding "Leftwinger" of the General Council, began by telling his audience that far from British Trade Unionism being played out it was just about to enter "its constructive period". In the following sentences he implied rather than described what this constructive period was to be. It was to consist of certain discussions with the employers. And the great advantage of these discussions was that they "would bring both sides face to face with the hard realities of the present economic situation".[1]

Nobody seems to have taken any particular notice of this passage in Mr. Hicks' speech at the time. Yet it was

[1] Report of the Trade Union Congress for 1927, p. 67.

one of the most significant announcements which have ever been made to British Trade Unionists. It was quoted and requoted by the spokesmen of the General Council when in the following year they were defending the policy for which Mr. Hicks' apparently careless sentences had been the preparation. In fact those sentences contained the germ of that whole policy of conformity to the new needs of capitalism which, in various forms, was to dominate the movement for the next decade. For what were those "hard realities of the present economic situation" with which conferences with the employers were to bring the movement "face to face"? The "present economic situation" was the economic situation of British capitalism. And the "hard realities" were that this situation was a declining one. Hence the real meaning of Hicks' words was that conferences with the employers would bring the workers to a realisation that all their demands for improvements were, in an epoch of declining capitalism, quite Utopian; that the only real prospect before them was one of successively abandoning the concessions which they had won in the past, but which British capitalism could no longer afford to allow them to enjoy.

Events were soon enough to prove that that was what Hicks and the General Council meant. But, of course, the delegates to the Trade Union Congress did not, and were not intended to, understand all that. Indeed, the essential tragedy of the British Labour movement was (and is) that the mass of delegates to both the Trade Union Congress and the annual conferences of the Labour Party, have in the past twelve years understood neither the new position which faced them, nor the policy by which their leaders were reacting to it. They have understood neither that they had entered a period of decline in the fortunes of British capitalism, and of counter-offensive on the part of the capitalists, nor that their leaders were proposing to meet that situation by quietly yielding on all really essential points, in order that, at all costs, a conflict which might drive the capitalists to extremes, might be avoided. For the greater part of the delegates to these two great annual conferences, which control the destinies of the British Labour movement, have lacked the analytic power to estimate the general trend of events and policies. They have lacked this analytic power, not because they have lacked intelligence; on the contrary, they have consisted of men and women of great shrewdness, experience and good sense; but because they have never been equipped with the body of knowledge and social theory which can alone make modern political life comprehensible. They have been almost helpless, therefore, in the hands of leaders who could and did take them along courses which, if they had realised whither they were going, they would not have followed.

In 1927, 1928 and 1929, there took place that series of conferences between the Trade Union Congress and an unofficial group of employers headed by Sir Alfred Mond (later, and consequently, to become Lord Melchett), which are known as the Mond-Turner Conferences. Mr. Ben Turner (later and consequently to become Sir Benjamin Turner) was the next year's President of the T.U.C. in succession to Mr. Hicks. The conferences themselves were wholly abortive; they petered out into endless sub-committees set up to examine pretentious and meaningless schemes for "reforming the Gold Standard" or "humanising rationalisation", or what you will. But the fact that these conferences were held; that conference with the employers was the method by which the leadership of the Trade Union movement proposed to rally the movement after the defeat of 1926, was all-important. The effect upon the Trade Union movement of the inauguration of the Mond-Turner Conferences was disastrous. The annual report of the 1928 conference tells us that the Congress had been the best, *and, it immediately adds, the smallest*, on record.[1] This was a new note, which could not have been struck before 1926.

These conferences were the first sign that the members

[1] Report of the Trade Union Congress for 1928

of the General Council had begun to doubt the possibility
of any further advance by the organised British workers.
They were a profound symptom of weakness, and were so
interpreted by both the workers and the employers. The
members of the General Council claimed that the conferences represented a first step towards the fulfilment of
the Unions' old claim to a voice in the control of industry.
But Sir Alfred Mond and his colleagues knew better than
that: they knew that the conferences represented, on the
contrary, a first step in the employers' new claim for a
voice in the control of the Unions. For the conferences
were not something which had been wrung from the
employers by the strength of the Unions; they were something, proposed by the employers, to which the Unions,
in the moment of their maximum weakness, had acceded.
The intention and effect of the conferences was to attempt
to make the Unions face up to the "hard realities" of
capitalism in decline.

But only a tiny minority of the members of Congress
realised what was happening. The delegates still believed
that they were living in an epoch of ascending capitalist
development, in which concessions might possibly be won
(instead of made) by sitting with the employers round the
conference table. The long list of proposals for the reform
of industry which the Mond-Turner Conferences were to
discuss, with its implications of all sorts of substantial
concessions to the workers, seemed to them quite capable
of fulfilment. Here, many of them felt, appears to be a
way, discovered by our General Council, by which real
progress can be made, and all without any necessity for
struggle. One voice was, however, heard in the Congress
to throw doubts upon this attractive prospect. One delegate
put forward the extraordinary and unwelcome view that
the real prospect for the coming years would not be the
winning "by scientific negotiations" of all sorts of concessions from a prosperous, and so benevolent, capitalism,
but hard and bitter battles to retain even what they had
got, against the ceaseless attacks of a capitalism made

desperate by its own misfortunes. This was the delegate of the Boilermakers, Mr. Harry Pollitt, who said:

"They believed they would find during the next three or four years that the whole strength of both sides of the movement would not be expended in getting better conditions for the masses, but would be expended in defending the miserable conditions which at present existed."[1]

There were members of the General Council who, as we have seen, had shaped their whole policy to meet, though by concessions instead of by defence, just such a prospect. But few, if any, of the delegates had any thought that so stern a period awaited them. If they had realised, if it had been possible to make them realise, that this was the real situation which, by one policy or another, they had to face, a majority of them would certainly have rallied to the policy of defence and resistance, and repudiated the policy of accommodation and retreat. But they were not equipped to perceive the general situation of British capitalism. Hence they allowed the General Council, the leading members of which did to some extent see the situation, to foist on them the policy of making concessions to capitalism, under cover of adopting a policy of obtaining, by negotiations, concessions from capitalism.

In 1928 when the Mond-Turner Conferences were being debated at the Trade Union Congress, the partial stabilisation of capitalism, which lasted through the twenties, had another year to run before the crash came. Though the strength of the Labour movement was visibly being dissipated, capitalism had not yet passed to decisive counter-attack. Indeed the political side of the movement continued to grow. The general election of 1929 recorded the high-water mark of the Labour Party. The movement as a whole was unaware, before the outbreak of the slump, that any storm impended, and even long after the storm

---

[1] It is significant that this delegate, who in 1928 showed sufficient insight to foresee the conditions of the next decade, was soon afterwards excluded, because of his political opinions, from taking part in the deliberations of the Trade Union movement of which he had been, and is, a life-long member.

had come, it failed to realise what was happening. The report of the 1929 Labour Party Conference is a document of extreme complacency. Mr. Herbert Morrison, its chairman, told his audience that "the conference to-day meets in high spirits; the party and the Labour Government are doing well. Success is not spoiling us". The report speaks of "the thirty wonderful years". The increase in the Labour vote had wiped out all consciousness that only three years before their leaders had allowed the power of the Trade Unions to be temporarily broken, and were steadily preventing revival by the Mond-Turner Conferences. The oldest of all lessons, that the essential, basic instrument of working-class strength is the Trade Unions, had been forgotten. The Labour Ministers, secure in the first inevitability; persuaded that British capitalism would tranquilly develop whilst they slowly transformed it, were sailing out on their fair weather voyage. The 1929 Labour Party Conference was held just a month before the beginning of the slump, and just two years before the Labour Government was routed at the 1931 elections and the Parliamentary Labour Party was reduced from nearly 300 to just over 50 members. It was not success which spoiled the British Labour Party.

The 1930 Labour Party Conference afforded a still more remarkable example of the inability of the movement to understand what was happening to it. The slump had been steadily deepening for almost a year. Already the whole reform programme of the Labour Government had been paralysed. Already it was becoming clear that the next step which any Government which intended to keep British capitalism in working order would have to take would be to begin revoking reforms already granted. The whole structure of assumptions on which British Socialism had been based was crashing to the ground. Nothing of all this was apparent to the leadership of the movement, however. The 1930 report is a document of unshaken complacency. The chairman of the 1930 Conference was, it so happened, Miss Susan Lawrence, a life-long Fabian.

Nothing could have been more revealing than her address. The whole world was reeling and crashing about her ears. Every day events posed more urgently the question: What is to be done? Shall the Labour movement, which forms the Executive Government of the country, which faces a great opportunity as well as a great crisis, show by its initiative, its willingness to take power and responsibility, its ability to clear opposition from its path, that the working-class movement can lead society out of the crisis? Or shall Labour show its impotence? In that case the only remaining way out will be the capitalist way out—the traditional way out, of restoring the profitability of capitalist production at the expense of the rest of the population. Unless they can be shown both an alternative, and also an organised party capable of leading them to that alternative, the people will support the capitalists in applying their solution, even though it involves heavy "cuts" in working-class standards : for men will always prefer even capitalist leadership to no leadership at all.

Faced with this crisis, Miss Lawrence did not lose her head, or get into a panic, or advocate retreat. On the contrary, she simply ignored the whole situation. The Fabian doctrines which she had learned had taught her that catastrophic crises do not occur. Social development invariably takes place in a decent and evolutionary manner. Hence no sensible or well-instructed person could suppose that anything really disturbing or unusual had occurred. Miss Lawrence simply cut the world crisis. But the storm raged inconsiderately on, and in a year had blown Miss Lawrence and her Government out of office, and, for most of its members, out of Parliament. The British Labour movement had been reduced, at the beginning of a key period of world history, to an impotence which it had not known for twenty years, and from which it has still only half recovered.

It cannot be said, however, that either the new leadership, which succeeded the absconding MacDonaldites, or the mass of the movement learnt any important lessons from the rise and fall of the second Labour Government. The rank and file as a whole stood bewildered and depressed as by an incomprehensible natural disaster. Or they put down the whole *débâcle* to the treachery of Mr. MacDonald, Mr. Thomas and Mr. Snowden. But this was to blame the sinking of the ship on the rats that leave her. The three ablest leaders of the British Labour movement only deserted because they had noticed that the whole ideology and policy of that movement had become bankrupt. Unlike Miss Lawrence and the other slower-witted, if more honest, members of the movement, the three absconding leaders had noticed the world crisis. They had realised that capitalism had entered a period of decline, and they had concluded that the future of such a Labour movement as they had built up, must, in the new period, be one of continued retreat, surrender, frustration and humiliation. So they joined the National Government. But the enormous majority of the members of the movement had no equipment to enable them to see anything more in what had happened than "the stabbing in the back" of the movement by three unscrupulous men. For there was little or nothing in British Socialism, still less in the diluted version of that ideology which had penetrated to most members of the movement, to teach men to look at the development of the economic and social situation as the final determinant of events.

The new men who succeeded to the vacant leadership of the movement did not adopt the policy of accommodation to capitalism primarily as a result of the fall of the Labour Government—though that event played its part. As we have seen, the General Council of the Trade Union Congress had already, with the Mond-Turner Conferences, begun to follow this policy as a reaction to the largely self-inflicted defeat of the General Strike. But neither the industrial nor the political leaders finally fixed the new line of policy till the year 1933. And they fixed it much more as a reaction to the coming to power of Fascism in Germany than as a reaction to the fall of the Labour

Government. Nineteen thirty-three was the year in which the policy of accommodation to capitalism was adopted by the British Labour movement. The whole period from 1926 to 1933 was taken up with the process of discarding British Socialism. That ideology had been built upon the premises of the permanent upward development of capitalism; upon a consequent lessening of the intensity of the class struggle; and upon an almost imperceptible building up of a Socialist economy within the shell of capitalism, accompanied by an equally imperceptible transference of political power from the capitalist to the working class. Every one of these premises had proved false. It had turned out that the course of capitalist development had turned downwards; that the class struggle was being enormously intensified; that not a step towards Socialist construction could be taken without the workers and their political allies first achieving predominant political power. British Socialism as an ideology was wholly bankrupt. Lip service was still paid to its principles by the leaders of the British Labour movement generally but many of them no longer believed in it.[1] The next chapter is devoted to a discussion of the policy, it is hardly comprehensive enough to call it an ideology, which they put in its place.

[1] This is, in my view, certainly true of many of the leaders of the Trade Union movement, but it is not, I think, true of Mr. Attlee, the leader of the Labour Party, who evidently still believes sincerely in the whole ideology of British Socialism. He still, it is evident, believes that we live in a period of upward social development, in which class antagonisms are being diminished, and opposition to Socialism is disappearing. Thus in his book, *The Labour Party in Perspective*, he writes:

"There is not to-day, as there was when I first entered the movement, a widespread and active opposition to the practical proposals which Socialism puts forward" (p. 280).

That it should have been possible, in 1937, at the height of the world-wide Fascist counter-offensive, in the period of the British National Government, for the leader of the British Labour movement to write this sentence may well become a classic instance for some future historian of the power of the human mind to believe what it desires to believe.

CHAPTER X

RESISTANCE OR ACCOMMODATION

THE PRECEDING CHAPTER defined briefly the policy which the British Labour movement adopted for meeting the admitted dangers of Fascism and the counter-offensive of capitalism in general. In one sentence, that policy has been an attempt to make the movement so to conform, on all really essential matters, to the requirements of capitalism, that a conflict which might provoke the British capitalists to attempt to destroy the movement would be avoided. This policy was adopted by the leadership of the movement as an alternative to a united defence of democracy, peace and the national standard of life.

It will be seen that the two policies are diametrically opposed. The policy of accommodation seeks to avoid conflict by allowing, with but mild protests, this or that worsening of the national standard of life, the impairment of this or that traditional liberty, or this or that principle of pacific foreign policy. As each concession is made, it is suggested that capitalism, thus appeased, will forbear to make any further demands; that the existing balance of power within British Society (in which the working class retains some ability to protect itself, since the Labour movement is undestroyed) can be indefinitely maintained. A first necessity for carrying through such a policy is to hold back the working-class movement from any over-vigorous activity; to prevent, for example, the appearance of formidable demonstrations against the imposition of cuts in unemployment relief, to induce the Trade Unions to accept the lowering of wages during the down-swing of the trade cycle, when prices are falling, and to refrain from strike action in the face of rising prices, during the up-swing of the cycle. Such a policy will almost inevitably divide a Labour movement. For many workers will not understand the strategy by which their leaders appear to be avoiding battle by voluntarily giving up the prize. They will protest and will attempt themselves to give a lead for the opposite policy of united resistance to all encroachments.

The policy of united resistance will, on the other hand, involve, for example, the mobilisation of the maximum possible demonstrations of resistance to cuts in unemployment benefit; it will actively encourage the Trade Unions to refuse demands for lowering wages; it will encourage them to demand increases, especially during periods of rising prices. It will demand the preservation of peace by genuine adherence to a system of collective security, even though the price of peace may be a united resistance which finally destroys one or other of the Fascist empires. Such a policy will, naturally, have an exactly opposite effect upon the Labour movement. It will unite where the other will divide; it will strengthen and increase where the other will weaken and shrivel. Moreover, it will bring allies to the Labour movement from sections of the population outside it who wish to defend peace, democracy and the national standard of life. For these things are manifestly precious in themselves and men will rally to their defence who do not agree that their preservation is now incompatible with the preservation of capitalism. Such men will defend these social treasures passionately, if blindly, and without regard to the effect of this defence upon capitalism.

Hence the policy of resistance will unite, bring allies to, and thus enormously strengthen the Labour movement. It is true that in so doing it cannot claim that it will avoid a conflict with the forces of capitalism. On the contrary, it definitely abandons the hope of making the Labour movement so innocuous that the capitalists will not trouble to destroy it. It plants the Labour movement, as the unyielding champion of peace, democracy and the national standard of life, square across the path to reaction which contemporary capitalism must travel. But in so doing, it

Fᴅ

gives the workers the assurance of winning the struggle which must result. Nor is it the policy of united resistance which makes social conflict inevitable. The opposite policy of accommodation to capitalism itself leads to the same conflict. The difference between them is that whereas the policy of united resistance leads to conflict on the most favourable ground possible, with the Labour movement at its maximum strength, the policy of accommodation leads to conflict on the most unfavourable ground, with the Labour movement discredited and disheartened. In a word, both policies lead to conflict; but the one leads to victory and the other to defeat.

The question of how the contemporary social conflict, which is going on all the time, can be prevented in Britain from degenerating into an armed conflict (and this must be an objective of all reasonable men and women) is an entirely different question from that of whether a struggle, however conducted, can be avoided to-day by the Labour movement failing to resist the encroachments of capital. Suffice it here to say that the present mobilisation of the maximum forces to resist by political and Trade Unions means the encroachments of Capital, is indispensable to the hope of being able to prevent armed conflict in the future.

It will be seen that the choice between resistance and accommodation to capitalism is at the same time a choice between a united and a divided Labour movement. In Britain during the last five years the question has been to a predominant extent discussed in terms of the question of the unity of the movement, very often without adequate realisation of the profound issue of policy which is inextricably intertwined with the question of unity. For the advocates of resistance have put forward the view that the first step to such resistance must be to reunite the Labour movements which, all over Europe were, in 1933, divided into Communist and Social Democratic, or Labour, parties. They have pointed to the frightful fate of the divided German Labour movement, which succumbed, without a struggle, to the onslaught of Fascism. In Britain they have asked the members of the General Council of the Trade Union Congress and the leaders of the Labour Party how they proposed to deal with the capitalist counter-offensive in general, and with Fascism in particular, if not by uniting the Labour movement in the defence of the elementary interests and liberties of the whole non-capitalist population. In 1933 they got their answer. In documents submitted to the Trade Union Congress and the Labour Party Conference, and in the speeches which introduced them, the leaders of our movements laid down the basis of their alternative policy of accommodation. This clearly was not a policy which it was particularly easy to get any Labour movement to accept. It could hardly be presented naked and as it was. It is instructive to observe exactly how the movement was persuaded, as it was, to adopt it.

In essentials the job was done at the 1933 Trade Union Congress. Sir Walter Citrine there introduced a document entitled *Dictatorships and the Trade Union Movement*. In this document, and in Sir Walter Citrine's speech, the new policy of the movement was put over. Both the memorandum and the speech prove that the charge, which is sometimes made, that our leaders had not realised the magnitude of the Fascist challenge is unfounded.

"They had to combat Fascism before it got to power," said Sir Walter Citrine. "They could not wait until it grew. They could not turn away their faces and say this was some inconsiderable thing of which they need take no notice, and something which would find a natural death. They had to expose Fascism and show how inimical it was to everything based on humanity. They had to show that it meant not only slavery of the intellect, but ultimately slavery of the working-class people of this country."

Our leaders (as every responsible critic has always acknowledged) were profoundly affected by the physical destruction of the German working-class movement. They were, rightly, far more impressed by this great and terrible event than by the collapse of the Labour Government in

Britain. They reacted strongly—but in their own way. They reacted by persuading, and if need be coercing, the British Labour movement down the path of accommodation.

Now in order to do this Sir Walter Citrine and his colleagues had to persuade the British Labour movement that the issue which confronted the movement was one of Dictatorship or Democracy, and not one of the rule of the capitalist class or the rule of the working class. Both the *Dictatorship and the Trade Union Movement* memorandum, and the manifesto which had been issued earlier in the year by the National Council of Labour, entitled *Democracy versus Dictatorship*, are devoted, from the first words of their titles to the last word of their texts, to this supreme purpose.

The *Dictatorship and the Trade Union Movement* memorandum tells us that we "must oppose equally all dictatorships whether of the Right or of the Left".[1] "It had been thought by some of the best people that they could give currency to the idea of dictatorship, provided it was a dictatorship of their friends, without weakening the forces of democracy. There was no such half-way house. Every support given to the institution of a dictatorship of whatever kind, weakened the fibre of their own people, and their belief in institutions to which they had subscribed," said Sir Walter Citrine in introducing the memorandum,[2] "The real point about the Manifesto," said Mr. Herbert Morrison in defending the *Democracy versus Dictatorship* manifesto at the 1933 Labour Party Conference, "is that we condemn dictatorship as such, whether that dictatorship is a dictatorship of the Left or of the Right, and the Conference must face up to that issue".[3]

Undoubtedly this is a root issue which every reader of this book must decide for him or herself. Does he or she really consider that the rule, or dictatorship, of "the Left" is as pernicious a thing as the rule, or dictatorship, of "the Right?" In seeking to answer this question we must,

[1] T.U.C. Report, 1933, p. 433.
[2] Ibid., p. 324.
[3] Report of the 1933 Labour Party Conference, p. 219

surely, first enquire what the words "Left" and "Right" mean in the political connection in which they are used in these documents and speeches. Now there can be no doubt that what is implied by a dictatorship of the Right, is a dictatorship of the capitalist class; and that what is implied by a dictatorship of the Left is a dictatorship of the working class. Hence we find that the main assertion of these documents is that the British Labour movement must be equally opposed to a dictatorship of the working class as to a dictatorship of the capitalist class. This is certainly a remarkable conclusion. For, after all, a dictatorship, however undesirable or pernicious a thing we may think it to be, is undoubtedly but one form of rule. Therefore, what our leaders are telling us is that the working-class movement must be as much opposed to one form of working-class rule as to this same form of capitalist class rule; that all that matters is the form of rule; that the question of which class exercises the rule is a matter of indifference.

The assertion of this principle is immediately followed, in all the documents and speeches which we are discussing, by the demand that the movement must have nothing to do with the Communists; for the Communists stand for a form of dictatorship to which the movement is no less opposed than it is to Fascism. For example, the Trade Union memorandum states that "there is some confusion of thought on these matters which has created a tolerant attitude to the dictatorship of the Left. This confusion of thought is reflected in the demands for a united front with the Communists against Fascism. . . . Such a demand, in effect, is asking those who believe in democracy to unite with those who believe in dictatorship to combat dictatorship".[1] Or again, Mr. Morrison at the 1932 Labour Party Conference said that "we should have been in a difficulty in fighting Fascist dictatorship by associating with the Communists, because they themselves believe in a form of dictatorship".[2]

[1] *Dictatorship and the Trade Union Movement*, T.U.C. Report, 1933, p. 432.
[2] Report of the 1932 Labour Party Conference, p. 219.

(On other occasions (though not as a matter of fact in the documents or speeches quoted above) leaders of the Labour Party have taken the line that what they mean when they talk about "a dictatorship of the Left", and declare that they oppose it every bit as strongly as they oppose a Fascist dictatorship, is not a dictatorship exercised by the working class, but a dictatorship exercised by a group or clique of wicked Communists over the whole of the rest of "the community". This attitude reveals so profound a misconception of the whole nature of contemporary human society that it is difficult to answer briefly. The truth is of course that the idea that particular groups of men and women can ever rule modern society except on behalf of, and in the interests of, one or other of the great classes is wholly false. For example, it is quite untrue, as is sometimes alleged, that the Fascists are simply a gang of criminals ruling Germany for their own benefit. They are a gang of criminals, but they are ruling Germany on behalf of, and in the interests of, the German capitalist and landowning class. Nor could the Nazis ever have got power, nor could they hold it for a month, if they ceased to represent the interests of this owning class.

In the same way the Communist Party of the Soviet Union rules on behalf of, and in the interests of, the Russian working class, and could never have got power, nor could hold it to-day, if it ceased to represent the Russian workers. We cannot forbear to apply to those who refuse to recognise these basic facts the words of the earliest political theorist of the British working class, Bronterre O'Brien, who wrote, nearly a century ago, of these who committed the error

"of imputing to individuals the glory and the guilt of those political acts and systems of Government, which are in reality the work of whole classes, and in the execution of which the individuals are but the chosen tools or instruments of these classes".)

In order to judge whether this theory is justified or not we may state briefly what is the Communist view on this basic question of democracy and dictatorship.[1] The Communist Party has always stood, and now stands, for the preservation and enlargement of every element of democracy (and it agrees that they are extremely important) which the working classes of certain capitalist societies, such as Britain and America, have won. In this respect it does not differ at all from the Labour or Socialist parties.[2] The difference—and it is a real difference—between the Communist and the Labour and Socialist parties arises upon the question of whether or not it will be possible to preserve, *for the capitalist class*, their existing democratic rights during the process of the transference of the means of production to public ownership and the subsequent organisation of Socialist production. Communists, let it be immediately agreed, believe that during this period of acute social crisis no working-class régime will be able to afford to allow those whose property in the means of production it is taking from them to organise resistance and opposition to the process.

Communists believe that owners of the means of production have always resisted their deposition with a passion so reckless, so hysterical, so ready to stick at nothing, that it is inconceivable that the process can be carried through without the imposition of definite restraints on the liberties of such classes. Those who would suffer such deposition are a tiny minority of the population of Britain and America. But they are an exceedingly powerful minority. For centuries they have monopolised not only the means of production but all the positions of political and military power in the country. Communists are convinced that to attempt to dispossess this class of its property and privileges, no matter how gradually or how rapidly, without making sure that the power to resist no longer remained in their hands, would be to invite the outbreak of a horrible civil war, such as now devastates Spain. They call the form of government which, they consider, can alone prevent the capitalist

[1] This subject is more adequately discussed on pp. 368–370.
[2] Lenin, for example, wrote that "only in the working class has democracy a champion without reservations, who does not waver, who does not look back". (*Selected Works*, Vol. I, p. 503.)

class from deluging their country in blood during the indispensable process of the abolition of capitalism and the organisation of Socialism, the dictatorship of the proletariat.

Once again, readers of this book must think over very carefully for themselves whether this view is true or not. They must consider for themselves the question of whether the British and American capitalists are likely to acquiesce in the loss of their money without attempting by any means, including if necessary desperate and bloody means, to overturn a Government, no matter how constitutionally elected, which is taking their money from them. Readers must decide whether or not they think it would be fair on the rest of the population for a Labour or progressive Government to allow the capitalists freedom to start a civil war in such circumstances. Communists are convinced that on the contrary such a Government would be criminally negligent if it did not take the steps necessary to make it impossible for the capitalists to strike at the rest of the population; and these steps undoubtedly amount to a dictatorship of the proletariat, or working class, and its allies.

Now the present leadership of the British Labour movement has laid it down that it cannot associate in any way with persons who take this view. Until we understand the reason for it this must surely seem very strange. For even if the Communists are wrong; even if they take a too pessimistic view of the possibilities of preserving normal democratic political conditions, even for the capitalists, and even during the acute phases of the transition to Socialism, there would seem, at first sight, no conceivable reason for refusing to associate with them in the immediately urgent task of protecting, not the capitalists' democratic rights at some time in the future, but our own acutely threatened democratic rights, here and now.

But the reason, in my view, is this. The refusal of the leaders of the Labour Party to allow of any joint action with the Communists whatsoever, and even for the defence of the most urgent working-class interests, *is designed to reassure the ruling class.* I believe that it is, whether or not the leaders of the movement realise it fully themselves, an urgent message sent from Transport House to the British ruling class. And the message reads:

The British Labour movement is not a threat to your vital interests. We do not desire more than to exercise a certain legitimate influence within the community. We do not desire to get such complete power into our hands as would even enable us to dispossess you. We will rigidly refuse to have anything to do with the Communists, because they do propose that the Labour movement should work for complete power. *So there is no need for you to destroy us. What we really want to do is to keep things very much as they are.*

What other reason than this can there have been for the above remarkable, and continually repeated, declaration that the British Labour movement is as strongly opposed to a dictatorship of the Left (i.e. of the working class) as to a dictatorship of the Right (i.e. of the capitalist class)?[1] How *could* a Labour movement really be as opposed to the rule, however exercised, of the working class—which must mean its own rule, since it is the instrument which the working class has organised,—as to the rule, whether through democratic or dictatorial institutions, of the capitalist class? Is it not clear that any such declaration on the part of a Labour movement can be nothing but a promise that the movement is no longer seeking power for itself; that it is no longer

---

[1] At the 1934 Trade Union Conference Sir Walter Citrine, in introducing a supplementary statement on Fascism, was at great pains to reiterate this declaration and, significantly, to call the attention of the capitalist Press to it. He said:

"I have observed in the Press during the last few days certain comments the purpose of which is to draw a peculiar significance from the fact tha this report deals with Fascism only. The assumption which writers have tried to draw from the fact that the report deals with Fascism only, is that in some way the Trade Union movement has receded from the position it took up and clarified last year. I think those of you who care to read the resolution will find in the last paragraph a very clear statement that the Trade Union movement is as much opposed to dictatorship from the Left as to dictatorship from the Right."

dangerous to the capitalists; that it is an innocuous sort of thing which nobody need worry to attack? Passionate and reiterated declarations that the Labour movement will never have anything to do with the Communists all have, in the last analysis, this meaning. The Labour leaders could not have described the Labour Party as "the spear-head of political power against Dictators, Fascist or Communist",[1] if their only objection to the Communists was that the Communists considered that in order to get Socialism it would be necessary to dictate to the capitalists. The real significance of these reiterated declarations was, and is, that the Communists do, undoubtedly, propose that the Labour movement should be willing and eager to take power, in order to lead society as a whole out of its otherwise insoluble crisis. For the leaders of the British Labour movement became convinced that it had become too dangerous even to try to get power; that to do so would provoke the capitalists to turn Fascist and destroy the Labour movement. Like the leaders of the nineteen-twenties, they felt a profound sense of weakness; a profound sense that it was quite impossible ever to challenge the power of the existing ruling class.[2]

In the following year (1934) Sir Walter Citrine went so far as to assure the capitalist world that not only would

---

[1] *Democracy versus Dictatorship*—the 1933 Manifesto of the Joint Council of the Labour Party and General Council of the Trade Union Congress.

[2] Mr. Attlee in his *Labour Party in Perspective* gives a somewhat different reason for the refusal of any common action with the Communists. For him the objection is that the Communists "think that the method of constitutional action is mistaken" (p. 134). This is a simple, straightforward, and I am sure, sincerely made, error of fact. As will be explained in Part III of this book Communists believe just as strongly as does Mr. Attlee in the need to elect a constitutional Labour or progressive Government. More generally they believe, and always have believed, in the absolute necessity of using to the very utmost every opportunity of constitutional action and of defending our constitutional rights to the last. The difference between them and Mr. Attlee is not as to whether *we* shall use constitutional action, but as to whether *the capitalists* will use constitutional action. I discuss this question more fully on p. 353. Mr. Attlee's error was no doubt perfectly sincere, for we must remember that he and his colleagues seldom or never read statements made by the Communist Party, taking their views of it almost exclusively from the capitalist Press. But it is sad that the official leader of the Labour Party should not take the trouble to inform himself on such an elementary point before making a considered statement in book form.

he have nothing to do with Communism, but that Communism everywhere, and in particular in Britain, had virtually ceased to exist.

"Communism has ceased to be, in almost every land, a serious menace to the Labour movement. Those of us who, some years ago, saw the implications of Communist philosophy, if one might say so rather in advance of some of our critics, realised that once the Labour movement's eyes were open to these implications, Communism in Great Britain, at least, would cease to be of any moment, and we have now arrived at that stage."

It was unfortunate for Sir Walter Citrine that those complacent sentences should have been uttered a few years before the Communist parties of Western Europe made incomparably their greatest advances. Since then the French Communist Party has grown in a single year from 34,000 to 300,000 members and the Spanish party has grown comparably, in the conditions of civil war. There and elsewhere the Communist parties have slowly but unmistakably emerged as the most persistent, tireless and indomitable units in the common struggle against the Fascist attack. In Britain also, almost from the moment when Sir Walter Citrine spoke, the Communist Party has made enough progress, at any rate, for the National Council of Labour to spend a high proportion of its time dealing with what in 1934 it denied was a question of "any moment". But again Sir Walter Citrine did not in 1934 really suppose that Communism had ceased to exist. What he was doing was to try and persuade the listening world of capitalism that the British Labour movement was virtually free of the terrible people who, in Lenin's words, still "dared to win". Everything was designed to the great end of persuading the British capitalist class that for them Fascism was quite unnecessary.

It is evident that a policy of accommodation to the needs of capitalism in decline involves the abandonment of any real attempt to achieve Socialism, whether gradually or rapidly, and by constitutional just as much as by revolutionary means. *It involves the retreat of a Labour movement from its third to its second stage of development; from Socialist to Trade Union politics.* If we examine the course along which that policy took the British Labour movement, in the light of a study of its previous history, we cannot fail to see that this is what was happening. The reaction of our leaders to the breakdown of British Socialism was not to examine Socialist theory afresh and see if any inadequacy in the British version of it was responsible for the breakdown. On the contrary, they in fact (though not of course in words) abandoned the struggle to abolish capitalism and set up a new social order. They turned back towards the stage reached by the movement in the early nineteen-hundreds, when the need for a separate political party founded on the Trade Unions had been recognised, but no need was felt to equip that party with any coherent social aims or distinctive social philosophy.

Sir Walter Citrine and his colleagues adopted the policy of accommodation in order to avoid a frontal attack by the ruling class upon the Labour movement. The essence of their argument was that if only the Labour movement does not challenge the capitalists' position, then the capitalists will not challenge the existence of the Labour movement. But, they warned, if we attempt to assert ourselves, even by a too vigorous and united defence of democracy, peace and the national standards of life; if above all we dare to unite with the Communists, then we shall be destroyed. Sir Walter Citrine in his basic speech to the 1933 Trade Union Congress expressed this view in these simple words: "Every time they made a Communist they made a Fascist."

This conception has been tirelessly repeated and developed by the members of the National Council of Labour and its speakers. Nor, to an audience unequipped with any comprehension of the structure and interactions of modern society, is it unplausible. The capitalists are represented as sleeping dogs whom it is vitally necessary to let lie; if members of the Labour movement become militant or Communist; if they begin (spitefully and unnecessarily) to challenge the capitalists; then of course—what do you expect?— the capitalists will reply in kind by becoming Fascists and destroying the workers with fire and sword. Therefore be quiet, be inactive, above all do not be too strong: strength —especially the strength of unity—is too provocative.

This view reveals an incomprehension of the nature and origins of Fascism. Fascism is regarded as a purely subjective phenomenon. Fascism, it is suggested, is produced by the wickedness of the workers in becoming militant. "Reaction of the Left (this is how Communism is described) is displaced by triumphant reaction of the Right", as the National Joint Council's 1933 manifesto on Democracy versus Dictatorship put it. If only the workers will stay with the Labour Party, is the implication, there will be no Fascism. But Communism does not produce Fascism any more than Fascism produces Communism. On the contrary, they are both the products of the social crisis caused by the disintegration of capitalism. Communism, or scientific Socialism, is the most complete and adequate summing up of the workers' reactions to the intolerable conditions into which they are plunged by that disintegration. In the same way Fascism is the organised expression of the determination of the capitalists to stick at nothing in order to stay in power despite that disintegration. How can we even reason with men who do not grasp this most basic of all the facts of the world situation to-day? For what these leaders are in effect denying is that the social struggle is conditioned by economic development. They are denying that the intensification of the class conflict (of which the appearance of Communism amongst the working, and Fascism amongst the capitalist class, are expressions) is the result of the bloody chaos into which the disintegration of the economic system is plunging the world. They continue to regard both Communism and Fascism as moods into which, for some unknown reason, the workers and capitalists have recently shown a tendency to fall.

This is the general attitude of our leaders. Underneath it it·is possible to discern, however, that Sir Walter Citrine and his colleagues have admitted, though in a semi-conscious, unthought-out sort of way, that if the economic situation of British capitalism continued to get worse, then it would breed increasingly severe class conflicts, which not even they could avoid. Sir Walter Citrine, in his 1933 speech had remarked, for example, that "if unemployment got more desperate no one, neither himself nor any member of the General Council, would be prepared to answer for the consequences". But the possibility of such a continued worsening is dismissed with this sort of alarmed side-glance—and then the movement's whole policy is laid down on the tacit hypothesis that either economic conditions will improve, or that economic conditions do not have any particular influence on men's political re-actions anyway.

It so happened that Sir Walter Citrine was immediately challenged on this very point during the debate which followed his speech to the 1933 Trade Union Congress. Mr. Aneurin Bevan, M.P., said:

"They had to ask themselves this plain simple question in order to make up their minds about this fundamental issue: What was their estimate of the future of private enterprise in Great Britain? Did they believe with the Germans that the economic conditions of capitalism were such that they were witnessing a slow and inevitable decline, or did they believe that it was possible for capitalism in this country to recover itself, to reorganise its economic life, and provide the circum-stances of an expansion of life similar to that experienced in the nineteenth century. Mr. Citrine's speech was based upon a profound belief in the possibility of capitalism to recover itself. Mr. Citrine had himself said so in his speech. Mr. Citrine had said that if unemployment continued and grew in Great Britain he could not answer for the result. What did that mean? If the statement of the President of the Congress was true that they were facing the inevitable decline of capitalism, then unemployment would grow and poverty would increase, and as poverty increased and unemployment grew the very foundations of democracy would be undermined and attacked not from the Left, but from the Right."

Here at last was a recognition that Fascism was not a fit of bad temper into which we might provoke the capitalists if we misbehaved, but was the expression of the imperative need of capitalism in decline to sweep away all democratic obstacles to its dictatorship. Sir Walter Citrine in his reply to the debate gave this answer to Mr. Bevan:

"Mr. Bevan stated that undoubtedly democracy would be attacked from the Right, whatever happened from the Left, and that unemployment would inevitably become worse because the capitalist system in process of decline must bring with it increasing unemployment and eventually some form of cataclysm. That was not a new theory to the delegates to this Congress. It was being preached when he first joined the Socialist movement. Its adherents had still to recognise that economic events were not the sole determining thing in the matter, that human beings had a strange way of reacting, apparently, to identical circumstances in different ways. He was not accepting the inevitability argument at all. In point of fact, the use of the inevitability argument in itself tended to produce the fatalism which shook one's faith, not only in democracy, but in any effort to raise the standard of life and the condition of the people."

Sir Walter Citrine here says two things. First, he says that the view that capitalism is declining, and will inevitably be forced to attack democracy, is not new; that it has always been current in the Socialist movement. Then he goes on to deny that it is true. ("He was not accepting the inevitability argument at all.") In other words, it was not inevitable that capitalism would continue to decline; and even if it did, it was not inevitable that the capitalists would react by going Fascist and the workers by becoming militant. People reacted in different ways to the same situation. The inevitability argument shook one's faith in democracy.

The issue was, then, posed, if somewhat obscurely. Sir Walter Citrine and his colleagues were acting on the basic assumption that the economic situation would not get worse; that no new slump would come; that there was nothing to show that capitalism was taking the world to war. Moreover, they asserted, even if things did get worse, that would not necessarily intensify the struggle between the workers and capitalists. The whole policy of accommodation was based, like the policy of British Socialism, which it succeeded, either on the hypothesis that economic conditions are of no importance, or on the hypothesis of the stability of capitalism. Was there ever such a steadfast faith? Nor wars, nor crisis, nor slumps, nor panics can shake the faith of the leaders of the British Labour movement in the stability of British capitalism. Long after the capitalists themselves have ceased to believe in their system, that faith endures.

What, we may ask, did the delegates at the 1933 Trade Union Congress think of Sir Walter Citrine's repudiation of the "inevitability argument"; of his repudiation, that is to say, of any coherent, Socialist estimate of what is happening in the world to-day, and of the social forces that these happenings must generate? The answer must be that they thought nothing in particular about it. The tragedy was that these shrewd, experienced men and women were not equipped to form any independent judgment either of the nature of Fascism or of the proper way to meet its menace. In the last analysis that is why it proved impossible at the 1933 Congress, as at subsequent Congresses, to make any effective challenge to the other spokesmen of the official view. The technical difficulties of making such a challenge are indeed enormous. Delegates are only allowed five minutes to reply to speeches which may have taken an hour to deliver. The men most capable of making adequate replies are systematically excluded from the Congress. But these difficulties could be, and would be, surmounted if a substantial section of the delegates had the knowledge and training necessary to have a view of their own on these matters. Standing Orders limiting speeches to five minutes could be suspended. The General Council could be forced to seat any delegate duly elected by his organisation. Anything could be done by delegates who had an independent view of their own. But the decisive majority of the delegates who attend the two great annual Conferences of the British Labour movement, do not yet have the basis of knowledge necessary to form an independent view.

In 1933, for example, they did not come to the Conference having made up their minds that Sir Walter Citrine's view of Fascism as the capitalists' punishment for a working-class movement which dared to aspire to power, and his consequent policy of accommodation to capitalism at all costs, was correct. They came to the Conference with no decided view of the nature of Fascism or of the way to combat it. Sir Walter Citrine put before them a thoroughly coherent, impressively documented, carefully reasoned, and totally false, view of Fascism and of the best way to meet it. What could they do but take his word for it? They had no alternative. Until they equip themselves with political knowledge; with, above all, an adequate, comprehensive, Socialist science, the men and women who do the hard daily work of the British working-class movement will always have to accept any policy which a small group of leaders at the top chooses to put before them.

Finally, we may ask whether the adoption by a Labour movement of the policy of accommodation to the needs of capitalism, if it were carried to its logical conclusion, could avert social conflict? There may be people who dread any form of social conflict so much that if it would, then they would be prepared to support it, even though it involved both the abandonment of any hope of Socialism and the progressive emasculation and division of the Labour movement. But the policy of accommodation cannot, even at this price, bring social peace. It is not possible to save either democracy or even a remnant of the Labour movement by trying to make them seem innocuous to the capitalists. The example of what has happened to German Social Democracy is decisive on this point. Accommodation to the needs of capitalism could not possibly have been carried further than it was in Germany. Even after Hitler came to power, right through the spring of 1933, the

German Trade Union leaders co-operated diligently with the Government. The Social Democratic Party voted for Hitler's Government in the Reichstag. The German Trade Unions took part in the Nazi May Day celebrations in 1933. Finally the German Trade Union leaders urgently telegraphed to the International Federation of Trade Unions in an attempt to prevent it, as an organisation of which they were still members, from protesting against the Nazi Government's murder and torture of many thousands of German workers. When the International refused to do this they resigned from it. The German Labour leaders did all this in the hope that the German ruling class would after all allow such harmless, such obedient, such grovelling Trade Unions to continue to exist. But in the conditions of the working-class struggle the policy of Uriah Heap is not merely loathsome, it is also unavailing. When the German Trade Union movement had utterly discredited itself by rolling in the mud before them; when it had lost every vestige of power to resist them, the Nazis contemptuously destroyed it. Grossmann and Liepart, the principal German Trade Union leaders, said the Nazis, may protest their loyalty to Hitler (as they did) but they are better in jail. And to jail they went, amidst supreme and universal contempt.

Such are the frightful consequences of basing the policy of a Labour movement on an attempt to placate the capitalists by "calming" the workers. The capitalists cannot be placated but the workers can be "calmed"—they can be calmed into a deadly indifference and despair which leaves the road clear for Fascism. The capitalists will never return the love which the Trade Union leaders lavish on them. "Take care," Lenin said to those members of the Russian Labour movement who wished, in 1905, to make the movement acceptable to the Russian Liberals, "take care you do not die of unrequited love." And it is of unrequited love of the British ruling class that the British movement would die if its present policy of accommodation were taken to its logical conclusion.

If the policy of accommodation cannot save even the remnant of a Labour movement, neither is it the way to prevent the social conflict from degenerating into a violent physical conflict. Time after time the leaders of the German working class forbore to defend some essential liberty of the German people, because they feared that to do so might mean an outbreak of armed struggle. But their successive surrenders have not spared Germany a single moment of armed struggle. On the contrary, they have made armed, as distinct from political or industrial, conflict, inevitable. What they did do was to cripple the working class so terribly that the struggle was turned into a massacre. The world saw a helpless working class attacked and beaten to the ground without organised resistance. It is only if we prefer massacre to struggle that the policy of accommodation can promise us anything. Even so, it can bind the hands of the working class for a time only. Who can doubt, for example, that the most violent struggles lie ahead of the German people? Now that the German capitalists have been enabled by the successive surrenders of the workers leaders to take every element of democracy from the German people; now, indeed, bitter and terrible civil war is inevitable. For nothing that the German capitalists can do, short of conquering the world (which would involve far greater bloodshed still), can ultimately arrest the disintegration of their system. The most abject surrenders cannot avert struggle. The workers must in the end be forced to struggle for sheer self-preservation. But the surrender of our existing liberties can transform, and transform immeasurably for the worse, the nature of that struggle. So long as the liberties and democratic institutions of the West are preserved, the social conflict can be conducted by political and industrial means. In these conditions there is always a possibility of transforming society without giving the capitalists any effective opportunity to resort to physical violence. But if liberty, democracy and all possibility of constitutional action have been given away beforehand, in order to placate the capitalists, then indeed the social conflict can only be conducted by physical force.

In either event the social conflict can, in contemporary conditions, only end in the victory of the workers. But if all the workers' vantage points, the strong bridge-heads of democratic rights and liberties, are given up, then the struggle will be a hundred times more difficult, more prolonged, more violent and more destructive. Nothing is more certain than that the way to minimise social violence is to refuse to yield one of our existing rights to the encroachments of capital; to mobilise the strength of a united Labour movement, and all its allies, to defend them. Nothing is more certain than that the road of surrender leads, through the massacre of a helpless and divided working class, to appalling civil and international wars.

In Britain the Labour movement has not yet been taken very far along the road of surrender, on which its feet were finally planted in 1933. Moreover, considerable forces have appeared from within the movement which are now demanding a halt to the retreat. But as yet, though with ever-increasing reluctance, the movement is still treading the fatal road. The main job of convincing the decisive majority of the movement of the fatal character of its present policy is still to do. I believe that there is a consideration not yet discussed in these pages which is hindering us from convincing the members of the British Labour movement of the necessity of adopting a policy of united resistance.

Now it is utterly untrue that the attitude of the capitalists to the Labour movement primarily depends upon our attitude to them. It is utterly untrue that even if we adopt a yielding, humble, pacifistic attitude, they will permanently tolerate the existence of a Labour movement. It is utterly untrue that the capitalists of Germany, Italy, Austria and the other countries of Continental Europe which have gone Fascist, have done so because "their" workers became militant. An examination of the historical facts of each case demonstrates that, on the contrary, it is precisely where the Labour movement has been most yielding and accommodating that the capitalists have most readily and successfully gone Fascist. For it is in these countries that the workers have despaired of their own movements, and that these movements have failed to rally the middle classes to the workers' side, and so have provided a rich soil for Fascism. To turn to some form of autocratic rule, of which Fascism is the contemporary model, is, I repeat, an absolute need of the capitalists to-day. The degeneration of their characteristic economic system leaves them no alternative. They will certainly attempt to make this turn whatever the Labour movement may do.

Sometimes, however, we (the advocates of the policy of united resistance, that is to say) have seemed, at any rate, to suggest that the attitude, the whole approach, of a Labour movement to its task of social transformation is not even a factor in determining the attitude and actions of the capitalists towards the Labour movement in question. Now this is clearly an over-statement. For example, as has just been described, the adoption of the policy of retreat and accommodation; the adoption of a soft, yielding, apologetic attitude by a Labour movement is certainly a factor in promoting and aiding the capitalists' turn towards Fascism. For it so rapidly destroys any Labour movement which adopts it that it leaves a vast debris of disillusioned, despairing, unattached men and women who are the perfect soil for Fascism. But, on the other hand, the adoption of a falsely revolutionary attitude; of a nervously and stridently aggressive attitude, by a Labour movement can play a part in aiding the capitalists' spontaneous turn towards Fascism. This is the grain of truth in the arguments advanced by Sir Walter Citrine and his colleagues to-day.

A consciousness in the minds of many members of the movement of the existence of this grain of truth in what Sir Walter Citrine and those who agree with him say, makes it difficult to convince them of the disastrous error of those leaders' position as a whole. For we of the militant sections of the movement have in the past given grounds for criticism in this respect. Some of us have shown, on occasions, this shrill, strident "aggressiveness for aggressiveness' sake" attitude. And this attitude can undoubtedly be almost, though never quite, as serious a liability to a Labour movement as the soft, yielding, pacifistic attitude. Lenin, all through his life, fought this "re-re-revolutionariness", as he called it. He defined it as the essential characteristic of the lower middle class, suddenly gone far to the Left, rather than the characteristic of the serious, sober, determined main body of the workers, marching steadily and unflinchingly towards their goal. It is imperative, if we of the Left would overcome the opposite, soft, pacifistic, accommodating attitude, which is literally killing our movement before our eyes, that we should wholly rid ourselves of this falsely aggressive attitude. For the average member of the movement is extremely quick to detect this false note in Left propaganda—and there is nothing that he more detests and distrusts.

Nor is his opinion unjustified. A Labour movement which approaches its vast, complex, arduous task of social transformation in a nervously aggressive spirit will gravely handicap itself. If a Labour movement approaches its job with the air of spoiling for a physical fight with the capitalists, it will probably get that fight in circumstances almost as unfavourable as if it approaches its job with sententious phrases on its lips about the impossibility of anyone being so wicked as ever to resort to violence in the furtherance of their political ends. Moreover it is true that silly, shrill re-re-revolutionariness in a Labour movement aids the capitalists in turning Fascist, by antagonising and driving away men and women who would otherwise be attracted to the popular forces. The Labour movement must approach its gigantic task with sobriety, with integrity, and with realism. Its attitude to the possibility of violent social conflict will be a factor of first-rate importance in its success or failure. If, on the one hand, it nervously denies the possibility of violent conflict, provoked by the present ruling class, or, on the other hand, nervously asserts that it is useless even to try to use the existing democratic machinery for the purpose of basic social change (and at bottom the two attitudes are opposite sides of the same coin; they are both nervous attitudes), it will fail. For in one sense the attitude, the approach, which the movement makes to its task is everything. If this is right everything else will come right. If this is wrong nothing can go right.

Fortunately, the Left has to-day almost completely freed itself from "re-re-revolutionariness". There is no trace of aggressiveness for aggressiveness' sake; there is nothing whatever shrill or strident about the work of the principal figures of the Communist Party of Great Britain —about the work of Pollitt, Campbell or Hannington— for example. But this may not be so completely true of all the work of all the members of the Communist Party, and it is, unfortunately, by no means true of some of the small Left-wing groups unattached, and indeed, hostile, to the Communist Party.

To sum up. The attitude of a Labour movement is not a primary factory in turning the capitalists towards Fascism. Even if the whole movement succeeds in adopting the ideal attitude the capitalists will still attempt to turn to some form of Fascism. But the attitude, the approach to its task, the style of the work, of the Labour movement is an important factor in either facilitating or making impossible the success of the capitalists' turn towards Fascism. Either the soft and accommodating, or the shrilly aggressive, attitude will help the capitalists. Moreover, Sir Walter Citrine and his colleagues are helped in taking the movement down the fatal road to surrender by the suspicion in the minds of many members of the movement that the Left is shrilly aggressive. Hence a vital task of those who stand for the policy of united resistance is to do so in all sobriety, integrity, earnestness and calmness.

CHAPTER XI

THE FRUITS OF ACCOMMODATION

THE YEARS WHICH have passed since the Trade Union Congress and Labour Party Conference of 1933 laid down a new policy of the Labour movement have been years of economic revival. The trade cycle has been in its ascendant phase. Unemployment has steadily diminished. The extreme pressure upon capitalism which in 1933 had brought the system to breaking point has been appreciably relaxed. The relaxation has been world-wide, but extremely uneven, being greatest on those capitalisms which needed it least (i.e. Britain) and least on those capitalisms which needed it most (i.e. Germany). Hence the constant increase, in spite of the economic recovery, in international tension.

This recovery has meant that British capitalism has had no necessity to attack, with intent to destroy, the British Labour movement. In turn, therefore, the movement's policy of accommodation on essentials has not hitherto necessitated the surrender of such vital popular interests as democracy or the depression of the national standard of life. But it has meant the, perhaps irrecoverable, surrender of positions which alone made it possible to maintain world peace.

It is true that even during this period of recovery British capitalism has felt impelled to make certain significant encroachments on the traditional liberties of the British people. The most important new anti-democratic statutes are the Incitement to Disaffection Bill and the Public Order Bill (often known as the Uniforms Bill). The first of these measures is designed to make it impossible for workers to influence members of the armed forces in favour of pacific or anti-capitalist ideas. The second makes the wearing of uniforms by political bodies illegal. Designed, according to the Government, to prevent the uniformed Fascist marches which were creating large-scale disorders, the Act takes the opportunity to curtail, in important respects, the right of assembly, one of the most precious liberties of the subject, and one without which democratic political life is impossible. These measures, however, have merely nibbled at our rights and liberties. Their importance is that they indicate the way the mind of the ruling class is working; they indicate that though no acute crisis either of war or slump faces British capitalism for the moment, yet quiet preparations for just such a crisis are being made.

It was, however, a tragic exemplification of the effect of the Labour movement's policy of accommodation that almost all effective opposition to both these measures came from bodies outside the official organisations of the Labour movement. Indeed in the case of the Public Order Bill the leaders of the Labour movement supported the Bill, in the belief that it would be used primarily against the Fascists, and, secondly, against the Communists. It is dreadful to have to write such words, but their public statements leave no room for doubt that some of the leading members of the Labour Party regard another part of their own movement, the Communists, with at least equal hostility to the Fascists, and are actually willing to use a capitalist government's aid in attacking it. Such a policy is not only base, it is also naïve. For every example shows that such measures as the Public Order Bill, though no doubt used at first mainly against the militant Left, are brought into action against the whole Labour movement as soon as the existence of that movement becomes intolerable to capitalism. Then the movement is pierced with a sword which it has helped to forge.

A more important struggle developed in 1934-5-6. Successive attempts were made by the National Government to depress the national standard of life by making alterations in the rules governing the receipt of unemployment relief.[1] These attempts were resisted with a very considerable measure of success. A series of hunger marches on London were organised and successfully carried through; gigantic demonstrations[2] took place in Sheffield, Birkenhead, and above all in South Wales. The Government was on several occasions constrained to modify drastically their original proposals to the advantage of the unemployed.

But again the whole initiative for this all-important movement of resistance came from organisations, such as the National Unemployed Workers' Movement, which have been excluded from affiliation to the Labour Party. It is true that this movement of resistance became so wide and deep that numerous units of the main body of the movement, Local Labour Parties, Trades Councils, and Trade Unions, were caught up in it. But not only did the central leadership play no part in the resistance, but to the very best of their ability the General Council of the Trade Union Congress and the National Council of Labour attempted to prevent any section of the movement from becoming active. In doing so they were applying logically their basic 1933 policy of accommodation to the needs of capitalism. If British capitalism needed, for its recovery, to depress the national standard of life, then the Labour movement must not offer more than a polite and parliamentary opposition; for to do more might make the position of British capitalism impossible and so provoke the ruling class to destroy the Labour movement as an intolerable menace to it. It followed logically that the most energetic efforts must be made to prevent units, or whole sections,

---

[1] It is a commonplace amongst economists that the rates of unemployment relief have in modern British conditions a profound effect on the general level of wages, and so on the national standard of life. If the unemployed are driven by starvation to accept any wages and conditions of work offered to them, it will be clearly impossible for the employed workers to maintain, still less to improve, their wage rates. Hence in contemporary Britain the struggle for the defence of the national standard of life is, to a considerable extent, fought out over the question of the rates and conditions of unemployment benefit.

[2] See Hutt's *The Post-War History of the British Working Class* for the best description of the events which reached their climax in the spring of 1935.

of the movement from following the lead of those who were organising the resistance. To this end determined attempts were (and still are being) made to exclude all militant individuals and organisations from the movement. As always the issue of policy, the alternative of accommodation or resistance, is inextricably interwoven with the issue of the unity or division of the movement.

In the event the movement, even though divided, and so at least half crippled, proved strong enough to wring very considerable concessions from the Government, though not to achieve the clear-cut triumph of abolishing the Means Test itself. The possibility of the divided movement winning even this partial success arose, to a considerable extent, however, because the British capitalists found that, after all, a wholesale depression of the national standard of life was not necessary to the revival of their system. The economic revival, greatly assisted by gigantic re-armament, proved strong enough to make it seem to the Government worth while to abandon the more drastic cuts proposed, rather than face the vigorous opposition which was developing. But the movement of resistance which in the spring of 1935 was growing rapidly, and was exercising a revivifying effect upon the whole Labour movement, was effectively prevented by the energetic efforts of the movement's national leaders from spreading from the single issue of the rates and conditions of unemployment benefit, either into the Trade Union, or into the directly political, field. The natural effect of both the considerable successes which were won in spite of everything, in pushing back the worst of the Government's attacks on the unemployed, and of the ever-growing revival of industrial activity, would have been a wave of Trade Union activity, involving the presentation of demands for better wages and improved conditions generally. But the leaders of the Trade Union movement judged it expedient to discourage any such activity from developing; and, though with ever-increasing difficulty, they have so far succeeded in doing so. Similarly the boycotting of the struggles of the unemployed prevented this success from reacting in the political field. Hence when in the autumn of 1935 a general election took place the Labour movement entered the electoral struggle, not as it would have done seven or eight months earlier, on the crest of a wave of militancy and self-confidence, but depressed and divided.

The election was lost. But I believe that this was almost certainly in accordance with the expectations of the leaders of the movement. Just as undue pressure upon capitalism in the industrial or economic sphere had, in their opinion, become too dangerous, so it was undesirable to disturb the National Government's period of office by an electoral victory. A considerable increase in Labour representation was desired and obtained. But it was felt that Labour was not yet ready to take office again.

I am aware that readers of this book may feel that this is a monstrous and unproven accusation. They will themselves have taken part in the 1935 campaign. They will have worked their hardest for Labour candidates. They will have seen the candidates themselves working hard for success. They may have worked for particular leaders of the movement and may feel convinced that these leaders were doing everything they could to bring success. How then can it be asserted that they did not try to win? This question raises a misunderstanding which often renders fruitless all discussion between members of the Labour movement belonging to different schools of thought. It is perfectly true that in the minds of some of our leaders, during the three weeks of the 1935 election campaign, there was a genuine desire to win. But nevertheless the whole policy of accommodation which they had been pursuing during previous years had been of such a kind as to result in the type of election campaign which in fact took place; a campaign in which the Government's policy was challenged on none of the vital issues of the day. Hence, objectively, and no matter what the ideas in the heads of some of the leaders of the movement may have been, there was, and could be, no fight to win.

Moreover, no one who reads the pronouncements of many of the leaders before the 1935 election can doubt that in their case, at any rate, they entered the campaign in a mood of conscious defeatism. The logic of the policy of accommodation could take them to no other conclusion. In the present world situation the British governing class would undoubtedly have been seriously perturbed by losing its direct and immediate control over the executive to a Labour ministry, however moderate. A Labour victory at the 1935 elections, just because it would have had immensely favourable consequences for the whole democratic cause all over the world, would undoubtedly have exacerbated the ruling class; would, in a word, have intensified the class struggle in Britain. Hence it might have led the ruling class, or sections of it, to turn towards the attempt to suppress the Labour movement by Fascist force. As the leadership had no confidence in their ability to defeat such an attempt; as they had, and have, a supreme confidence in the ability of the ruling class to impose its will upon society, they desired above all things not to do anything which might incline their rulers to such courses. At the 1935 General Election our leaders gave a supreme example of the tactics of those who do not dare to win.

The culminating example of the failure to challenge the National Government upon essentials in 1935 occurred upon the issue of foreign policy. The foreign policy of the National Government had been strongly endorsed by the spokesmen of the Labour movement only a few weeks before the election, under the extraordinary impression that that policy was anti-Fascist. This appalling error was the most important single factor in ensuring the Government's success. We discuss it below, pages 191–205.

Since 1935 the economic revival has turned into a typical, if particularly unstable and inflationary, capitalist boom. Hence any necessity to attempt to depress the national standard of life by direct cuts in unemployment benefit or wages has disappeared. A steady rise in prices has, however, set in, so that unless wages rise as steadily and as

rapidly, the national standard of life falls automatically
The test of the capacity of a Labour movement to resis
the encroachments of capitalism during such a perioc
must consist in the ability of the Trade Unions to take the
offensive and secure, either by strike action or by the threa
of it, concessions on wages, hours and conditions which
will at least offset the rising cost of living, and which certainly
should take some share in the truly gigantic profits which
are always made in such periods. For many months afte
the development of boom conditions the British Trade
Union movement seemed unable to take any appreciable
advantage of its opportunity. Uneasiness and the desire
for a forward movement has now begun in the Unions
however. Of the consequences of this movement it is stil
too early to write. But once again it is apparent that the
initiative has come from the mass of the movement itsel
and not from the leadership. That leadership shows al
the signs of adhering, in the present (1937) boom condition
of rising prices, to its basic policy of abstaining from putting
any serious pressure on capitalism, either by resistance on a
falling market, or by demands on a rising market.

Indeed the series of unofficial strikes; of strikes, that i
to say, which are opposed by the leaders of the Trade
Unions concerned, which have occurred during 193'
are an indication of the vigour with which the Genera
Council is holding the rank and file of the Unions bacl
from taking the offensive. For the occurrence of unofficia
strikes is always the sign that the rank and file of a Trade
Union movement is pressing forward, while its leaders ar
pressing back.

Some readers may have an objection to the abov
argument in the back of their minds. "It is all very well,'
they may be feeling, "to criticise the leaders of the movemen
for retreating both in the industrial and in the politica
field during the past few years. But are there not period
when one must retreat, periods in which to put up a figh
is merely to invite disaster? Sir Walter Citrine, Mr. Ernes

Bevin and their colleagues are experienced men, may they not have come to the conclusion that this is just such a period, and may they not be right?"

Now it is perfectly true that there are periods in which it is impossible for a Labour movement to act on the offensive. In fact it is agreed in principle that this is such a period, for our main proposal is essentially that the movement should defend every position that it already occupies.

The essential criticism which has been made of the leadership of the British Labour movement is precisely, that they are not defending their positions. It is true that in the present world situation an unyielding defence of peace, democracy and the national standard of life by the British Labour movement would result in very heavy political and industrial struggles with British capitalism. For British capitalism must in the long run attack these three basic interests of the British people. But immense forces can be rallied by British Labour for the defence of these three interests. Moreover, for the moment, British capitalism is attacking only one of them—namely peace—with any great determination. In the case of democracy and the national standard of life the defence has hardly yet been tried. Nothing is more certain, however, than that the movement's power of defence on this home front will be tried, and that very soon. But before devoting our attention to the situation which will then confront the British Labour movement, we must follow up the effects of the policy of accommodation on the third great interest of the people of Britain, namely the maintenance of peace.

The economic revival which has been going on since 1933 is, I repeat, world-wide. But it has been far more marked in Britain than in the desperate, ravenous capitalisms of Europe. In the Fascist states especially, in Germany and Italy, it has been to a considerable extent merely a change in the nature of the pressure to which these capitalisms are subjected. Instead of facing mass unemployment and industrial paralysis, as they did five years ago, they now have industries working to capacity, predominantly upon the basis of rearmament, but with an accompanying shortage of every kind of raw material and foodstuffs, and consequently ever-increasing pressure upon an over-driven population. In these circumstances, European capitalism could not halt its counter-offensive against the European Labour movements. For it remained essential to its existence that its ability to depress the national standard of life, and to make war, should be unquestioned by any independent force whatever. Hence each year since 1933 has seen a major assault made by European Fascist-capitalism upon the defences of peace, democracy, the standard of life, and their one effective protector, the European Labour movements.

The rest of this chapter must be devoted to a description of the reaction of the British Labour movement to each of the major Fascist aggressions of the past few years. It is inevitable that such a description should be controversial and critical. Many of the readers of this book may wonder whether much is to be gained by "raking over" these issues which, so recently and so painfully, divided our movement. The answer must be that it is precisely because we have always refused to study the past of our movement; because we have always flinched from careful and objective estimates of the effect which particular decisions have had, that we have learnt so little from experience.

Above all, we have never been able to believe that the criticism of the actions of individuals was useful or necessary. Lacking any solid foundation of economic and political science from the objective standards of which the actions of individual leaders could be judged, we have almost always ascribed such criticism to motives of spite or envy. The following pages will certainly be considered to be of this character by those who wish so to consider them. They are written, however, in the conviction that until we learn to take note of what have been the consequences of the recent divisions of the movement; to judge, calmly and objectively, what, in the light of events, have been the results of the actions of individuals, we can have no hope of making wiser decisions in the future.

In 1934 the last Labour movement of Central Europe was destroyed and a Fascist régime set up in Austria. In 1935 Italy annexed Abyssinia, and in so doing was allowed to destroy (until such time as it is rebuilt, at any rate) the system of collective security under the League of Nations which had been the main obstacle to the outbreak of the next war. In 1936, the German and Italian Governments, using General Franco and the Spanish officer caste as their agents, launched their attempt to destroy the newly-founded Spanish democracy and to establish themselves, with all the immense strategic implications which this would involve, in Spain and Morocco. In 1937 Japan invaded China. Now in the most important of these great events the attitude of the British Government has been decisive. In turn, a decisive factor in determining the attitude of the British Government has been the attitude of the British Labour movement. Let us see how the leadership which had in 1933 adopted the general policy of accommodation reacted to these foreign emergencies.

Of the four the crushing of the Austrian workers was the most difficult for the British Labour movement to influence. It was not easy for the British Labour movement at the last moment to save the Austrian workers. Moreover, Sir Walter Citrine was able to report to the 1934 Trade Union Congress that he and the General Council had not been idle in the matter. He described to the Congress what the British movement, as part of the International, had done.

"I am proud to say that the international Trade Union movement has lived up to its highest ideals in the fullest possible measure in regard to the assistance rendered to our Austrian comrades. First we had our meeting in October in Vienna. We went to Vienna because we wanted everybody who was forming part of our meeting to realise the conditions on the spot. At that meeting I repeated what I said in the case of Germany: 'Comrades, our International is formed upon the

GD

principle that every one of its units has complete autonomy. There is no dictatorship here. Yours must be the responsibility to take the decision as to how you shall combat the menace of Fascism in your country, but I would remind you that you have not only a domestic obligation, but you have an international one. If your decision is taken to resist this menace, then you may depend that so far as is humanly possible the organised Trade Union Movement, despite its enormous difficulties, will rally to your support with its fullest power.' The Austrian comrades said: 'Yes, we are going to resist,' and immediately committees were formed as to how that detailed resistance could best be organised. I am talking in the presence of the Press, and I must measure my language very carefully. When I came back to Great Britain, I came here for the purpose of raising an immediate sum of £10,000 which was the allotted quota of this country for the purpose of helping our Austrian comrades. They contemplated that they would have to embark upon a general strike, and they knew that the first effect of that general strike would be to cut off supplies not only from the Government, but from themselves. Consequently we gave them every help we could, to prepare not only for that general strike in the way of provisioning, but for such other contingencies as the Government might force upon them. I make no apology for what we did. The Austrian Government, I repeat, is to-day, and was at that stage, a dictatorship without authority, electoral or of any other kind, from the people of Austria, and when your constitutional right is taken away from you, when you have been proceeding along the path of democratic procedure and the Government blocks the way to you, then you would be less than men if you did not take what remedies were open to you."

This declaration is worthy of attention in two respects. In the first place it shows that in this instance the principle that it was the duty of the British Labour movement to go to the assistance of another Labour movement fighting with its back to the wall against Fascist assault was, so lately as 1934, fully accepted by the General Council. It is, as a matter of fact, common knowledge that Sir Walter Citrine and his colleagues did not stop at raising money, but, to their honour, attempted, at any rate, to arrange for the supply of arms to the Austrian Socialists. Secondly, Sir Walter Citrine makes a declaration of principle as to when the use of force is justifiable for a Labour movement.

"When," he said, "your constitutional right is taken away from you, when you are proceeding along the path of democratic procedure and the Government blocks the way to you, then you would be less than men if you did not take what remedies were open to you."

It is important to realise that every Communist would accept this statement in its entirety. They would agree wholeheartedly that so long as constitutional, democratic, peaceful means of working-class action are open, a Labour movement should and must use these means to the very full. They would agree that it is only if and when the Government, or governing class, "blocks that way", that a Labour movement must find other methods of struggle. *In a word Communists, in the present world situation, ask nothing more of the leaders of the British Labour movement than that they should live up to these words of Sir Walter Citrine.*

At the 1935 Trade Union Congress and the 1935 Labour Party Conference the great question at issue was the impending Italian invasion of Abyssinia. It was clear that if Italy was allowed to conquer and annex another member of the League of Nations, then collective security under the guarantee of the League Covenant would be at an end. And if the system of collective security was destroyed, then a principal obstacle to the aggression towards which the Fascist states are impelled, by their very structure and nature, would be removed. Once again the attitude adopted by the leaders of the movement was in principle correct. Both to the Trade Union Congress and to the Labour Party Conference they pointed out the necessity of opposing Fascist aggression. The opposition was led at the Conference by the pacifists, headed by Mr. Lansbury, and Sir Walter Citrine was particularly severe upon those who flinched from opposing Fascist aggression because a risk of war was involved. He said:

"The irrefutable facts are: Italy has accepted the covenant; Italy has denounced, in effect, war; Italy is preparing for war; Italy is attacking a defenceless nation. We must act.

We must do something to restrain the bully. There is only one way of dealing with a bully, and that is by the use of force. . . . Some of you, I know, think this is a very serious matter. I agree with you. I overheard a delegate say at the commencement of my speech 'It means war'. It may mean war, but that is the thing we have to face." (*Trade Union Congress Report*, 1935, p. 349.)

Mr. Robinson, the chairman of the 1935 Labour Party Conference, said that:

"Labour cannot now flinch. It must not shrink from the logic of its considered policy. If the League fails in this crisis in its history, it destroys itself and the hopes of the nations. Lawlessness will stalk across the world. Under its cover, naked imperialism and militarism will hold sway. Dictatorship will flourish. Every aspiration which Socialists have nursed in their bosoms will be crushed."

Dr. Hugh Dalton, in moving the official resolution, was still more explicit:

"A threat of sanctions may be enough to prevent war. If not, the actual use of sanctions, economic and financial, without any military or naval action, may be sufficient to re-establish peace even if Mussolini breaks it.

"If not—face all the facts—it is hard even now to believe it, but if Mussolini be so lunatic as to resist the united League of Nations by force, then so be it. He will order the firing of the first shot, and he will take the consequences of that order."

It was perfectly clear that the fear of war did not in 1935 restrain the leaders of the British Labour movement from opposing Fascist aggression. In this our leaders were perfectly right. Unfortunately, however, they put forward this correct policy in a disastrously misleading way. *It was put forward in the form of demanding that the Labour movement should support the National Government in resisting Fascist aggression.* There was a complete assumption that the National Government had decided effectively to oppose Mussolini's invasion of Abyssinia. The only issue which came before the Trade Union Congress and Labour Party Conference was whether or not the movement should support the National Government in this supposed determination.[1] But within two months it had become undeniable that this was a false, indeed a non-existent, issue. It had become manifest that the British Government had no intention of effectively opposing Fascist aggression. Hence the issue of supporting their alleged efforts to do so could not arise.

To sum up. In 1935 on this vital issue of saving the system of collective security, our leaders adopted the right policy, but did so under the mistaken impression that they were thereby supporting the National Government. Thus their willingness to support, if necessary, the application of military sanctions to Fascist Italy in 1935 cannot be considered to have been a deviation from the policy of accommodation. For they believed sincerely, though mistakenly, that in so doing they were merely backing up the National Government. Far from attempting to force the Government to apply effective sanctions, they supported its non-existent determination to do so. In so doing they not only failed to expose, but immensely reinforced, the Government's declarations of support for the League, which did so much to win it the 1935 election. It would no doubt have been extremely convenient and satisfactory if the National Government had decided to resist Fascist aggression in 1935, and if, therefore, all that the Labour movement had needed to do was to proffer its loyal support. It is easy to understand how earnestly the leading figures of our movement, who were sincerely anti-Fascist, but were at the same time determined to co-operate with the National Government, wished this to be the position. For then they could have combined anti-Fascism with co-operation with the British ruling class. Their wish was evidently so strong that it soon over-rode all considerations of fact. It begot the thought without a moment's hesitation. And from then on the idea that in order to resist Fascist aggression abroad it was necessary ceaselessly to oppose the National Government

[1] The *Daily Herald*, it will be recalled, went so far as to say that Sir Samuel Hoare in his speech to the League Assembly on September 11th, spoke with the voice of England.

at home could be put far out of sight as a piece of silly Communist scare-mongering.

The crushing of the Austrian Socialists in 1934, and the rape of Abyssinia in 1935, were, however, merely preliminary manifestations of the onward march of the Fascist offensive. In 1936 that offensive reached a far higher degree of intensity by the large-scale invasion of Spain by German and Italian men and material designed to enable General Franco to crush the Spanish people in general and the Spanish Labour movement in particular. The Spanish civil war, after a year of furious fighting, is at its height while these pages are being written, and its outcome is still uncertain. But it is now clear that upon its result, far more than upon any single event so far, depends the successful defence of peace, democracy and the standard of life of the peoples of the world against the Fascist-capitalist offensive. No one, surely, can any longer doubt that this is an immensely important turning point? If Fascism engulfs Spain, then the struggle will become fiercer and fiercer, engulfing one nation after another in war and civil war. The defenders of civilisation will have been driven back. The forces of night will have gained much ground. The victory of the Spanish Government, of which the Spanish Labour movement is the core, would, on the contrary, have an immense and immediate effect upon the whole world. It would in all probability turn the tide of Fascist aggression, save democracy and rebuild dominant and united Labour movements in the whole of Western Europe. It might lead to the rebuilding of a collective security system which could yet prevent world war.

Here then was the critical test for the British Labour movement. Should it use its great resources to mobilise resistance of every kind to this culminating instance of Fascist assault? It had done so, to some extent, at any rate, in the case of Austria, and to a considerable extent, in intention, at any rate, in the case of Abyssinia. Moreover, it soon became apparent that the British Labour

movement occupied a position of extreme strategic importance. The situation so developed that the British Government's acquiescence in German and Italian aid for Franco,
and its determination, not only to give no aid to the Spanish
Government, but to prevent France from doing so either,
became crucial factors in the war. This policy of unilateral,
or one-way, non-intervention on the part of Great Britain
could only be carried through successfully, in view of its
dangerous and dubious character, even from a strictly
Imperialist standpoint, if it could command the support of
the British Labour movement. I have myself no doubt
that the British Labour movement could, both by direct
help in men, in money and in supplies, and even more by
making impossible the British Government's one-way
non-intervention policy, have ensured the victory of the
Spanish people during the autumn of 1936.

What the British Labour movement did is still fresh in
our minds. The 1936 Trade Union Congress met a little
more than a month after Franco had struck. Sir Walter
Citrine, in the name of the General Council, persuaded
the Congress explicitly to support the British Government's
adherence to the non-intervention pact, although the Fascist
powers had already been detected in sending formidable
supplies of arms to Spain. (As when Italian bombers on
their way to Spain crashed in French North Africa.)

The British Labour movement also persuaded (though
with great difficulty) the Labour and Socialist International
and the International Federation of Trade Unions to support
non-intervention. Mr. Attlee in his recent book, *The Labour
Party in Perspective*, records this decision as follows:

"The two bodies decided, while maintaining the right of the
Spanish Government to obtain arms and munitions, to acquiesce
in the policy of non-intervention provided that it was worked
fairly and made effective."

It is impossible not to tremble for our movement when
our leader's very good intentions cause him to write such a
sentence as that. Is it not somewhat as if Mr. Attlee had

told us that the Internationals, while maintaining the right of the Spanish people to breathe, had acquiesced in the policy of attempting to stifle them, in a fair and effective manner? (For every one agrees that, even apart from violations, non-intervention in 1936 grossly penalised the Spanish Government as against the rebels.)

It is an ungrateful task to point out these painful inconsistencies within a sentence written by the leader of our movement.[1] But unfortunately this kind of refusal to face hard alternatives, this belief that you can both retain a right in theory and surrender it in practice, is so easy and so fatal that it must be pointed out. In another place in his book Mr. Attlee uses the phrase "when Republican Spain has won her fight". Alas, alas, fights are not won by acquiescing in the things which bring defeat, while maintaining the "right" to victory. Fights are won by fighting. It is the hardest of all lessons. Shall we of the British Labour movement learn it in time? At the 1936 Labour Party Conference, the Executive proposed and carried the same policy. But before the close of the Conference feeling against non-intervention became so strong that an emergency resolution was carried pledging the Executive to repudiate non-intervention if it was proved, by further investigation, that the agreement "had been definitely violated" by the Fascist powers.

Since then an unknown number, usually computed at not less than 40,000[2] or more than 200,000, Italian troops, with full equipment, including machine-guns, artillery, tanks, bombing and fighting aeroplanes, have invaded Spain. Flight after flight of German aeroplanes have accompanied them. Whole towns, such as Guernica, have been razed to the ground by the aeroplanes of the Fascist non-interventionists. Whole battles, which have been graphically described by the Press of the world, have taken place in which the rebel forces have been exclusively composed of

---

[1] As this book is passed for the press Mr. Attlee is performing a memorable service by visiting Spain as the guest of the Spanish Government.
[2] This is the official figure admitted to by Mussolini.

Italian troops. During 1936 the sole reaction of the National Council of Labour was to issue a single, short, and somewhat colourless statement, withdrawing formal and explicit support from the Non-intervention Agreement. Neither substantial activities for the direct assistance of the Spanish people, nor any campaign against the British Government's continued adherence to one-way non-intervention were promoted. The original fund which was opened, much more on philanthropic than on political grounds, for sending medical stores to Spain has indeed been actively campaigned for, has raised considerable sums of money, and has covered the country with "Aid for Spain" Committees. But so lukewarm was the support given to the Central Committee of this fund by the leaders of the movement that the main work fell onto the shoulders of men and women excluded from the Labour Party. So marked did this cold-shouldering of the Spanish Medical Aid Committee on the part of some of the leaders of the movement become that some Labour Members of Parliament actually came to the point of complaining that the Spanish Medical Aid Committee was a "disruptive" Communist organisation which should be banned by the Labour Party! During the summer of 1937, however, the Spanish policy of the National Council of Labour was changed. Support of one-way non-intervention was definitely abandoned, and several statements of increasing strength, were issued demanding that the right of the Spanish Government to buy arms in the markets of the world should be restored to it. No campaign designed to exert such pressure on the National Government that it would have to abandon one-way non-intervention was, during the summer of 1937, however, undertaken. An imposing campaign for the revival of the Labour Party was announced for the autumn of 1937. But this campaign had no specific relation to Spain, or indeed to any other of the major issues of the day. In the autumn, however, after the 1937 Labour Party Conference, held at Bournemouth (see the next chapter), a Spanish sub-committee of the National Executive was appointed. An active, and most successful,

G1

campaign against the now ever more openly pro-rebel policy of the National Government were undertaken, and the large-scale resources of the movement for itself giving direct aid for Spain, in the form of supplies of milk and foodstuffs, through the Co-operative movement, began to be mobilised. Every member of the British Labour movement must be profoundly thankful that this direct work on behalf of the Spanish Government has now been undertaken by the movement as a whole. It is the most encouraging of a number of signs, which we shall note below, that the fundamental policy of the movement will not long remain that of accommodation to the will of the British ruling class on essentials.

But we pray that this major reversal, in one sphere, at any rate, of the policy of accommodation, has not come too late. If, in August 1936, the British Labour movement had adopted its present policy in regard to Spain; if, instead of officially endorsing, as it did, the National Government's policy of non-intervention, the movement had, as it is now doing, undertaken both a national campaign demanding the restoration of the right to buy arms to the Spanish Government, and had itself organised large-scale direct aid for Spain, there is no doubt that the Spanish civil war would long ago have ended in the victory of the Spanish Government. The whole international Socialist movement was then held back, with great difficulty, from organising aid for Spain by the determined support of non-intervention which the British movement was giving. The international situation at that time was such that a change in the Spanish policy of British Labour, such as has now been made, would almost certainly have tipped the balance of forces decisively. No such immediately decisive results can now be expected. The policy of the British Government has now hardened into solid support, including *de facto* recognition, for Franco. The Fascist powers, and in particular Italy, have been allowed to commit a whole army to the Spanish hazard. Successive French Governments have been blackmailed into repeated retreats before Fascist threats. It is to-day (November 1937) a hundred times more difficult for British Labour to save Spain than it would have been fifteen months ago.

Hence it is imperative that we should examine the arguments which induced the British Labour movement actually to support non-intervention at the critical moment, during the first three months of the civil war. For analogous, and still more vital, situations will certainly arise in the near future; analogous arguments for inaction, or, as in this case, for actual support of the National Government's policy will be used; these future arguments will seem as plausible as did those in favour of the support of non-intervention in 1936. Unless we have been willing to learn the lesson taught us by the terrible consequences of the acceptance of non-intervention in 1936, we shall accept those future arguments; and we shall be finally destroyed.

If we turn to the speeches in which our leaders explained their support, during 1936, of the National Government's Spanish policy, we shall find that a number of reasons were put forward. As usual, the most lucid and comprehensive explanation of the official view was put forward by Sir Walter Citrine. Sir Walter Citrine, at the 1936 Trade Union Congress, began by describing the situation of the Spanish Government, against the authority of which 90 per cent, he estimated, of its armed forces had mutinied.

"It was quite clear in those circumstances that the great need of the Spanish Government, and our comrades there, was to be supplied as rapidly as possible with war material, and to be able to obtain that material in conformity with the rights of constituted Governments from such other countries as the Spanish Government were able to apply to. The Government's task was, shortly, to improvise an army to find some means of replacing those people who, within a short few months of having affirmed the oath of allegiance to the Republic, had broken their oath and had left the Government in its hour of dire distress to take up arms against the properly constituted authority of the people. Another urgent need was the need for pilots. Fortunately, news of the revolt came to the Government in sufficient time for them to be able to prevent the larger part of their air fleet going over to the rebels. But the pilots to the extent of about 75 per cent deserted and joined the rebels. It was quite clear, therefore, that the need for military equipment on the part of the Spanish Government was so urgent that it was necessary that every ounce of assistance which could be given by sympathisers abroad should be rendered at the earliest possible moment.

"Now what was the difficulty?"

The difficulty was, Sir Walter Citrine went on to say, that the British Government had told them that if they demanded that the Spanish Government should be allowed to buy arms, Europe would be divided into blocs, and there would be a risk of war. Therefore, Sir Walter Citrine concluded, the British Labour movement must refuse to do anything to save its Spanish comrades.

Let us now justify the grave allegation that this was what Sir Walter Citrine said with further quotations from his speech. He followed the above passage, describing the desperate needs of the Spanish Government, with an analysis of the motives of the French Government in proposing the non-intervention pact. The French Government's motives were, he said, also based upon a fear of the Fascist powers making war on it. He went on to deal with the question of how the steady stream of Fascist munition which was even then pouring into Spain could be stopped. If that stream were stopped, the Spanish Government would still be gravely penalised by non-intervention (since the rebels had 90 per cent of the arms) but at any rate non-intervention would not mean in practice intervention exclusively on the Fascist side.

"It was known that Hitler and Mussolini were supplying arms to the rebels. There was no secret about that. The precise quantity of arms that had been sent in was not perhaps known, but the fact that they were being supplied was patent to everybody."

How could this be stopped?

"How could you prevent Hitler and Mussolini from supplying arms to the rebels in Spain if they desired to do that? There is only one answer, and that is to place a naval blockade round the coasts of Spain. Now think it over when you come to debate the matter. Just face up to that point. Think about it for yourselves, and I am perfectly sure if you can make any suggestion or contribution which will afford light to the General Council on matters that have hitherto been dark they will rejoice in it."

And so, Sir Walter Citrine concluded, it could not be done, for a blockade of Spain might provoke the Fascist states into making war. The members of the General Council had seen the British Government and had pondered its advice.

"*The greatest fear of all was this, the British Government had said to us : You would have the Powers divided into blocs, and you would have incidents which it would be impossible to escape.*"

Meanwhile, Sir Walter Citrine continued, the Non-intervention Agreement was being negotiated. Therefore, even though Fascist munitions were pouring into Spain, nothing should or could be done.

"Could we do anything at that stage which could revoke that agreement or get a sufficient public opinion behind it to cause its revocation? We felt it was dangerous even to try."

"We felt it was dangerous even to try." Is that to be the epitaph of European democracy?

In 1936 our leaders felt that it was dangerous even to try to save the Spanish people and the Spanish Labour movement. But why did they come to this extraordinary and terrible conclusion? Was it because they were afraid that if they did try to help Spain the Fascist powers would make war on Britain? It cannot have been that, for exactly a year before they had, as described above, shown themselves eager to stand up to Mussolini over Abyssinia, even, as they specifically explained, at the risk of war. Why did they make this startling change between 1935 and 1936? Why did they, in 1935, berate the pacifists in the Labour movement, and dismiss Mr. Lansbury from the leadership of the Labour Party, for refusing to oppose the Fascist invasion of Abyssinia, and then, in 1936, adopt the full pacifist line themselves over Spain? Why was it right and proper in 1935 to refuse to desert Abyssinia in face of Mussolini's threat of war (see Dalton's speech quoted above, p. 196), but absolutely necessary, in 1936, to desert the Spanish Labour movement, because of Mussolini's threat of war?

I am afraid that the only possible answer to this question is that the change was due to the fact that in 1935 our leaders believed, erroneously but sincerely, that the British Government was in favour of stopping the Fascist invasion of Abyssinia, while in 1936 they knew that the British Government was against stopping the Fascist invasion of Spain. Consequently, standing up to the Fascists in 1935 did not violate their fundamental policy of accommodation to British capitalism, while standing up to the Fascists in 1936 would have done so. That was why they felt that "it was dangerous even to try". It was dangerous even to try to bring effective help to the Spanish people, for to do so would have brought the Labour movement into opposition to the will of the British capitalist class on a matter of first-rate importance. And this is what the leaders of our movement were determined to avoid.

There were, no doubt, contributory reasons for our leaders' intense unwillingness to try to help the Spanish Labour movement in 1936. I believe that two of the contributory factors were: first, a fear of losing the Catholic vote in such cities as Liverpool and Glasgow[1]; and, second, dislike of supporting any movement or Government with which Communists were in any way associated. To suggest that these considerations influenced our leaders in their refusal to move on the Spanish question during 1936 is, I realise, to make a very grave allegation. For, if it is true, it means that in the first place our leaders have put the narrowest (and, as a matter of fact, most fallacious) electoral calculations before the duty of saving one section of the world-wide forces of democracy, on whose struggle our own lives probably depend; and, secondly, and this is far graver still, that in their hearts many of our leaders would rather risk, at any rate, the greatest triumph which Fascism has had since Hitler was given power than aid a Labour movement which had not excluded the Communists from its ranks. If this was even a contributory cause to the British

[1] Roman Catholics in Britain form about 8 per cent of the population and of the electorate.

Labour movement inaction over the Spanish issue it suggests a fanaticism, a virulent, unreasoning, uncontrollable hatred of the Communists on the part of some of our leaders such as must have, if it is not effectively checked, a devastating effect upon any Labour movement. It seems as if on this subject some of our leaders are so far removed from all reason that they are willing to sacrifice the most vital interests of all of us, and of themselves, in order to pursue their vendetta.

Yet I cannot resist the impression that, for example, Sir Walter Citrine's totally different reaction to the peril of the Austrian and of the Spanish Labour movements was affected by the consideration that the Austrian Labour movement contained very few Communists indeed while the Communist Party of Spain was a comparatively small, but active and important, section of the Spanish movement. It is not, however, suggested that these were more than contributory causes. Undoubtedly the main, overriding cause of the refusal of the leaders of the British Labour movement to do anything effective to help the Spanish people in 1936 was due to their determination not to challenge the policy of the British Government on a first-rate issue.

With the series of decisions which the movement took upon the Spanish question in 1936 the policy of accommodation entered a new phase. Hitherto no point essential for the defence of peace, democracy or the national standard of life had been given up. But the decision to defer to the wishes of the British Government over Spain in the critical early months of the war meant that (unless the help of the Soviet Union, and, above all, their own indomitable courage, enables the Spanish people to crush Fascism nevertheless) an essential position in the struggle to defend peace was gone. For who can doubt that with Fascism triumphant in Spain, with Italian and German air and submarine bases established on the Atlantic, with France surrounded on three sides by Fascist states, and her communications with Africa severed, world peace would not be worth a month's purchase?

CHAPTER XII

THE PRESENT ISSUE

IN 1936 THE Labour Party Conference met at
Edinburgh. "It was not a good conference," remarked
Dr. Hugh Dalton, Chairman of the Labour Party for
1936–37. No one will venture to disagree with him. For it
was at the Edinburgh Conference that the effects which
three years of the policy of accommodation had had upon
the movement first became apparent. From one end of the
British Labour movement to the other, the proceedings
of the Edinburgh Conference spread bewilderment and
dismay. Thousands of the noblest men and women in
Britain; men and women who had given their whole lives
to the British Labour movement, suddenly realised that
some disease was sapping the vitality of the organism
which they had created. The representatives of the Press
unanimously reported, either with alarm or with satisfaction,
according to their political complexions, the extreme sickness
of the Labour Party. Thus Mr. A. J. Cummings, the foremost political commentator of the democratic Press, wrote
of the Conference and the Labour Party as follows:

"Yes, what has happened to it? (the Labour Party). What
is to be its political fate? Will any Labour man or woman
over the age of forty live to see a Labour Government in power
again in England?

"These are among the many anxious and depressing questions
delegates were asking themselves and each other long before
the Edinburgh Conference had come to an end. . . .

"As a Labour politician remarked to me in melancholy tones
in the Caledonian Hotel: 'The Government has us now at its
mercy.'

"He expressed the view, widely shared by the rank and file,
that as a national Opposition and a constitutional alternative

to the present Government Labour has put itself out of court for a generation, or at least until the next world slump, with or without a world war."

The *Observer's* comments on the Edinburgh Conference were equally instructive. The *Observer* is a journal with pronounced Fascist sympathies. It has pronounced sympathies, that is to say, not so much for the British Union of Fascists, as for the German and Italian Governments, with which it constantly advises the British Government to ally itself. The correspondent of this newspaper thus described the effect of the 1936 Conference upon the leadership of the Labour Party:

"The acute differences that have been consuming the movement underneath were clearly exhibited in the Conference itself. No one who has attended the meetings could have failed to notice the moments when the block of trade union seats would be sitting motionless and silent, while the delegates representing the local parties were wildly cheering and gesticulating. The antagonism between the two reached such a pitch on the second day that the non-trade union delegates were actually talking of tearing up their voting papers and leaving the hall in a body.

"This is the pass to which the platform has reduced the party. It is impossible not to feel after this Conference that the movement is morally disintegrating, a process that must have begun years ago, but is only now beginning to appear. Outwardly things remain the same. There are the same brave words, the same gestures The showman still stands outside the door, beating the drum. There is the same patient and tired crowd But the tragedy is that there is no show. There is only a moth-eaten marionette, going mechanically through the gestures and motions once made by living men and women."

Thus there can be no question of the appalling character of the Edinburgh Conference being a vile imputation of disgruntled Communists. By the Chairman of the Labour Party himself, and the whole Press, that character is agreed. Yet the Edinburgh Conference could come as a shock only to those who had not observed either that the movement had allowed its leaders to adopt the policy of accommodation, or the effect that this policy was having. The official organ of the movement, the *Daily Herald*, which was tirelessly engaged in popularising this policy, did not itself pretend that there was any health in the movement.

"The fact had better be candidly faced that Labour's dynamic drive forward as a national force stopped in 1929. Since then it has on balance held its ground, but no more."[1]

No one who remembers the spirit of the British Labour movement in the nineteen-twenties, no one who lived through that glad, confident morning of the independent political activity of the British working class, can fail to be profoundly affected by this calm admission of the official organ of the party that for eight years it has made no progress. The Edinburgh Conference did in a sense bring home these terrible facts to the members of the movement. It spread dismay and, unfortunately, something very near to despair, amongst those life-long Trade Unionists, those deeply loyal co-operators, those tireless canvassers, secretaries, women workers and out-door speakers in the Local Labour Parties, who in a very real sense *are* the Labour movement.

The reaction of these all-important men and women was strong, but, unfortunately, it was almost wholly negative. They felt that something was very wrong with their movement. But they did not know what. Therefore they could not tell what could be done to put things right. And so they were all too inclined to sink into indifference and despair. For even now these tens of thousands of men and women, who are the core of the British Labour movement, do not possess the necessary equipment or training to enable them to analyse what has made their movement sick unto death. Even now these key men and women, instinctive and

---

[1] The *Daily Herald*, Nov. 6th, 1936. Mr. Marchbanks, a major Trade Union leader (General Secretary of the National Union of Railwaymen), has made the same admission. Writing in the *Railway Review*, he said:

"The plain fact is, and we had better face it, that the Labour vote is not expanding. We are not making converts. Our hold is strong upon the faithful supporters who stand by the party in fair weather and foul; but we are not making headway."

emotional Socialists to their very bones, have never been enabled to grasp Socialism as a science, to understand the nature of the mighty social struggle in which they are so deeply engaged. Hence when their movement is led down the wrong road; when they see it visibly wilting as it departs further and further from its essential tasks and functions, they are almost helpless. They *feel* what is happening, but they do not know the cause and therefore cannot even begin to look for the remedy. Marxists have often pinned high hopes on the shock which such events as the Edinburgh Conference give to the movement. But unless a decisive number of the members of the movement are equipped to understand what is happening, and so to see the remedy, the effect of such shocks, though great, is merely to depress, to drive into indifference and apathy, not to galvanise for revival. Yet these basic members of the movement have only to be shown what is wrong, and what is the way out, to be fired with all their old passion for the cause of Labour. And when that passion returns, it will have been hardened by the searing experience of all that the movement has suffered, and deepened by the acquisition of the knowledge of what is the remedy.

The Edinburgh Conference revealed what the policy of accommodation to the needs of capitalism does to a Labour movement. Briefly, it kills it. It is designed to avoid the necessity of engaging in any serious conflicts with the ruling class; and it actually may, for a time, enable the movement to avoid any major struggles. It is then seen that a Labour movement which has ceased to fight has ceased to live.

The Edinburgh Conference made four major decisions. First it revoked the existing constitution of the Labour League of Youth, taking away from that organisation almost all independence and all right to voice opinions on policy. This was avowedly done because the Labour League of Youth had declared in favour of unity and the policy of united resistance. Second, the application of the Communist Party for affiliation was rejected, as an essential part of the policy of accommodation. Third, support for the National Government's non-intervention pact on Spain was, as already related, passed unconditionally, and then made conditional on its observance by the Fascist powers. Fourth, a resolution which has resulted in the Labour Party withdrawing its opposition to the Government's rearmament programme was passed. (In July 1937 the Parliamentary Labour Party abstained from voting against the arms estimates.)

One has to describe this last event in the above somewhat indirect way, as the resolution itself neither supported nor opposed the armaments programme. It read as follows:

"That in view of the threatening attitude of Dictatorships which are increasing their armaments at an unprecedented rate, flouting International Law, and refusing to co-operate in the work of organising Peace, this Conference declares that the armed strength of the countries loyal to the League of Nations must be conditioned by the armed strength of the potential aggressors.

"The Conference, therefore, reaffirms the policy of the Labour Party to maintain such defence forces as are consistent with our country's responsibility as a Member of the League of Nations, the preservation of the people's rights and liberties, the continuance of democratic institutions, and the observance of International Law.

"Realising the relationship between foreign policy and armaments, and having regard to the deplorable record of the Government, the Labour Party declines to accept responsibility for a purely competitive armament policy. It reserves full liberty to criticise the rearmament programme of the present Government, and declares the continuance of vested interests in the private manufacture of arms to be a grave contributory danger to the Peace of the World.

The Conference accordingly pledges the Labour Party to unceasing efforts, both by exposing the present Government's record of incompetence and betrayal of its Peace pledges and by expounding our own positive International Policy, to secure the return of a Labour Government to power."

This resolution defied all attempts at interpretation. Dr. Dalton, in introducing it, assumed that it meant that the party would support rearmament. Mr. Herbert Morrison, in supporting it, assumed that it meant that the party would not support rearmament. Mr. Ernest Bevin bitterly complained that he had understood that the resolution committed the party to support rearmament, but now Mr. Morrison had said that it did exactly the opposite.

The decision, or rather non-decision, of the Conference on armaments was perhaps less immediately crucial than were the decisions which it took on unity and on Spain. But it was the armaments debate, with its tragic confusion and cross-purposes, even within the leadership, which did the most serious damage to the reputation of the party. Above all, the fact that the Executive had been unable even to formulate a resolution which took up any definite attitude on an all-important issue of the day revealed the dreadful condition to which the movement had been reduced. For this is the very nadir of leadership.

The despondency, if not despair, which settled on the British Labour movement in the autumn of 1936, and which, if it had long continued, must have led to steady disintegration, was met and to some extent overcome by strenuous and determined efforts at revival during 1937. These efforts were made, however, by men and women who were then, though happily they are not all now, outside the official leadership of the movement.

The Communist Party of Great Britain undoubtedly performed its greatest service, so far, to the British Labour movement when it organised the sending of a British battalion to fight in Spain. For if that had not been done, a frightful sense of impotence and frustration must have settled upon every member of the movement. Moreover, effective work for Spain was undertaken by many groups and individuals outside the Communist Party. A network of local committees, set up for the collection of money and supplies for Spain, under the auspices of the Spanish Medical Aid Committee are an example of the sort of activity which kept the movement alive. Again, the series of mass meetings held by the signatories of the Unity Manifesto during the spring of 1937 had a markedly tonic effect. The growth of the Left Book Club began to pump a steady supply of new blood into the movement. But, with the notable exception of Mr. Attlee's message of encouragement to the Left Book Club, these all-important activities owed little or nothing to those who controlled the great resources of the movement as a whole. Some of its leaders (as Dr. Dalton, for example, apparently did in the autumn of 1936, *see p.* 208) recognise the serious condition into which the movement had fallen, But they either failed to recognise that the reversal of the policy of accommodation will alone effect a revival, or if they did recognise this, refused to pay the price in conflict with the ruling class which such a reversal would necessarily have involved. Others of our leaders were, it seems, quite genuinely unaware that anything was wrong.

In the summer of 1937, for example, the national leader of the Labour Party issued through the Left Book Club a volume in which he expressed his political philosophy and programme (*The Labour Party in Perspective*). It must have come as a profound shock to many of its readers to find nowhere in the clearly and pleasantly written pages of Mr. Attlee's book any indication that the position of the Labour movement, was anything but wholly satisfactory. Just as Mr. Attlee showed that he did not consider that any critical situation in the world's affairs was "imminent" (and would be prepared to reverse his attitude to the question of a People's Front if he did, *see p.* 310 *below*) so, he did not see anything amiss with the position of the party which he led.

The 1937 Conference of the Labour Party was held at Bournemouth. Writing in November 1937 it is already possible to make a tentative estimate of what happened at this extremely important conference.

The truth, it is becoming clear, is that two separate, and indeed contradictory, things happened at Bournemouth. On the one hand, the Executive Committee, elected at the previous conference, carried the policy of accommodation many steps further. And on the other, a new Executive Committee, the election of which, many presume, will lead to the abandonment of the fatal policy, came into being as the result of a reform of the methods by which the Conference elects its Executive.

It is extremely important to evaluate both these events. There has been a certain tendency in the discussion of the Conference to concentrate on one of them to the exclusion of the other. Both, however, are of the highest importance. Let us consider them in turn.

The policy of accommodation was reaffirmed and reapplied at the Bournemouth Conference in two essential respects. First, the demand for the unification of the movement by the affiliation of the Communist party to the Labour Party, or by any other suitable means, was again refused; and second, the movement's policy on rearmament was changed from one of indecision and abstention to one of avowed support.

In one other respect accommodation had been, as we have seen, abandoned: during the summer of 1937 the movement declared itself opposed to one-way non-intervention in Spain. But it was not until after the Conference and the election of the new Executive that steps were taken actively to oppose the National Government's increasingly pro-Fascist policy. Unfortunately, however, the decision to support the National Government on rearmament outweighed the decision to withdraw support from the National Government upon Spain. Thus so far as its policy decisions went the Bournemouth Conference undoubtedly registered a further, and considerable, stage in the application of the policy of accommodation.

The second and contradictory event consisted in the election of the main leaders (Sir Stafford Cripps and Professor Laski) of the Unity Campaign to the new Executive combined with the acceptance of the new method of the election of a section of the Executive by the vote of the local Labour Parties alone.

The question on which the whole future of the British Labour movement depends is simply this: Which of these contradictory tendencies is going to predominate? The reform of the method of the election of the Executive and its immediate fruits in the appearance of new members on the Executive has undoubtedly proved an immense stimulus to the spirits of the movement. Indeed, the stimulus has proved so great that there has been a certain tendency to assume that the battle has already been won; that the policy of accommodation is now a thing of the past.

It is, however, obviously impossible to take this view. What has happened is that those within the Labour Party who have opposed, and who will certainly continue to oppose, the policy of accommodation, have greatly increased their strength. But the struggle itself, by which the fatal policy can be changed, still lies ahead of them—and of us.

What will be the test by which in the coming year we shall know whether the British Labour movement has abandoned the policy of accommodation? The test is a very simple one. We shall know this by whether the movement opposes the will of the National Government on essential issues, and whether it does so half-heartedly or whole-heartedly.

The coming year will see great and simple issues raised in both home and foreign affairs; issues upon which the Labour movement will have to make up its mind whether it is to accommodate itself to, or oppose, the National Government. These will be momentous issues; they will be issues on which the National Government will be determined to have its way; issues on which the National Government will, if it meets whole-hearted opposition from the Labour movement, enter upon a stern struggle with that movement.

We delude ourselves if we think that there are not still very powerful forces within the leadership of our movement which wish at all costs to accommodate the movement to the National Government's wishes on these essential issues, in order to avoid the grave struggle which will undoubtedly develop if the movement decides to oppose with any vigour. On the other hand, the issues themselves will be of so simple, indeed of so elemental, a character that those forces which wish to oppose the National Government will be in an exceedingly strong position; for accommodation would inevitably involve a startling surrender of much that the British Labour movement has always stood for.

Let us see what these issues are likely to be. In the first place, there is the great issue at home: the issue of the defence of the standard of life of the British people. That issue will force itself more and more strongly upon the movement. It is at present arising in the form of the workers', and above all the unemployed workers', reaction to rapidly rising prices. This is the most elemental of all political issues. A Labour movement which will not fight both industrially and politically on this issue will fight on nothing.

Moreover, this issue of the defence of the national standard of life is likely to arise in a changed and still more acute form during the course of the next twelve months. It is highly probable that well within that period the slump will come (indeed it may well already (November 1937) have begun). We should not suppose that we shall necessarily be faced by a catastrophic collapse comparable to that of 1929. It is possible, in view of certain counteracting factors, such as the rearmament programme, that there will be instead a slower, longer, dragging depression. In either case, however, a downward turn of trade (and the possibility is not excluded that it will take a catastrophic form) would end the rise of prices. But it would only do so at the cost of enormously increasing unemployment. (This increase appears to have begun.) The workers' standard of life would be cut into, not indeed as at present by rising prices, but far more sharply by a decreasing number of wage-earners per family. Nor, of course, would the depression have gone far before demands for reductions in wage-rates would be made.

In this case the question before the Labour movement would be this: Should the leaders of both the industrial and political sides of the movement co-operate with the National Government in attempting to meet the depression by means of measures which must, in the very nature of things, be based on sacrifices from the working class, however disguised these sacrifices may be? Or should they genuinely oppose the National Government and defend the national standard of life? And if the movement chooses this latter course of opposition, how should this opposition be carried on? Should it be confined to a polite, formal and parliamentary opposition, or should it be a real and formidable opposition? Should it be conducted, for instance, by means of stubborn Trade Union resistance to wage-cuts? Should the resistance of the unemployed be mobilised, not as was done (and even in those conditions with considerable success), with the aid of the small resources of the Left, in 1933, 1934, and 1935, but with the great resources of the movement as a whole? Should the defence of the national standard of life be made, as it obviously could be made, an overwhelming political issue at every election?

If the movement takes the latter course; if it begins to oppose with its full strength the declared will of the National Government on essential issues, very serious struggles will result; but the movement will live again. Moreover, the prospects of success in those struggles, however severe, are exceedingly bright. The truth is that the National Government is bound, whether by means of rising prices in a continuing boom, or by rising unemployment and falling wages in a new slump, to attempt grossly to lower the national standard of life in the next two years. A Labour movement which has not surrendered its independence can hardly fail to win in such a situation.

The issue of accommodation or struggle is the same, and is even more urgent, in foreign affairs. Unfortunately, in this case it is not quite so simple. I have no doubt that when the majority of its leaders persuaded the Labour Party, as they did, to some extent at Edinburgh, and fully at Bournemouth, to endorse the rearmament programme, they did so because they assumed that British armaments would always be used to restrain the Fascist aggressors. They could not even comprehend the criticism that, on the contrary, British armaments would be used to strengthen and buttress the position of the Fascist aggressors.

It was by no means difficult to have illusions on this score a year ago. But to-day such illusions should be impossible. For the Labour Party's full endorsement of the National Government's rearmament programme at Bournemouth has unquestionably been used by the National Government as a demonstration of national unity on a policy which is becoming one of full co-operation with the Fascist powers. The *de facto* recognition of Franco, Mr. Chamberlain's reiterated approaches to Germany and Italy, the National Government's evident desire to serve the interests of Japan in the Far East, are startling and terrible evidence that what we have endorsed is the strengthening of the power of a Government which has every intention of turning the existing Berlin, Rome, Tokyo triangle into a Berlin, Rome, Tokyo, London quadrilateral. Surely this fact is now beyond argument.

The practical question is this: Will the Labour movement now effectively oppose the pro-Fascist world policy of the National Government? A genuine beginning has been made. The appointment by the new Executive of the Spanish Committee to carry on a large-scale campaign in favour of arms for Spain is a real advance. If this had been done a year ago, it would have had a decisive effect on the history of the world. But it is a hundred times better that it should be done now than not at all.

There is, however, one thing, and one alone, however hard it may be to do it, which would be taken by the world as a signal that the British Labour movement had come out in genuine opposition to the pro-Fascist world policy of the National Government. And that thing is a formal pronouncement on behalf of the movement that, in view of the startling developments in the National Government's foreign policy since the Bournemouth Conference, the Labour Party, both within and without the House of Commons, must reconsider its support of the Government's rearmament policy; that henceforth it will oppose that policy until, by deeds as well as words, the Government shows that it has abandoned connivance and co-operation with the Fascist aggressors and is implementing a peace policy of solidarity with the democracies.

The uproar which such an announcement would make would, of course, be colossal. The heavens would ring with cries that the British Labour movement had committed suicide; that it was asking a disarmed Britain to fight the world, etc. etc. But through all the sound and fury the facts would steadily emerge. The very uproar itself would, for the first time, enlighten the British people as to the essential issue at stake. That issue is this: Shall the might of Britain be thrown on the Fascist or the anti-Fascist side?

I have not the slightest doubt that the Labour movement, using the great means of publicity which it now has at its command, could, within the space of a few weeks, make its position clear to the British people; show that it was opposing rearmament simply because it was now clear that the influence of British arms was being used to make Fascist aggression everywhere possible; that, as soon as a reversal of the world policy of the National Government had taken place; as soon as, for example, the British Government had restored the Spanish Government's right to buy arms, had begun to co-operate with, instead of to rebuff, the United States in the Far East, and in general was implementing a policy of collective security, the movement's policy towards rearmament would again be reconsidered.

In sum, the question is: Will the British Labour movement, over the coming months, oppose the National Government on essentials, or will it continue and intensify the policy of accommodation which it has pursued over the past four years? If it does the former, it will live. If it does the latter, it will die. The Bournemouth Conference in itself carried on, and carried further, the policy of accommodation. But, at the same time, it put into the leadership of the movement new forces which are opposed to that policy, and which have already, made their influence felt to some extent. What they are able to accomplish depends, of course, not merely on them, but on us. Every single member of the British Labour movement who realises the position must work as he or she has never worked before to see to it that our movement, instead of agreeing and dying, as it was doing before the Bournemouth Conference, shall now fight and live.

Nor have the living forces within our movement unlimited time in which to effect its revival. A new period of intenser social crisis is coming back to Britain. (The crisis never lifted from Continental Europe.) The crisis may come back in the form of slump or in the form of war, or of both successively. If, when the next crisis strikes us, we allow our leaders to cause the Labour movement to retreat before the onslaught upon the vital interests of the British people which capitalism will then be forced to deliver, our movement will go down to inevitable and deserved ruin. The mighty and terrible crises which now periodically rend the capitalist world ought to be periods of supreme opportunity for Labour movements. Then, at the very height of the storm, when the confidence of millions of men in the stability and permanence of capitalism has been shaken, is the time for Labour movements boldly to step forward and proclaim how the crisis can be overcome, not as always before at the expense of the people, but by sacrificing some, at any rate, of the gigantic property rights of the ruling class. The first Labour movement which has the courage to do that will ride the storm to power and to victory. But to Labour movements whose leaders regard these recurrent crises of capitalism with incomprehension and terror, who are always astonished at their onset, and who can think of nothing to do to overcome them but to yield up everything which the ruling class demands, these periods of crisis are fatal. They do not survive them, and they do not deserve to do so. We shall not know until the next time of trial is upon us whether the British Labour movement is still, as it certainly was in 1931, of this latter helpless, hapless type. But then we shall know. For it will not survive unless it has become, or unless, at any rate, during the period of crisis it becomes, a Labour movement of a different type and temper, such as can alone survive the social tempests of our epoch.

CHAPTER XIII

THE END OF THE ROAD BACK

WE HAVE TRACED the emergence of the modern British Labour movement through its various stages. Consisting originally of Trade Unions which were almost unconscious that their activities had any political implications, it became a movement of Trade Unions which actively promoted their political interests by putting pressure now on this, now on that, capitalist party. Then the political needs and interest of the Trade Unions became so important, and the Unions became so subject to capitalist attack, that, encouraged by the early Socialists, they found it necessary to found and foster a political party of their own.

This new working-class political party possessed at first no distinctive ideology of its own. Gradually, however, an ideology which we decided, with some reluctance, to call British Socialism, came to dominate the thinking of the majority of both its leaders and its rank and file. We analysed this ideology, first in its original form as it appeared in the minds of the Fabians, and then, under the title of the three inevitabilities, as it was actually applied in the post-war period, during which it dominated the movement. We saw that this ideology was unable to offer adequate guidance to a Labour movement faced by the formidable social conflicts of the post-war world. We saw how British Socialism broke down; how in the immediate post-war years it frittered away the then predominating strength of the Labour movement, so that by the nineteen-thirties political initiative had returned to the capitalists and the workers were everywhere on the defensive. In the new situation British Socialism became not only erroneous but irrelevant. It has been in fact, though never in form, abandoned by the leadership of the movement. In 1933 this leadership induced the movement to accept the policy of accommodation to capitalism, which it pursued steadily until the autumn of 1937, but the continuance of which is now in the balance.

This policy of accommodation to capitalism was in effect an abandonment of the independent ideology of the Labour movement; it was a return to non-Socialist, Trade Union politics. A movement which has regressed to pure and simple Trade Union politics, while it gives the impression of having no ideology, inevitably passes under the domination of the current capitalist ideology. No one who reads the speeches of, in particular, the two predominant British Trade Union leaders, who reads the speeches of Mr. Ernest Bevin and Sir Walter Citrine, can doubt that they have relapsed into a full acceptance of current capitalist ideas. At present they are, it is true, at the second stage of Trade Union Politics; at the stage in which the Unions have recognised the need to maintain a political party of their own. But the logical next step to their tacit repudiation of British Socialism, and of any other distinct working-class ideology, is to return to the view that Trade Union interests are best served, not by the maintenance of a separate Labour Party, but by putting pressure on the existing capitalist parties. For what is the use of maintaining, at great expense and by ceaseless efforts, a separate Labour Party if that party is to have no distinctive point of view?

In a word there is no halting place in the road back on which the feet of the movement have been planted. Once the bankruptcy of British Socialism had become evident, an inescapable alternative faced the movement. Either it had to secure a new and adequate Socialist ideology, which could only be scientific Socialism, or it had to go back to a pre-Socialist, pure and simple Trade-Unionist ideology. Thus the wheel has come full circle. Because the British workers did not find the right road forward, the road which they have taken is leading them back to their beginnings. Only a fresh start, made in the light of the rich experience which they have accumulated during this sixty years' journey, can now prevent the uninterrupted decline of the British Labour movement. Nor, as we have seen, has there been anything fortuitous about the whole cycle of development and decline which the movement has been through. No Labour movement which failed to equip itself with an ideology far more adequate and comprehensive than British Socialism, could hope for any other destiny.

The British Labour movement was in 1933 headed back towards its beginnings. But it must not be supposed that it is suggested that the conditions of 1855 can be reproduced in 1937. It may be that Sir Walter Citrine and his colleagues suppose that it is possible to return, first to pre-war, and ultimately to nineteenth century, conditions of only partially political Trade Unionism. But this is a dream. Neither that nor any other feature of the pre-war world can be restored. A return to non-Socialist, and ultimately non-Labour Party, Trade Unionism could be to-day but a brief transition stage in a return to a new form of non-political Trade Unionism. For that is the only form of Trade Unionism which contemporary capitalism will ultimately tolerate. Hence that is the goal towards which the policy of accommodation is leading us.

But non-political Trade-Unionism in its contemporary form is merely one feature of that new capitalist régime, designed to meet the desperate needs of capitalism in decline, which we call Fascism. This fact was perfectly illustrated by an elder statesman of British capitalism during a recent visit to Hitler. Mr. Lloyd George, in an interview with Mr. A. J. Cummings, describing his impressions of Fascist Germany, spoke in high praise of the German Workers Labour Front—the Nazi equivalent to Trade Unionism. Several German workers (one can imagine the types!) were produced for the foreign statesman's interrogation.

"More than one of them said to me," Mr. Lloyd George reported, "that it was a good thing to have got rid of what they described as the political Trade Unions. They preferred to keep questions affecting conditions of their working life out of politics. John Burns, Henry Broadhurst, Thomas Burt and most of the old Trade Union leaders were strongly of that opinion when it was decided to incorporate the unions in a political party" (*News Chronicle*, Sept. 21st, 1936).

The sharp and approving eye of the capitalist politician had detected that an essential purpose of Fascism was to drive back the workers to the primitive type of organisations which they had alone possessed fifty years ago. For, needless to say, "keeping questions affecting their working life out of politics" means, precisely, accepting the needs of capitalism as an absolutely governing and overriding consideration, which cannot even be questioned, in the settlement of the wages, hours and conditions of the wage-workers. In a word the policy of accommodation to the needs of capitalism in decline means the regression of movement, not merely to its starting point but to conditions of much more highly organised servitude to capital than those suffered by the British workers in the first half of the nineteenth century. The real contemporary equivalent to the non-political Trade Unionism of the last century is Fascist Trade Unionism. Accommodation to contemporary capitalism will ultimately mean, if it is not abandoned, accommodation to Fascism. For Fascism is the most systematic and adequate expression of the needs of capitalism in decline.

Naturally Fascism will not always be called Fascism. For example, the present policy of the British ruling class appears to be leading towards an attempt to establish its unchecked autocracy; to the attempt to sweep away all such opposition as a free Labour movement might offer, without resorting to a special demagogic Fascist movement. The British capitalists appear to intend to use the existing State machinery, and their existing methods of securing mass support, to get rid of the restraints of democracy.

HD

This programme probably involves the expectation that the British Labour movement will not have to be destroyed or driven from the field. Our rulers noted with the highest satisfaction the adoption of the policy of accommodation. They believe that if that policy is pursued with sufficient consistency, the British Labour movement will itself voluntarily retire from the political arena, and in so doing lose nine-tenths of its size and strength. Their ideal is, in a word, the self-liquidation of the Labour movement. They rely, for the moment, upon its leaders being able to carry the movement to the end of the road of surrender.

What is it, the reader may ask at this point, that makes those leaders who are pursuing what must necessarily be an unpopular policy of retreat, so strong that, hitherto, they have been able to maintain themselves, against all criticism? Is it that they are extraordinarily able? On the contrary, they are for the most part very ordinary men, without strongly marked characteristics of any kind. Their strength is a borrowed one. Their strength lies in the enormous and never withdrawn support which the whole capitalist world gives to them. The strength of the ruling class, so long as it maintains its monopoly of the means of production, is vast, and it is this strength which is lent, in a hundred ways, to the leaders of any Labour movement who will pursue a policy of accommodation to capitalism.

This is why those who stand for the alternative policy of united resistance can always be made to seem a handful of comparatively powerless critics. Everything they do is relentlessly opposed by the whole weight of the capitalist class. Everything done by those who follow the path of accommodation is applauded, aided and rewarded. No wonder those who pursue the path of accommodation seems strong. Who would not seem strong when he had the power of the old world behind him?

There is, however, another factor, and one which is perhaps of more practical importance, since, unlike the former, it is within our control. And that is the occasional failure of those who oppose the policy of accommodation to make their attitude to the Labour movement clear. The supporters of united resistance are constantly accused by the supporters of the policy of accommodation, of disloyalty to the Labour movement. And we have not always known how to express ourselves in such a way as to avoid giving colour to this accusation. The British working class has with immense difficulty and sacrifice created an extensive and highly developed Labour movement. The politically conscious workers, even in their moments of maximum disappointment with it, feel intense loyalty to that movement. Consequently they regard with hostility anyone who appears to be weakening or damaging it. The workers are entirely justified in this attitude. For the creation of an organised Labour movement is a historic achievement which no working class can afford for one moment to take lightly. We have seen in the early chapters of this book how long and arduous was the struggle by means of which the British workers created their movement. Nor can any working class ever create two such movements in any given period. A class is only capable of so much creative effort. The workers know instinctively that whatever may be the faults and limitations of the movement which they have created, it is all they have. Those critics who seem, by the bitter, harsh, shrill character of their criticism, intent not to improve but to destroy the Labour movement are, whatever their intentions, doing a terrible disservice to the working class. For experience has shown that the destruction of a Labour movement, in which this type of criticism from within the movement has played a part, even when that criticism was itself justified to the full, has not led to the creation of a new and better movement, but to the collapse of almost all forms of working-class organisation. Hence it is a primary necessity for all those who believe that, for instance, the policy of accommodation must lead the British Labour movement to destruction to show by everything that they do, and above all by the way they express their criticism of that policy, that their whole purpose is to save the movement.

Nor is it sufficient for them to know in their own minds and hearts that their purpose is wholly constructive. In politics intentions count for little. They must, above all, see to it that the actual effect of their criticism of existing policies is constructive. They must see to it that the effect of their words is to encourage the whole membership to put right what is wrong and not either to retire in despair or to drop into the fatal attitude of the professional critic who is up against everybody. Nor will it always be easy to prevent criticism, however well founded, having these disastrous effects. Men and women who have not made a close study of politics are only too apt to jump to the conclusion that, for instance, those who severely criticise the Labour Party, are "against" that party. By no means all of even the politically active British workers yet think sufficiently in class terms to realise that criticism of the policy of the Labour Party and the Labour movement is necessary just because that movement is the historic, irreplaceable creation of the British workers, which must at all costs be saved.

The by no means happy story of the development of the British Labour movement must be studied. For unless we study our mistakes we shall never mend them. But in doing so it is a thousand times necessary that every spokesman of scientific Socialism should prove his or her perfect loyalty to the Labour movement—or else no one will pay any attention to what they say. Moreover they must pay equal attention to the task of presenting their criticism in such a way that it is stimulating and constructive; that it leads onward to the reconstruction of the movement. For even the most justified criticism, if it be expressed in such a way as to seem biased, rasping and personal, can have a merely destructive effect.

In my opinion a failure to allow for these considerations —a kind of inhumanness—has hitherto been the principal flaw in the methods of the spokesmen of scientific Socialism. Their indispensable contribution to the thought of the Labour movement will not be fully effective—and the movement cannot revive until it has become fully effective —until they remedy this deficiency in the way in which they present their case. Nor is this a small or subsidiary question concerned merely with their manner, style and tone of voice. It *is* a question of manner, style and tone of voice; but these things reveal the basic attitude of a writer or speaker to what he is discussing. That is why the workers are perfectly justified in attaching a high importance to this question. It will not be until all the spokesmen of scientific Socialism have satisfactorily adjusted their own attitude to the Labour movement that they will succeed in carrying the workers with them.

What then is to be done? Preceding chapters have carried the implication that the one indispensable thing is to provide the British Labour movement with an adequate instead of an inadequate socialist ideology; to replace the now bankrupt ideology of British Socialism with scientific Socialism.

This is an indispensable task which must be undertaken by every one who cares for the survival of our movement. But if the question is asked, is this the only thing necessary to our salvation, we can give only a conditional assent. In one sense it is true that the substition of scientific, for Fabian, socialism as the ideology of the movement is all that is needed. If and when this is accomplished the British Labour movement will be in a position to perform its historic function of leading the British people out of the decay of capitalism into a new civilisation. But the acquisition of scientific Socialism as its ideology implies a change in the very structure of a Labour movement. It will not suffice—and indeed it is not possible—for the existing movement, just as it is, to acquire the new ideology. The tasks which have to be accomplished are too formidable for that. A basic change in the very structure of the movement is indispensable. For such an organisational change is inseparably associated with the acquisition of scientific Socialism as the ideology of the movement. Before going on, in the third part of this book, to discuss the prospects which the adoption of scientific Socialism will open up, we must turn our attention to this question of the structure of a Labour movement. For it is of the first importance.

PART II

THE NEW MODEL

CHAPTER XIV

WHAT IS A PARTY?

"THE TRANSFORMATION OF the world is a great, complicated and painful process," remarked Joseph Stalin.[1]

No one doubts it. But equally almost no one in the Labour movements of the West has faced this fact. Or, rather, they have not realised that the aims of their movements, which are simple enough in themselves, since they consist in the provision of decent conditions of life, of security and of peace for the working populations of their communities, cannot be achieved without a transformation of the world. This enormous underestimate of the task before them, amounting almost to unconsciousness of its existence, has, above everything else, hitherto stultified the efforts of these movements. For a consciousness of the magnitude and character of their task alone forces men to create adequate instruments of their will. And such adequate instruments of the will of the working class the Labour movements of Britain and America have not hitherto become.

Now any class which is impelled by the social pressures exercised upon it to attempt to remould the world creates a political party as the vehicle of its collective will. Social classes which have interests to defend, or purposes to achieve, form political parties; for that is the only way in which they can do the job. *Hitherto, however, they have done so more or less unconsciously.* And this has led to endless mystification. Social classes have not been by any means fully conscious of themselves. Therefore it has been impossible for the members of this or that class—or subdivision of a class—of the landlords, of the industrial entrepreneurs, or

[1] In his interview with Mr. H. G. Wells

of the wage-workers, for example, to come together, saying self-consciously: "Look, we are a distinct class with interests of our own. We herewith found the such-and-such political party to promote our interests." Nothing like that has ever happened.[1] And yet a series of political parties, each one of which reveals itself, when we examine its actions, to have been the political instrument of a particular social class, has come into being. But how can these parties have been created, if their creators did not know what they were doing?

The method by which particular social classes have created political parties to represent them has been this. The most active and advanced members of some class have begun to voice their opinions. They have said what they thought ought to be done. They have defined what they held to be *right*—and consequently what they asserted were their *rights*. The rest of their class, after longer or shorter delay, has heard their voice and discovered that it agreed with them. Gradually the most energetic members of the class in question have got together in some sort of association designed to promote the ideals which they have found that they had in common. The association or party thus formed has been created round the body of ideas and ideals which the most energetic members of the class find that they have—as if by chance—in common. Thus each and every political party has been created to establish democracy, or, conversely, to preserve religion, or to protect the family, or to aggrandise the Empire; in short, to promote some particular ideal. It has not been the conscious instrument of class interest.

The members of such parties protest, and genuinely believe, that it is an association of like-minded (and, of course, right-minded) men and women who all happen to hold the same opinions on the fundamental political issues of the day. And so it is. *But what its members have never guessed is that they hold this group of opinions—amounting to*

---

[1] Except, perhaps, in the case of some of the Farmers' movements of the Western States of America, and, as described below, in the case of some Labour Movements.

what we have called an ideology—because they belong to the same class, and therefore have the same basic interests. They may belong to the class the interests of which the party of like-minded people is promoting by adoption and not by birth. For instance, talented adventurers have often risen from the working class into the capitalist, and even, in the past, into the feudal classes, and have acted as efficient servants of their adopted class. Similarly, members by birth of the capitalist class, or more often of the intermediate sub-class of independent intellectual workers (doctors, lawyers, preachers, merchants, civil servants, etc.), have often served the working class in its parties—and some of them (e.g. Marx, Engels and Lenin) have done so supremely well. No reasonable student of human history can now deny that this is the nature of political parties. They are not simply groups of men and women who, by some extraordinary accident, all think alike on all the major questions of the day. They are the organisations formed (though unconsciously) by particular and distinct social classes for the promotion of the common ends of the class.

This fact—of cardinal importance for the understanding of human history—has, however, only been grasped during the past half century. For it is only in our epoch that men are gaining any conscious understanding of human society and its process of development. A common feature of all hitherto existing social systems, of servile society, of feudalism, and of capitalism, has been that in them men were socially unself-conscious. They did not know that they were living in a servile, a feudal, or a capitalist society. They just knew that they were living. Their social environment seemed to them almost as immutable as their natural environment. It was not until capitalist society was firmly established in the middle of the last century that social self-consciousness began to appear. Gradually and gropingly men began to ask questions as to the nature of their basic social institutions. Still more gradually and gropingly they have begun to find answers to these questions. It may be worth while to give an example of the need both to ask such sociological questions, and to answer them, from the related but distinct sphere of economics. For the whole idea of dragging into consciousness the nature of our basic economic or political institutions is both a strange and a quintessentially important one.

Sir Robert Peel in introducing the Bank Act of 1844 (one of the essential statutes completing the legal framework of British capitalism) to the House of Commons asked the famous question: "What is a pound?" Neither he nor any honourable member was able to provide an answer. For capitalism is the last of a series of unselfconsciously constructed economic systems. Under capitalism the division of labour necessary to the existence of any community is effected automatically and unconsciously by means of exchanges made possible by a medium of exchange which we call money. But nobody within capitalist society knows what this money is. It is, to be sure, one particular commodity—lately gold or silver—set aside to serve as a medium of exchange. Thus historically a pound sterling is a pound weight of silver. Peel, no doubt, knew this perfectly well. But this piece of historical knowledge did not help him much in his bewilderment over this extraordinary thing, money, which his new Act was (he hoped) to regulate; this thing which was evidently a linch-pin in the economic life of society; which could dislocate that life catastrophically if it got out of control; this thing which everybody both used and worshipped, but which nobody understood.

In the long period during which men had used money, very few people had ever asked Peel's question: What is this stuff? It was a sign of the dawning social self-consciousness of man that the question was asked. But it could only be answered by men who had achieved a much wider degree of social self-consciousness, who had realised that capitalism, with its unconsciously effected division of labour, by means of exchanges mediated by money, was but one transitory type of social system. Once that was realised it became plain that money could be nothing but a unit of the thing which was being divided up, or apportioned, amongst the working population, viz. their labour—their available working time. The thing being divided up was human labour. That is what any highly organised economic system has to enable the community, consciously or unconsciously, to do.[1] It has somehow or other to enable men to divide up the necessary work of the world amongst the available workers.

A pound, then, is a unit of so much human labour. When you spend a pound you apportion, do you not, so much human labour to such-and-such a task? If you spend the pound on a pair of shoes, you order that such-and-such a number of man-hours shall be spent on shoe-making. If, instead, you spend the pound on chocolates, you order that the same number of man-hours shall be spent on producing chocolates. But since all this is done without anybody understanding it—since it is done unconsciously —your pound cannot be just a written order for so many man-hours' worth of shoes or chocolates; it has to be an actual, tangible embodiment of that amount of human labour, or a paper certificate that you possess such a tangible embodiment of human labour. That embodiment can be nothing but some commodity which it takes—on the average —that amount of time to produce, viz. a pound weight of silver, or so many ounces of gold, as to-day. For the possession of, for instance, one ounce of gold, which it takes, on the average, X man-hours to produce, is the proof that you have the right to apportion X man-hours of labour to such-and-such a task.

That is a pound. It is some one, socially selected, commodity which it takes—on the average—a particular, given

[1] More primitive societies, consisting of self-sufficing peasants, have clearly no such need, for in them each family does its own work. The only division of labour which is necessary is a division of labour within the family. Such societies cannot be said to possess an economic system. It is only as and when the hitherto self-sufficing peasants begin to specialise in producing this or that, and consequently to exchange this *with* that, that it becomes necessary somehow or other to apportion out the necessary work of the community amongst the available households. And this gets done, quite unconsciously, of course, by the process of exchange, which will be, in such societies, based strictly on the amount of human labour which has been devoted to the production of the things exchanged.

amount of man-hours of socially necessary labour time (to give it its proper name) to produce. Pounds are units of embodied labour-time which can be thrown now here, now there, as our ceaseless exchanging of commodities apportions (exceedingly badly, as a matter of fact) society's available amount of labour-time to all the different, necessary tasks of society.

Peel asked, and Marx answered, the question: What is a pound? In the same way we must question every major social phenomenon. We can take nothing for granted. If we are ever to comprehend, and so control, our social life we must know what things are. For example, we must ask not only what is a pound, but what is a party? The answer to this latter question is, I repeat, no longer in doubt. A political party is not an association of like-minded individuals; it is the instrument of the common will of a particular social class. (Or, to bring the two conceptions together, it is an association of individuals like-minded because they are members or agents of a particular social class.)

This interpretation of the nature of political parties has only become undeniable in our epoch. In past epochs of human history the class structure of human society has been of great complexity. Coalitions of classes, and sub-classes, have formed political parties and they have done so in complete unconsciousness. The apparent basis of parties has been religious and ideal. They have seemed to stand for Protestantism, limited or absolute monarchy, liberty, equality, fraternity, or what you will—for anything but the interests of a particular class. Hence it was, and to some extent still is, a matter of controversy whether, for example, the seventeenth or eighteenth century parties were really organisations of particular classes. When we come to the nineteenth century, however, it would now be a most eccentric historian who would deny that in Britain, for example, the Conservative Party had represented, on the whole, the interests of the landlords, and that the Liberal

Party had represented, on the whole, the interests of the industrialists. But even then the interplay of class interest was complex. For these two sub-divisions of the ruling class (they were no more) had much in common. They both owned means of production. They quarrelled bitterly, but it was to some extent a family quarrel. They could strike many a mutually satisfactory bargain. Hence their respective parties could not be, and were not, unswervingly consistent representatives of their respective class interests. For example, a Government based on the Conservative Party, when it repealed the Corn Laws in the middle of the century, served the interests of the industrialists as against the interests of the landlords, though it broke the Conservative Party in two in doing so.

In Britain it was not until the twentieth century itself that the class nature of political parties became fully plain to all. (It has not become so even yet in America.) For it is not until the wage-workers form their own political party that it becomes finally undeniable that political parties are the organisations of distinct social classes. But then it does become undeniable. For the working class forms its political organisations with a far higher degree of self-consciousness than any previous class has possessed. Even now, however, the process has not become fully conscious. Many of the political leaders of the British, and still more of the American, workers do not feel themselves to be the representatives of a particular class in society. They often still speak and feel as if they were individuals who just happened to believe in certain political ideals, viz. this or that social reform, or this or that conception of Socialism. Spokesmen of the British Labour Party, in particular, continually suggest that it is "not a class party". If they meant that the Labour Party should, and does, represent the interests, not only of the manual workers, but of the whole 85 per cent of the population which has no substantial ownership of the means of production, they would be wholly correct. But they mean, rather, that the Socialism for which the Labour Party declares itself to stand is not the particular interest of the workers, but it is an abstractly desirable ideal which may be expected to appeal equally to capitalists and workers.

In suggesting this they can do nothing but confuse and distort the palpable facts of the case. It is perfectly true that a substantial section of the working class has not yet become sufficiently conscious of itself and its interests to support the Labour movement. It is equally true that a tiny handful of men and women from the capitalist class support that movement. But to suggest that this constitutes any appreciable qualification, even, to the assertion that the Labour movement is the movement of the wage-workers is to fly in the face of all sense and reason. In just the same way, though rather less obviously, it is apparent that the Conservative Party is the party of the class which owns the means of production. It is perfectly true that in a capitalist community which maintains democracy it is necessary for such a party to obtain the votes of a substantial section of the wage-workers. It is perfectly true that in Britain, at the moment, it often succeeds in doing so. But no one who has the slightest acquaintance with the character of, for instance, the British Conservative Party, could possibly doubt that it was the party of the owners of the means of production. Indeed, the fundamental reason why it can still get the votes of the more backward sections of the British wage-workers is precisely because they know it to be the party of the ruling class. For this section of the wage-workers still consciously accepts the leadership of that class. Moreover, though the Conservative Party must attract the votes of many workers, it attracts them to vote for strictly capitalist-class candidates. The Conservative Party consists in its active personnel, in the men it sends to Parliament and still more to office, of members, either by birth or by adoption, of the capitalist class. (A Conservative working-man is occasionally permitted to stand for some unwinnable constituency, and one is usually elected to the executive of the Central Conservative Association—with no other object, apparently, than to be a living exception, professionally engaged in proving the rule.) The final test is, however, as usual, financial. Whence comes the money which respectively supports the two parties? One has only to think of how inconceivable is the idea of a Socialist Party which drew its main financial support from the capitalists, or of a Conservative Party which drew its main financial support from the workers, to be convinced that contemporary British political parties are the instruments of the wills of distinct social classes.

In the first part of this book we described how the British working-class movement came to found its own political party. We then traced the story of this party's rise, and discussed its present tendency to decline. One of the lessons which can be learnt from this tragic story is that, bound up with the inadequacy of the ideas of the movement, was a corresponding inadequacy in the kind of political organisation which the movement created. The acquisition of an adequate Socialist ideology—of, in a word, scientific Socialism—would have necessitated the creation of a basically different type of political organisation.[1] For, again, the organisation is conditioned by the task which it sets itself.

The British Labour movement never became adequately conscious of the magnitude and difficulty of the task which confronted (and still confronts) it. It realised but dimly, if at all, that it must accomplish a colossal task of social transformation or perish. Hence the movement felt no necessity to evolve any specially efficient or highly developed political party as an instrument of its will. A knowledge of scientific Socialism alone could have made the movement conscious of the job it had to do, and so of the type of political instrument needed to do it.

For a knowledge of scientific Socialism, and this alone, could have guarded the slowly growing political consciousness of the British working class, and its organisations,

[1] Though this different form of political organisation would, in my view, have had to have been an addition to, not a substitute for, the Labour Party (see below).

from the formidable influence of the Imperialist environment in which they necessarily developed. Above all,
scientific Socialism could alone have enabled the movement
to have become conscious of the critical urgency of its task.
It alone could have enabled the movement to realise that
a certain point must come in its development, and in the
growing difficulties of British capitalism, when either
the Labour movement must transform its environment or
be destroyed by it.

The Fabian Socialists saw in a sense the need for social
transformation. But they seem to have regarded its
accomplishment as a very ordinary affair which, since it
would be prolonged over several centuries, during which
the existing social system would serve mankind well
enough, called for no new or special form of organisation.

In the event, the British Labour Party was built much
on the lines of the existing capitalist parties. Such parties
(the then existing Liberal and Conservative Parties in
Britain, for example,) were, historically, parties consisting
of Members of Parliament. In origin, they were associations
into which the persons elected to Parliament had sorted
themselves out in the course of parliamentary debate. For
when these parties had been formed, the franchise had been
exceedingly restricted. Hence the parties which had emerged
had had the character of opposing parliamentary groups,
each representing a subdivision of the ruling class. By
the end of the nineteeth century the British franchise had
become relatively wide and the character of the existing
political parties had been to some extent modified. They
had remained groups, and at bottom parliamentary groups,
representing particular subdivisions of the ruling class,
but at the same time they had become large-scale vote-
gathering machines. One of their primary functions was to
return a majority of the Members of Parliament at general
elections. Accordingly they had added to themselves local
associations, one for each parliamentary constituency.
These associations were, and are, the only popular units of
the capitalist parties. They are controlled, moreover, by

powerful party headquarters. For the capitalist parties do not, of course, merely gather votes in the abstract—they gather votes for the benefit of the capitalist class, or the particular section of it which they represent.

The Labour Party resembled these existing capitalist parties in the respect that its object was to elect Members of Parliament. Its original name, the Labour Representation Committee, shows that this was its original, and in practice, unique object. As the party grew to national dimensions its structure also became more and more that of an association of local parties, one for each parliamentary division. This is its character to-day. Nor could any other form of organisation arise from Fabian conceptions. For the Fabians thought of political action as essentially consisting in the election of the maximum possible number of members to Parliament and other governing bodies.

It is true that it was not possible to make the Labour Party a replica of the capitalist parties. For after all, the Labour Party was a party of the working class, and it was therefore impossible to finance it from the same sources as the capitalist parties, viz. the subscriptions of rich individuals. No Labour Party can hope to be financed except from working-class organisations, of which the Trade Unions are the essential examples. (In Britain the Co-operatives play some part in financing what are, to all intents and purposes, Labour candidates.) Hence a Labour Party cannot help remaining a party of the Labour movement. As such it must have a formal and avowed connection with the interest, i.e. the working class as organised in Trade Unions and Co-operative Societies, which it is designed to promote. The capitalist parties are designed to promote the interests of the owners of the means of production, and they never cease to do so. But the capitalists, being a small class, can act as individuals. Hence there is no need for the capitalist parties formally to affiliate themselves to, or to accept affiliation from, the characteristic organisations of the capitalist class, as, for example, the Federation of British Industries. This enables the capitalist parties to maintain the outward pretence that they are not class parties at all, but disinterested guardians of the common weal, and, very ludicrously, to attack the Labour Party for its avowed organisational connection with the Trade Unions.

The leaders of the Labour Party were convinced that a parliamentary and vote-gathering organisation was all that the working class needed in the political field. Or, rather, they never conceived of a political party of any other kind. *The lesson of experience is, however, that this kind of political party can never by itself do the job of social transformation which every Labour movement must, when it reaches a certain stage of development, accomplish or perish.*

The British Labour movement is to-day confronted with the menacing prospect of frustration and decline, not only because of the policy of accommodation instead of struggle, the nature of which we analyzed in Part I, but also because—and this has been inextricably associated with this policy of accommodation—the only political organisation which it has hitherto adequately developed has remained of the simple parliamentary or vote-gathering kind. It is this organisational deficiency, as well as its failure to acquire the ideology of scientific Socialism and the policy of working-class struggle, which has brought our movement to its present pass.

In fact the three deficiencies are really one. For an essential part of the science of Socialism, as it has been developed to-day, is a conception of a new type of political party differing in decisive respects from the capitalist parties and from the working-class parties which have been modelled on them. The new wine of Socialism cannot be poured into the old bottles of a political party of the old exclusively parliamentary, vote-gathering type. The experience of the modern British Labour movement during the whole half century of its existence proves (as does, for that matter, and even more clearly, the experience of the Western European Labour movements) that we have reached one of those points in history when the forces of progress can only win if they can create new forms of organisation adequate to the task which confronts them. They must create, on pain of their stultification and destruction, a new model.

Such situations have frequently arisen before in history. An example comes from the English Great Rebellion. In 1643 the Parliamentary cause seemed faced with total frustration. It had had to rely upon what were fundamentally amateur armies, based on the London trained bands. They had proved incapable of destroying the Royalist forces. Then Cromwell organised his New Model Army. It was still an army, be it observed. But it was something different from, and more than, any army which the world had hitherto known. It was not merely that it was professional; that it achieved a level of training and equipment equal to that of the forces opposed to it. It was an army which had equipped itself not only with arms and technical skill but with, to use our modern term, an ideology. It was an army better educated, more conscious of what it was fighting for, and better, and yet more voluntarily, disciplined than any yet seen. It was an army which in the hour of victory combined the destruction of the enemy with keen political debate as to the kind of society which should be set up. (See the Clarke Papers for an account of the New Model's profound debates on the relationship between property and democracy, for instance.) It was almost a political party as well as an army. It proved adequate to its historical task; it conquered. It has bequeathed us the conception of the new model; the new instrument forged for the accomplishment of new tasks.

No sooner do we begin to reflect on the present frustration and decline of the British and Western European Labour movements than the need for the development of a new type of political party, if they are ever to win, positively leaps to the eye. For the task of social transformation which they must accomplish, if they are to triumph instead of being destroyed (and there is no third alternative) is the most gigantic which has ever faced any association of men in the history of the world. The transformation of the world, undertaken consciously and purposefully, in order first to make life tolerable, and then endlessly to develop it, for the immense majority of the human race is indeed a great, complicated and painful process. In particular, the transference of the means of production from the individual ownership of the few to the collective ownership of the whole people, and this is the indispensable condition for everything else, is a colossal undertaking. For it inescapably involves, as experience has shown, the transference of the power of the State from the hands of the capitalists to those of the workers. Nor is this the full extent of the task. For again experience has shown that the organised workers cannot simply capture the State machine and use it for their own purposes. Once they have power in their hands they have to discard the existing State machine and build up a new one of their own. For the existing State machine was built up for the specific task of maintaining the rule of the capitalist class and has proved incapable of performing any other.

These tasks of social transformation are in themselves gigantic. Moreover, the transformation is being, and will be, resisted by the existing ruling class with all its might. Such resistance is natural and inevitable, for no one likes to have immense wealth and privileges taken from him. Sometimes this wealth and these privileges have been acquired by their present possessors by superior intelligence, cunning or diligence in the course of the ceaseless struggle for personal power and leadership which goes on within the capitalist class. In these cases they seem to their possessors the hard-earned rewards of personal merit. In other cases equally great privileges and wealth have beeen acquired without any effort at all, merely by the accident of birth. In these cases they seem still more precious and sacred, for they appear to their possessors to be part of the natural order of things. There is, however, something frantic, something hysterical and beyond reason, in the lengths to which the capitalist class has, hitherto, at any rate, shown itself ready to go in order to defend its possessions. This frenzy is partly accounted for when we remember that the modern property owners, like all other ruling classes, have genuinely persuaded themselves that there is no alternative to their rule. The majority of the modern capitalists sincerely suppose that they are defending human civilisation itself; for they confuse human civilisation with their unearned incomes.

But what at bottom gives the resistance of the richest and most securely established members of the ruling class so frantic and stick-at-nothing a character, is fear. These topmost members of the ruling class are usually farthest removed from any contact with the actual processes of production. Many of them are now members of the increasingly influential *rentier* sub-class of purely passive owners of the means of production. I believe that many of them are, more or less unconsciously, convinced that they would immediately perish if they were deprived of their property derived incomes. They simply cannot imagine that it is possible for people to exist by earning their livings.[1] Hence to them, to their deepest selves, the threat of the deprivation of their unearned incomes is nothing more nor less than the threat of death by starvation. They show by their whole outlook and conduct that this is how they regard the proposal to socialise the means of production. This is why the greater number of them have always hitherto allowed themselves to be persuaded by their leaders that, in the name of religion, the family, morality and public order, they are fully justified in attempting anything, including mass murder, and the destruction of whole cities and countrysides, in order to keep their money. Thus the struggle of the working class to socialise the means of production is necessarily a desperate one. For the class

[1] Since some 90 per cent of the population must in the nature of things always exist by earning its living, this statement will seem fantastic and incredible to most workers. But from a fairly wide knowledge of the class that lives by owning I assure them that this is the case. We are here dealing, not with conceptions which are open to rational considerations, but with the fantasy life of the possessing class.

which will resort to almost anything to retain its claim to derive unearned incomes, is the ruling class in existing society. It possesses immense power; its hands are on every lever of social control. It is deeply entrenched in the central citadel of power in modern society, the State.[1]

In the first number of the journal in which he was to begin to develop the conception of the new model political party Lenin wrote of the power of the old ruling class.

"Before us, in all its strength, towers the fortress of the enemy from which a hail of shells and bullets pours down upon us, mowing down our best warriors. We must capture this fortress, and we shall capture it if we combine all the forces of the awakening proletariat with all the forces of the Russian revolutionaries into a single party that will attract all that is virile and honest in Russia."[2]

Lenin was writing of the struggle of a Labour movement in an autocratic society. In such societies the need to take power—to acquire the power of the State—as the prerequisite of everything else is obvious and undeniable. An essential lesson of the post-war history of the West is that this is no less true, though it is far less obvious, in capitalist democracies. The existence of democracy does, indeed, change the task which faces a Labour movement. But if in some ways it makes that task much easier, in others it makes it more difficult, in the sense of more complex. The bonds by which those who own the State control the rest of the population, mentally as well as physically, are in capitalist democracies much more pervasive, just because they are so much less apparent and tangible, than they are in capitalist autocracies. It may be (and we must do everything in our power to ensure that it shall be) that these bonds can, in capitalist democracies, be loosed without the capitalists being given any opportunity of provoking armed conflict.

---

[1] Mr. Attlee, the present leader of the Labour Party, believes, however, that the Labour Party will "secure the acquiescence of the greater number of its opponents in the changes that will be brought about". (See below, p. 353, for some discussion of this view.)

[2] *Selected Works of Lenin*, Vol. II, p. 14.

This will be, if we can achieve it, an immense gain. But to achieve it will require, not less, but much more, skill, knowledge, self-discipline and organised power on the part of the Labour movement. Thus our struggle in Britain and America is at present, and may remain, of a different kind from that which faced the Russian Labour movement. But in many ways it is an even more difficult, as it is certainly a more complex, struggle. In order to win it we need, as an absolute condition of victory, a new model party.

In regard to America we can only make this assertion on the basis of the experience of the older and more highly developed Labour movements of Western Europe. In Britain we know that it is true. For we have been trying for fifty years to do the job without the adequate development of such a party, and we have not succeeded.

The second part of this book is devoted to a description of this new type of political party. If such a new kind of political party did not exist we should have to invent one—or rather very slowly and painfully to evolve it by trial and error. For nothing is more certain than that the old exclusively parliamentary, vote-gathering type of working-class party can never, by itself, do the job. How could it? Once the magnitude of the task before a Labour movement has been realised no one can really suppose that the old, loose, broad, vague kind of party—the greater part of the activities of which consists in the single task of attempting to elect local councillors and Members of Parliament—is up to the job. Fortunately, however, we do not have to go through the long, toilsome and costly process of evolving out of our own heads the new model which can alone bring victory. A party of the new type was evolved, though not without extreme difficulty, in Russia in the first twenty years of the present century. It proved capable of taking power from the capitalists, and holding it for the workers. It did transfer the means of production from the individual ownership of the capitalists to the collective ownership of the whole community. For the past twenty years it has been engaged in building up a new type of human civilisation called Socialism. Moreover, in the course of those last twenty years efforts have been made, more or less successful according to local circumstances, to build up parties of this new type in almost every capitalist state in the world, and such parties, embryonic in some cases, large, highly developed and influential in others, exist in sixty-eight states to-day. Lenin conceived of this new kind of political party, and built the first sample of it. This new kind of party should engage our closest attention. For the development of a party of this new type is an indispensable part of the measures by means of which alone the British Labour movement can escape from the frustration which is to-day threatening to destroy it. Similarly, the adequate development of such a party in the United States of America is an indispensable part of those measures by means of which alone the American Labour movement can prevent itself from treading the dreary cycle of growth, indecisive maturity, frustration, and inevitable decay which the British movement has so far trod.

CHAPTER XV

CHARACTER OF THE NEW MODEL

THE DISTINGUISHING CHARACTERISTICS of political parties built upon the new model are as follows.

First they possess the ideology which we have called scientific Socialism. Such an ideology amounts to a full realisation of the nature, methods and purposes of the struggle into which the working class finds itself impelled by the conditions of life which capitalism imposes upon it.

The basis of scientific Socialism is an understanding of capitalism. Unless we understand the nature of the existing economic system, we can never free ourselves from it. It was, we saw, primarily because they never achieved an understanding of the nature of capitalism that the Fabian or British Socialists proved such disastrous guides for the working-class movement. If those who guide a working-class movement do not understand the nature of capitalist exploitation, that movement is doomed. If in particular they do not realise that the inescapable tendency of any system in which the means of production are owned by a small class, is to appropriate for that class the whole of the huge mass of surplus wealth (of wealth in excess of what is needed to maintain the rest of the population, that is to say) which is created by modern means of production, the movement will never be able to foresee and to prepare for the conflicts which will confront it. Conversely, if this one fact is really grasped, the whole twentieth century development of capitalism can be comprehended. That development leads, through Imperialism and its wars for the redivision of the markets of the world, to extreme unevenness in the development of the rival Empires, and a frontal attack on all the rights and interests of the mass of the population. Fascism and the destruction of human civilisation are the logically necessary and fore-seeable goals if this whole chain of development is not intercepted. When once the basic nature of capitalist exploitation has been grasped, it becomes inescapably clear that the present line of capitalist development is taking us, not upwards to a halcyon period of gradual and beneficial reforms, but downwards to a dark night in which civilisation founders amidst endless violence and war.

Similarly, if the direction of the development of modern capitalism has once been grasped, then the nature of the task which confronts the working-class movements will become apparent. That task is not, unfortunately, one of co-operating with an ascending capitalism in the improvement of human life; it is one of opposing flatly the down-thrust of a capitalist system in decay; of breaking off the present line of social regression and starting a new ascent from a new foundation. This realisation should in turn make it apparent that the working-class movement can do comparatively little until and unless it gets power; until and unless, that is to say, the power of the State passes out of the hands of the owners of the means of production, where even in the capitalist democracies it undoubtedly resides to-day, into the hands of the 85 per cent of the population who are non-owners. It should further become apparent that the State cannot remain as it is during this transition; that the existing State is part and parcel of the class which owns it, and that consequently its transference to another class involves its more or less complete abolition and the construction of a new kind of State, suitable to the needs of the new ruling class. From this it should be evident that, however gradual the building of a Socialist economic and political system must be, the transference of power from one class to another must, in the nature of things, be a relatively short and decisive process. Thus a sufficiently profound understanding of capitalism will reveal the character and magnitude of the task which confronts a Labour movement in the twentieth century, and will, therefore, indicate the type of organisation which can alone hope to do the job.

Such, in briefest outline, is the scientific Socialism which a political party of the new model will have made a very part of itself. Such a party must consist of, and above all be guided by, men and women who have completely mastered the whole body of political and economic science indicated above. This knowledge must have become a part of them, so that they instinctively think and act upon its basic premises. Thus the new model political party is, in one of its aspects, the vehicle, the incarnation, of scientific Socialism.[1]

Parties based on the new model have another, and to many people a far more surprising, ideological characteristic than this, however. Not only do they possess the ideology known as scientific Socialism; they possess no other ideology. In a word, they do not tolerate within their ranks the co-existence of more than one ideology. This somewhat startling characteristic was in a sense the first feature of the new model to become apparent. The original example of a political party built upon the new model came into existence in Russia between 1900 and 1917. But, like everything else in the world, it was not entirely new. Indeed, its supporters first began to differentiate themselves from other contemporary Socialists by a demand to return to the theory and practice of the original type of Socialist or working-class parties. These original working-class parties had been founded in Germany, France and many other European countries, on the basis of the exposition of scientific Socialism by Marx and Engels, during the second half of the nineteenth century. It is clear that Marx and Engels intended that these parties should be of a new kind; that they should not resemble the capitalist parliamentary parties, and in particular that they should be founded upon one scientifically arrived at body of social

[1] It is more usual to call this body of doctrine Marxism. But to do so is to neglect the development of Marxism made by Lenin and Stalin. Hence the science is often now alluded to as "Marxism-Leninism"—an appallingly clumsy term.

theory, from which they should not permit their members
to depart. For a time the new Socialist parties succeeded
fairly well in embodying these concepts. But towards the
end of the century they began to degenerate. In the last
analysis this tendency represented the influence exercised
upon the middle class and the top section of the workers
by Imperialism. Before his death in 1895 Engels found
himself struggling hard against the rottenness which,
he said, he felt was gaining ground in the German party.
This was the beginning of that "revisionism" to which
we have already referred.

Now the revisionists began by making the claim, not
that the whole Socialist movement should come over to
their point of view, but that the advocates of this point
of view should have "freedom of criticism" of scientific
Socialism. It was against this tendency that Lenin launched
his full powers. He demanded that the movement preserve
inviolate both the scientific ideology and the well-defined
organisational structure of the original Socialist parties.
He was writing, however, mainly in respect of the Russian
movement. And in Russia a Socialist Party had not yet
been fully constituted. Hence Lenin's demand was that
the new Russian "Social Democratic Labour Party" should
reject the current innovation of the period (which was the
loosening tendency of revisionism) and should be built
upon the "old model" of Marx and Engels. But, as so
often in history, the result of Lenin's ultimately successful
struggle to preserve the old, produced a far greater innovation than anyone had dreamt of. It produced the new
kind of working-class political party, which history has
shown to be indispensable for victory.

Lenin's famous book *What is to be Done?* answers the
question of its title by saying in effect—start building a
Russian Socialist Party genuinely capable of leading the
Russian people in its struggle with autocracy. And for this
purpose, Lenin went on, far from it being advisable, as the
revisionists are claiming, to allow greater freedom of
criticism, it is above all necessary to clarify and unify our

ideas, so that we may have an unshakable basis of common assumptions on which we can all work. For is not, asked Lenin, this demand for freedom of criticism a very queer one? Does it not in effect deny that Socialism is a science at all? If Socialism is a science, then those who believe that one of its theories is erroneous must point this out and demand that the old theory be scrapped and a new one put in its place. If they ask this then we will all examine the new theory, see whether the old is really defective, and, if it is, make the substitution, but if not, not. But the revisionists are demanding, not that we scrap the old, but that we put a new and quite incompatible theory alongside the old, and that some of us, *in the same party*, should be free to subscribe to the old theory and some to the new. They are asking, said Lenin, "not the substitution of one theory for another, but freedom from any complete and thought-out theory".[1] This, Lenin declared, would be fatal. No Socialist Party which really meant business could possibly allow this. This way lay disintegration. This way lay what he called "the marsh". By the marsh he meant those people—and they exist in every Socialist and Labour Party—who do not see, and do not want to see, the importance of questions of theory. Such people cannot and will not comprehend that the whole fate of a working-class movement nearly always depends upon the kind of Socialism which it adopts. Such people have not the slightest realisation of what a Labour movement is up against. Therefore they see no need for clarity, for thinking things through to their ultimate conclusions, for discipline, for self-restraint, for the sacrifice of personal predilections. Lenin described the damage which these often well-intentioned persons may do in one of the most famous passages which he ever wrote:

"We are marching in a compact group along a precipitous and difficult path, firmly holding each other by the hand. We are surrounded on all sides by enemies, and are under their almost constant fire. We have combined voluntarily, precisely for the purpose of fighting the enemy, and not to retreat into

[1] *Selected Works*, Vol. II, p. 46.

the adjacent marsh, the inhabitants of which, from the very outset, have reproached us with having separated ourselves into an exclusive group and with having chosen the path of struggle instead of the path of conciliation. And now several among us begin to cry out: let us go into this marsh! And when we begin to shame them, they retort: how conservative you are! Are you not ashamed to deny us the right to invite you to take a better road! Oh yes, gentlemen! You are free not only to invite us, but to go yourselves wherever you will, even into the marsh. In fact, we think that the marsh is your proper place, and we are prepared to render *you* every assistance to get there. Only let go of our hands, don't clutch at us and don't besmirch the grand word 'freedom'; for we too are 'free' to go where we please, free not only to fight against the marsh, but also against those who are turning towards the marsh."

With what immense force does Lenin reveal the magnitude and gravity of the task which faces a Labour movement! The path is precipitous and difficult; we are surrounded by very formidable enemies, who will not be moved, as he says elsewhere, by "patient appeals to become subdued"; we are under their constant fire. That is why we must have a new kind of political party, something far more closely knit, both in the opinions which its members hold and in its form of organisation, than anything which the world has hitherto seen. Just as mountain climbers must rope themselves together when they attack considerable peaks, so the attack upon the supreme peak of capitalism demands that the workers' party should be roped together by the strong ties of one single organisation, the members of which possess a unanimously adopted, really understood, social theory.

Nor is there anything in the very least unfree, slavish, pedantic, or reactionary about such self-imposed discipline. All these epithets, which the inhabitants of the political marshes of present-day Britain and America, no less than the inhabitants of the political marshes of Russia forty years ago, throw at the supporters of the new model, miss the point so simply put by Lenin in the words "we have combined voluntarily, precisely for the purpose of fighting the enemy". No one can be forced into accepting the discipline of the new model. Everyone is perfectly free not to join. But its members claim the freedom to impose this discipline upon themselves, for they know that it is the only way by which Socialism can be won. To those who feel that their personal opinions are so important, exclusive and precious that they cannot possibly let themselves become part of a group engaged in forming one unified collective opinion, even though such a refusal of intellectual co-operation must bring defeat to the cause which they are pledged to support, we can only say with Lenin: You are perfectly free to choose as you like—only let go of our hands.

But, it is objected, may not the discipline of a party with one single unified ideology be abused? May not "a disease of orthodoxy" arise in which all new ideas will be killed? Yes, this discipline, like all other disciplines, may be abused. But the possibility that it may be abused does nothing whatever to remove the necessity for it. The plain fact of the matter is that capitalism is incomparably too strong to be abolished by a working-class movement which fails to create for itself a disciplined new model political party. If our critics can persuade the capitalists to retire gracefully from the social scene then indeed we can dispense with the self-imposed discipline which our critics find so monstrous. Otherwise we must inform them that not only do we mean to maintain it, but that no one who refuses to submit to it can expect to be considered a full partici-pant in the struggle of the working class to save human civilisation. Moreover, the acceptance of one, single, clear-cut, fully defined ideology does not exclude discussion. On the contrary discussion within new model parties, both on the principles of scientific Socialism, and on their application to the particular situation which confronts the movement at this or that time and place, is continuous. There is, as a matter of fact, incomparably more such discussion within parties of the new type than ever takes place within the loose, broad parties of the old type, the members of which are only too often almost completely disinterested in questions of theory. But from time to time

ID

new model parties must arrive at definite decisions which, until and unless they are revised by the party as a whole, are binding on all their members. For the peaceful cohabitation within the party of two contradictory views on some vital issue is never tolerated.

In this refusal to tolerate the co-existence of incompatible opinions, the new model parties are simply asserting the claim that Socialism is scientific. They are claiming that the way to agreement on basic questions of social theory is not for everybody to make concessions from his or her own personal point of view, and so reach a colourless, characterless, lowest common denominator of Socialist theory. They are asserting the view that the only satisfactory way to agreement is by such intensive study of the facts that the true view will emerge and be acceptable by all. The claim is definitely made that the body of knowledge, and the method of social investigation, which we now possess, makes it possible to arrive at substantially certain, verifiable conclusions in sociological and political affairs. Thus the era of uncertainty, of guess-work, when one opinion was as good as another in such matters, since none could be verified, is over, and an epoch of genuine scientific investigation, in which facts and deductions can be tested and established, has opened.

The claim that the original new model party should have one unified ideology outraged almost all the prominent European and Russian Socialists. It only gradually became apparent to them that Lenin really meant that in the Russian Social Democratic Party there should be no room for conflicting opinions on essentials. But when it became unescapably apparent that this was just what he did mean, not only the great majority of the most prominent Russian Socialists of the period, but all the leaders of Western European Socialism, including the most militant, were appalled. Many of these leaders were engaged at the time in combating, some like Kautsky, it is true, increasingly half-heartedly, but some, like Rosa Luxembourg, perfectly sincerely, the revisionists. The revisionists, led by Bernstein and the then prominent French Socialists, Millerand and Briand, were, as we have seen, attempting to induce the Labour movements of their respective nations to abandon scientific Socialism in favour of a version of what was really British or Fabian Socialism. But not even the most vigorous of the European defenders of scientific Socialism ever dreamt of suggesting that Bernstein, Millerand, Briand and their friends had not the right to remain in the Socialist Parties, while advocating what were, in the ultimate analysis, their anti-Socialist views. Hence they were deeply shocked when Lenin advocated their expulsion. They were still more shocked when in the case of the Russian Socialist Party, and whenever he was able to get a majority to agree with him (which was by no means always), he actually expelled all persons who advocated similar views. As Popov, the historian of the Communist Party of the Soviet Union, puts it, almost everybody but Lenin and his supporters, both inside and outside Russia, demanded that the Russian Socialists should create a "decent party on the European model, in which the most varied tendencies and currents, including out and out opportunism, could peacefully live side by side".[1]

But Lenin would not do it. With almost inconceivable pertinacity he stuck to the concept of the new model. At times he was left with a mere shred of organisation in his hands. About 1910 the Russian Social Democratic Party was declared on all hands to have ceased to exist. The whole numerous, if heterogeneous, company of Russian Socialists, who were opposed to Lenin and his ideas, proclaimed that there was no question as to whether the new model party, to the building of which Lenin had devoted the preceding decade, was correct or not, for it had already ceased to exist. Just before the outbreak of the war all these men, and the groups which they led, appealed to the Socialist International to order Lenin and his colleagues to readmit them to the Russian Social Democratic Party. Nor is there any doubt that such a tribunal would have vehemently condemned

[1] *Outline History of the C.P.S.U.*, Vol. I, p. 218, Lawrence & Wishart.

the very idea of a party which insisted upon ideological unity. But at that moment the war broke out. In the event it was history, and not the Western European Socialists, which passed judgment on the new model as the instrument for the accomplishment of the mission of the working class.

The second of the distinguishing characteristics of the new model consists, not in the ideas which its members hold, but is innate in its very structure. Parties built upon the new model are constructed very differently from any other political parties which the world has so far seen. A phrase which Lenin used at what was in effect the inaugural congress of the original new model party reveals very strikingly this new conception of organisation.[1] In a speech delivered at the Congress of the Russian Social Democratic Party in London on August 15th, 1903, Lenin said: "We must strive to raise the calling and the significance of a party member higher, higher, and still higher."

Party membership as a calling, a vocation; as a vocation of the very highest significance. Here is obviously a new conception of the nature of a political party, a conception quite foreign to the Labour and Socialist parties of the old model. For example, it would be impossible to speak of membership of the British Labour Party as a calling of the highest significance. Such membership is held, for example, by several million Trade Unionists, some of whom take no part whatever in political life except (and that only presumably) to vote for Labour candidates at elections. To vote in a certain way once every five years is not a vocation. As will be described below, there is, in the conditions of British and American democracy, a definite, and indeed essential, place for such very wide, very loose, political parties of the working class. All we are intent

[1] I am referring to the 1903 Congress of the Russian Social Democratic Party held in London. This was technically the second Congress of the Party, a largely abortive Congress having been held in Minsk in 1898. (It was abortive as almost all those who participated in it were at once arrested.) It is agreed, however, that the London meeting was the real inaugural Congress. (See Popov's *Outline History of the Communist Party of the Soviet Union*, Vol I, p. 52.)

to do at this stage is to distinguish them clearly from parties built up upon the new model.

To put what is essentially the same point in another way, a political party built upon the new model must consist of professionals who give their lives to achieving the purpose for which the party is formed, not of amateurs who give their spare evenings. But if we put the point this way we must immediately qualify it. Only the full-time, paid staff of a new model party can, it is obvious, actually devote the whole of their time to party work. The overwhelming majority of the party's membership will consist of men and women who must devote the greater part of their working time to earning their livings. And yet this qualification is not by any means so considerable as it may seem at first sight. It is true that by far the larger part of the party's membership must spend anything from seven to ten hours a day in some employer's factory, mine, office, or farm. But that does not mean that during those hours they will have ceased to live as members of the party. In Britain and America most of us shallowly conceive of political activity as something cut off from everyday life; we conceive of politics as a sort of hobby which a man may take up as, say, a substitute for gardening or postage stamp collecting. But the politics of the new model parties are a way of life. They should infuse, colour and condition the working time of every party member no less than the rest of their lives.

It is perfectly true that it is often no easy task for particular individuals to find a way of achieving this ideal. Certainly they will not do so by ill-timed and ill-thought-out propaganda "on the job", however genuinely self-sacrificing they may be, and however often they may leave their employment by so doing. It may be that a party member will exercise his or her influence at their place of work rather by what they are than by anything which they do or say. Indeed, if they really have become members of the party in the fullest sense of the word they will not fail to exercise such an influence. Thus the party as an organisation of men and women who are professionals in the sense that they devote themselves wholly to the cause of the working class, is fully compatible with by far the greater part of the party membership being engaged in earning their livings in the ordinary way. Indeed, it is incompatible with anything else. For the party must never narrow itself down to a sect of professional politicians, however skilful and however devoted. It must always predominantly consist of ordinary men and women pursuing their normal avocations. This is why all comparisons (and they are frequently made) between parties of the new model and the old orders of preaching friars and the like miss one essential aspect of the new type of association.

Another approach to this question of the composition, and consequently structure, of parties of the new model is to ask the question, who is to be considered a party member? Is it to be anyone who in general agrees with the party and works and votes for the same social ideals, or is party membership to be confined by a clear cut, distinct line of demarcation, to those who are members of one or other of the groups affiliated to the party? It was on this exact point that the new model first differentiated itself. At the aforementioned Conference in 1903 the Russian Socialists assembled in London debated the question of what were to be the rules of their party. Two drafts were submitted for Point 1 of the rules, which defined party membership. A Russian Socialist named Martov, who had up till this moment worked closely with Lenin, submitted this text for Rule 1.

"A member of the Russian Social Democratic Labour Party is one who recognises its programme and supports the party materially as well as working under the control and guidance of one of the organisations of the party."

Lenin, on the other hand, proposed these words:

"A member of the Russian Social Democratic Labour Party is one who recognises its programme and supports the party materially as well as by personal participation in one of the organisations of the party."

Martov's wording, as Lenin pointed out, made it possible for well-intentioned but quite unsuitable persons (for anyone who participated in a strike, for example, or for people who had given a subscription to party funds) to call themselves party members. To use the terminology of Britain and America, it confused participation in the Labour movement as a whole with membership of the party as such. Lenin's wording, on the other hand, made it possible to say with absolute precision that so and so was and that so and so was not, a member of the party. For in order to be a member of the party you had to be, not a member in the abstract, but a member of some particular, functioning group, or other unit, of the party. It was on this issue that Lenin and the supporters of the creation of a new model political party first became differentiated from the other Russian Socialists. To outside observers (if there were any) the division must have seemed to be over a hair. Yet in fourteen years it led to the opposite side of desperate civil war.

No sooner did the Russian Socialists find that they were divided over this issue than they discovered that they were divided on almost every other issue of importance also. The camps into which they divided have come to be called in history the Bolshevists, or majorityists, and the Mensheviks, or minorityists. These, as Lenin once said, not very appropriate titles, arise from the fact that on most of the decisive issues, though not, as a matter of fact, on the above issue of the definition of party membership, Lenin and his colleagues were in a majority at the inaugural London Congress of 1903. But that majority was a very narrow and very impermanent one, so that during the next fourteen years the Bolsheviks and Mensheviks struggled unceasingly, and with varying success, for the leadership of the Russian Labour movement. And one of the essential things over which they struggled was to the very end what it was at the very beginning. Should the Russian Social Democratic Party be allowed to go the way which the existing Western European Socialist parties were rapidly going or should it become a new kind of political party such as the world had never known before?[1]

It must have seemed, indeed we know from their scornful comments that it did seem, to outside observers that the Russian Socialists were the most impractical and futile people in the whole world. There they were, a tiny band, numbering in 1903 and again in 1910[2] only a few hundreds, facing what seemed one of the most powerful autocracies in the world. And yet they seemed to spend nine-tenths of their time and energies in fighting each other! For example, the 1903 inaugural Congress went on for no less than forty long sessions of passionate discussion. And then it ended in an apparently hopeless stalemate between the Bolsheviks and the Mensheviks; a stalemate which ripped the new party into two irreconcilable factions from its very foundation. Patronisingly and pityingly the "practical men" of the Western European Socialist movements looked down on these endlessly disputatious Russians. But the Russian Socialists, or rather the central body of them grouped round Lenin, knew what they were doing. Those forty sessions of endless debate in the hot August of the London of 1903 were not wasted. For they produced a political *novum*. A new star swam into the firmament of the twentieth century. A political party of a new kind was born; a political party which when the test came alone showed itself capable of victory. In order to bring this new kind of organisation into being it was worth while, Lenin and his associates were passionately convinced, to devote, if need be, seemingly endless time and energy to controversies within the ranks of the movement. Again and again Lenin had to refuse to listen to specious, plausible, persuasive

[1] Intensely important divisions over programme and policy were of course indissolubly associated at every stage with this basic difference on organisation. In just the same way the organisational question of unity is in Britain to-day intertwined, as we have seen, with profound issues of policy.

[2] See *The Outline History of the C.P.S.U.*, Vol. II, p. 238.

appeals to unite the party, at the cost of letting it degenerate into a party of the contemporary Western European kind. Again and again he had to give apparent colour to the accusation that he was a hopeless sectarian, far keener on fighting with his fellow Socialists than against Tsarism.[1]

Grimly, fiercely, with endless pertinacity, through the black, ghastly years of reaction after the defeat of the 1905 revolution, when some of his closest associates gave way, Lenin held on his course. In 1917 when the hour of supreme opportunity struck, there existed in Russia, as nowhere else in the world, a working-class party capable of victory.

A third distinguishing characteristic of a party built upon the new model is that it undertakes any and every kind of activity on behalf of the working-class movement. Its members regard all forms of working-class activity, from the proper conduct of a Co-operative Society, recruiting for a Trade Union, calling or settling a strike, to the election of a municipal councillor or a Member of Parliament, as being merely different aspects of one single and indivisible struggle of the working class for power.

This may seem to be an extremely obvious, even plati-tudinous, conception. But it is a conception to which the British, and still less the American, Labour movements have not yet by any means risen. It is hardly too much to say that these movements are crippled by an ultra narrow conception of political activity. The British movement often fails to realise that there exists any form of political activity other than preparations for local and parliamentary elections, or these elections themselves. It is no uncommon

---

[1] In 1913, for example, Trotsky wrote thus of Lenin:
"And what a senseless obsession is the wretched squabbling systematically provoked by the master squabbler, Lenin . . . that professional exploiter of the backwardness of the Russian working-class movement. . . . The whole edifice of Leninism at the present time is built up on lies and falsifications and bears within it the poisoned seed of its own disintegration." In a Letter to Chkheidze, quoted by Popov, *Outline History of the C.P.S.U.*, Vol. I, p. 289.

thing for local Labour Parties in Britain composed of first-rate, keen and militant workers, and living in periods which cry aloud for the most manifold and intense forms of political activity, to feel that they have literally nothing to do—and actually to tend to go to pieces through inactivity—because neither a local or a national election is in immediate prospect. During the Summer of 1937, for example, there was in Britain a desperate urgency both for a national campaign on behalf of Spain and for intense political work and propaganda in favour of the wage claims which the Trade Unions were putting forward, just as a year or so before there had been a desperate urgency for mass agitation, centred round the hunger marchers, on behalf of the unemployed and their life and death struggle against the Means Test. It is true that in each of these instances the National Council of Labour, in pursuance of the general policy of accommodation described above, urged local Labour Parties to remain inactive. But local Labour Parties had themselves a difficulty in seeing the need for such activities. For they were founded, and still largely conceive of themselves, simply and solely as vote gathering organisations. They have never grasped the conception of political activity as a many-sided, diverse, continuous process in which the fighting of local and national elections is simply one important part. They have never realised that their electoral activities themselves cannot be fully successful unless all the other forms of extra-electoral political activity are being vigorously undertaken.

Since the first draft of this chapter was written illuminating examples of this inability to conceive of extra-electoral political activity have been given us both by an individual and by the national leadership of the Labour Party. One of the most energetic of the younger intellectuals of the Labour Party, Mr. Richard Crossman, after unsuccessfully contesting, during the summer of 1937, the West Birmingham division at a by-election wrote an article in the *New Statesman and Nation* in which he asked for a truce to all inner party controversies in order that all Socialists should concentrate on the task of building up the electoral organisations of the party, now in many constituencies fallen into decay. Mr. G. R. Strauss, M.P., and others of the most politically conscious members of the Labour Party were quick to point out the connection between a policy and activities which inspire the workers with hope and confidence, and the standard of electoral organisation which a political party can hope to achieve. But the correspondence which followed Mr. Crossman's article made it clear that even now only a small minority of the members of the Labour Party have realised that there is a connection between the policy of general accommodation to the needs of capitalism which the Labour Party has pursued since 1933, and the admitted decay of the party's electoral machinery, which they were deploring. Their failure to realise this was, above all perhaps, due to the fact that they were quite unaccustomed to conceive of any possibilities of political activity between elections.

Yet once the question is raised who can doubt but that if, since 1933, the whole British Labour movement, under the leadership of the National Council of Labour, had thrown itself into (1) the struggles of the unemployed against the Means Test; (2) had in 1936 undertaken a nation-wide campaign for the restoration of its right to buy arms to the Spanish Government, and had itself organised a British contingent to the International Brigade; (3) had in the Summer of 1937 undertaken nation-wide propaganda activity on behalf of the claims of the Trade Unions and (4) had refused to support an arms programme undertaken by a Government which was step by step destroying every one of the guarantees of peace, the whole level of party life, including electoral organisation, instead of being in admitted decay, would be more vigorous and flourishing than ever?

The second illustration is far more important. As a remedy for the admittedly grave situation of the Labour Party its then leaders, instead of leading the movement in sustained agitation on the above vital and immediate issues, decided to launch during September 1937 a propaganda campaign to get another million votes per year for the Labour Party at the next general election, which will probably take place in or about 1939 or 1940. This campaign was certainly better than nothing, for all activity was to be welcomed. Every supporter of unity and resistance did everything possible to aid it. But the campaign was hamstrung by the abstract character of its appeal. A million more votes a year were to be given to Labour— for what? The answer had to be for the Labour Party's new short-term programme. The British Labour movement needs such a programme, and there is no necessity to make objections to this one.[1] But no programme of future activity by a Labour Government in the nineteen-forties is a substitute for political activity here and now in the nineteen-thirties. The new short-term programme will not bring the Spanish Republic back to life if in the meanwhile it has been allowed to perish at the hands of International Fascism with the virtually unchallenged connivance of the British Government: the unemployed would be far more moved to vote for a party which *had* fought for them by supporting, instead of doing everything in its power to hinder, their marches and demonstrations over the *past* three years, than for one which promised them *future* help in *three years' time*. Support for the principle of collective security by a Labour Government of the future will not stop its destruction now. And so on through each of the urgent issues of the day.

Nothing could better exemplify the two differing conceptions of political activity held by parties of the old and the new model than this campaign of the Labour Party. The 1937 campaign was precisely and explicitly a vote-getting campaign. Its declared purpose was to attract a million more votes a year to the Labour Party. It showed that the leaders of the Labour Party still regarded the collection of votes as the only conceivable form of political activity. Now our criticism of the campaign was not that

[1] See Chapter XX for some discussion of this programme.

it was designed to win the next election. The winning of general elections is unquestionably a matter of first-rate importance to a Labour movement. Our criticism was first that we deluded ourselves if we thought that the winning of general elections was the only thing that mattered, and secondly that *this was not the way to win elections*. The real way for the Labour Party to win the next election is to have earned the votes of the workers by its record of activity, upon such urgent issues as the fight of the unemployed, the fight to save Spain from Fascism and the struggle of the Trade Unions, in the four or five years since the last election. Then the votes will come. They will not come automatically even then. It will still be of great importance to perfect electoral organisation to the highest possible degree; it will still be of great importance to put forward a suitable short-term programme on which all the progressive forces of the country can unite. But in contemporary conditions neither of these things will avail, unless the record of the party is one of active, honest, vigorous struggle on behalf of the essential interests of the mass of the population since the last election.

The policy of accommodation which the British Labour Party adopted in 1933 made such struggle impossible. It was this policy which was killing the British Labour movement, and which will continue to do so if it is continued. No efforts at constituency organisation, and no short-term programme, can save us if the policy of accommodation is continued. One of the most important obstacles, not merely to the repudiation of such a policy, but to the very realisation that the movement is pursuing a policy of accommodation, consists in the deep-rooted inability of most of us in the British Labour movement to conceive of the possibility of extra-electoral political activity. Hence the extreme importance of stressing the, in itself platitudinous, conception, which is an integral part of the whole political outlook of new model parties, of the many-sidedness, and yet at the same time the indivisible unity, of the activities of a Labour movement.

The very deep, very crippling, British, and above all American, tradition of the undesirability of combining Trade Union and political activity is a special case of this inability to conceive of politics as the all-sided struggle of the working class. This is clearly a remnant of that specifically Trade Unionist ideology which, as we saw, dominated the movement right up to the war period. Not all the leaders of the British Trade Unions have even now fully realised that the wage struggles in which they engage have political implications. Hence they still regard a campaign undertaken by the political, propagandist side of the movement on behalf of their members' claims as "unwarrantable interference" with their authority. This attitude is in contemporary conditions almost sure to have disastrous consequences for the success of the workers in industrial struggles. Every big strike or lockout to-day has profound political implications. The Government almost always intervenes in the dispute in one form or another. Almost the whole Press, and the other vast propagandist forces, of the governing class as a whole are as a matter of course used unsparingly on behalf of the employers from the first day of the conflict. What chances have the workers got if they are mad enough to refuse to use their own propagandist organisation, which is of nation-wide extent, on behalf of their own cause?

A Labour movement which had accepted the political conceptions of the new model would utilise, in every major industrial conflict, every local Labour Party, every Co-operative Guild, every branch of every Trade Union not itself engaged in the dispute, every one of the movement's newspapers and other forms of publicity, to carry on an unceasing campaign on behalf of the workers engaged in the dispute. But this would be fighting to win. And this many leaders of the movement have considered it dangerous even to try to do.

Thus for Britain, and even more for America, where the mass of the organised workers are still further from this conception, the insistence of the new model upon a co-ordination and unification of the various forms, political and industrial, which the workers' struggle takes on, is an indispensable contribution to the success of the movement in the conditions of the twentieth century.[1] It is impossible to exaggerate the revivifying effect upon a Labour movement which can be exerted by this conception of the unity of the many-sided struggle of the wage-earners against the conditions of their lives under capitalism. Yet just because this conception is in itself so simple and so obvious, just because it is never resisted in principle, though particular reasons are continually produced to show why it cannot be applied in this or that instance, it is very difficult to bring it home to the members of the movement. Yet this is an essential task which every supporter of the whole new model conception of politics must persist in undertaking.

Nor is it necessary to preach this co-ordination and unification of the many-sided struggle to the right wing of the movement alone. As we described in Chapter VII, there grew up in the pre-war period, as a result of the inadequacy of the Socialism of that time, a left-wing sub-variety of Trade Union politics—which in some countries blossomed out into the distinct ideology of Syndicalism. Hence there are many extremely militant and potentially valuable workers, especially in South Wales and Scotland (and many more of course in America, with its deeply Syndicalist traditions), where the Syndicalist influence was relatively strong, who have quite failed to grasp the many-sided unity of the workers' struggle. For them industrial disputes *are* that struggle. All the rest is mere inessential superstructure. Taking this point of view they naturally come to feel that the Trade Unions are the only important working-class organisations. They feel no

---

[1] The question was one of the issues which divided the Bolshevists and Menshevists during the whole period during which the former were desperately striving to develop the new model. The Menshevists "considered that the Trade Unions must maintain a neutral attitude towards political parties. In their opinion the Party and the Trade Unions each enjoyed full competence, but each in its own field (the Party must confine itself to the political struggle and the Trade Unions to the economic struggle.") (*Outline History of the C.P.S.U.*, Vol. I, p. 193.)

need for a political party on the new model—or indeed of any kind. This profoundly erroneous view has undoubtedly been a most serious barrier to the development of parties of the new type in particular areas in which, owing to the militant tradition of the local working-class movement, we might otherwise have expected a rapid growth. Nothing but the tireless, patient, thorough explanation of the conception of all-sided political activity conducted under the unifying control of a new model party, can remove this most hampering misconception.

CHAPTER XVI

CHARACTER OF THE NEW MODEL
(*continued*)

THE FOURTH DISTINGUISHING characteristic of
new model parties consists in the centralised nature
of their structures. A major controversy occurred during
the evolution of the original new model party as to
whether any party constructed on these principles could be
truly democratic. Lenin, in particular, was violently
assailed by all the opponents of the new model as an
unprincipled autocrat, who was attempting to enslave
every other Russian Socialist. Immediately after the
inaugural Congress described above, at which the outline
of the new model began to show itself, Axelrod, a leading
Russian Socialist of the period, published an article in
which he alleged that Lenin was inspired with "ambitious
phantasies" and by the "traditions of the dictatorship";
that he had set up "an omniscient centre" which "at its
personal discretion disposes of party members who have
turned into screws and cogwheels"; that the Congress had
set up "innumerable ministries, departments, sections,
offices, workshops"; that the Russian revolutionaries were
being transformed by Lenin "into heads of offices, clerks,
sergeant-majors, N.C.O.'s, privates, watchmen, artisans";
that the whole conception of the new model was an "organisational Utopia of a theocratic character"; that it
was "the triumph of a bureaucratic centralisation in the
Party organisation". (See Lenin's *Selected Works*, Vol. II,
for this whole controversy.)

The founding of the first party on the new model provoked
this kind of frenzied opposition on the part of the great
majority of the leaders (though it was accepted by the

majority of the actual workers) of the Russian Socialist movement. It is particularly interesting to read these strictures to-day. For exactly the same things are said of the new model parties which have come into being in Britain and America. In particular the accusation is repeatedly made that these parties are bureaucratic, autocratic and generally undemocratic. As soon as many Labour politicians begin to realise what the new model is; as soon as they realise that not only in its ideas, but in its very structure, it is a quite different kind of thing from the old type of party; as soon as they see that it is a far more closely knit, disciplined and centralised body; that it is a weapon, not a vote-getting organisation or a debating society, they recoil from it in positive horror. For such an organisation does undoubtedly demand of its members, and more especially, of course, of its staff of full time, professional, political workers, a sacrifice of long-established, easy-going habits, such as have almost always grown up amongst the politicians who direct the older type of Labour and Socialist parties. Not only does the new model demand, as we have seen, unity of ideology; it also demands practical unity of activity, so that all its forces can be thrown, for example, into one decisive phase of the general struggle at a given moment.

The original new model, it must be remembered, was created in the conditions of Tsarist autocracy in which, except for two years during the semi-freedom of the 1905 revolution, the party was an illegal organisation. In such conditions the construction of a formally democratic party in which all the leaders, national and local, were elected by vote of the members, and major questions of policy were submitted to a referendum of the entire membership, was simply out of the question. Any attempt to adopt such a form of organisation would have meant immediate discovery by the Tsarist police. Nevertheless the opponents of the new model actually proposed to organise the party on these lines. Lenin had to spend a good deal of time attacking what he called "toy democracy". The more, he said, you write into your party rules the most elaborate system of democratically elected Committees, control by the rank and file and the like, the more unworkable will you make the whole organisation. In conditions of illegality the only possible way in which the party can work is for leaders to emerge by a process of natural selection. That is to say, men and women appear who, by their activities, their writings, their speeches, their power to organise, etc., etc., actually do begin to lead. As soon, no doubt, as stable local organisations have been formed these must appoint delegates to periodic Congresses, in which the policy and construction of the party must be decided by majority vote. And this was done at the 1903 and all subsequent congresses of the new model. Nor was it ever Lenin who refused to abide by the vote of such congresses, when he was outvoted, as he frequently was. On the contrary, it was the opponents of the new model who from the very beginning refused to accept the vote of Congress when it went against them.

Moreover, Lenin insisted, a further principle of organisation was indispensable if the new model was to accomplish its colossal task. It must be centralised. The Central Committee of the party, that is to say, though the leaders who compose it will of course be elected by the democratic vote of the party Congress, must, while it holds office, have disciplinary power over the lower, local organisations of the party. This principle of organisation has come to be known as "democratic centralism". It is democratic in that the central body in which these powers are vested is democratically elected. It is centralised in that during its period of office this Central Committee—or whatever you may choose to call it—has power to make decisions which are binding on the whole party, and so to use the whole strength of the organisation, unimpaired by inner disputes, in the most critical phases of the struggle at any given moment.

What are we to say to this principle of democratic centralism, which is so strangely different from the principles of organisation on which most Socialist or Labour organisations have hitherto been formed? (though Trade Unions are in effect usually organised on this principle). The first thing to say about it is that, whether we like it or not, it is indispensable. No one who has any real experience of the workings of Socialist or Labour organisations not based on this principle can possibly believe that they can ever become capable of leading the working class to victory. No one who has any real knowledge of the strength of the capitalist class, its instinctive cohesion, its determination to remain in power at all costs, can believe that a fully disciplined and highly centralised body can be dispensed with by its opponents. Thus, even if we regret its necessity, we must, *unless we do not at heart believe in the possibility of achieving Socialism at all*, accept the principle of democratic centralism as indispensable to any new model party. There is, however, very little to regret in the abandonment of much, at any rate, of the ostentatiously democratic, decentralised, and therefore loose and vague, forms of organisation characteristic of so many Labour and Socialist organisations. Anyone who has worked in such organisations, and who has been really intent to get things done, will have come to the conclusion that many of their characteristics, even in present-day British and American conditions of legality, are really pieces of "toy democracy". Such organisations often set up so many safeguards and checks and balances against the risk of autocracy on the part of their leaders, and give such enormous opportunities for procrastination and the avoidance of decisions, both to the type of member who is constitutionally "against everything", and to the sincere but inexperienced member who finds it extremely difficult to come to definite decisions on complex political questions, that they become entirely incapable of effective action.

Moreover, the most elaborate constitution and safeguards do not by any means always succeed in preserving a genuinely democratic spirit in an organisation. Painful experience shows that both political parties and Trade

Unions may become intensely bureaucratic and autocratic, while preserving, in form, a severely democratic constitution. (No one who knows the British and American Labour movements to-day need lack for examples.) Real as opposed to toy democracy often consists as much, or more, in the general spirit and temper of an organisation—in a unity of practice and theory between the leaders and the rank and file—as in the terms of the constitution or rule-book. Finally, parties of the new model have it always in their minds that the legality which they enjoy at certain times and places, such as Britain and America to-day, is precarious and possibly transient. They value that legality very highly and believe that a democratic, united and clear-sighted working class movement can preserve the legality of all its parts. But experience shows that whenever and where-ever this ideal type of Labour movement is not achieved in time, the ruling class, as the struggle grows more severe, attempts to withdraw the legality of first one and then another section of the movement, and that it is almost certain to start with the new model party. Hence the party must be prepared at a moment's notice to work in conditions of illegality. At any time the whole controversy over whether the structure of the party is sufficiently democratic may become as grotesquely inappropriate as it was under the Tsarist autocracy in Russia, or as it would be in the case of the new model parties of Germany and Italy to-day. For centralisation is quite patently the only possible principle of organisation for any political party which is forced to work secretly, in conditions of illegality. This ever-present possibility of illegality is in itself a sufficient justification for the distinctive structure of all parties built upon the new model.

It must not be supposed, however, that such parties make themselves into closely knit, highly disciplined, centrally controlled bodies merely for this reason. They do so principally and essentially because a high degree of organisation is the characteristic weapon of the working class in its struggle for power. In the course of the desperate controversy which the mere outlining by Lenin at the 1903 Congress of his conception of the new model provoked, a certain Russian Socialist, signing himself "Practical Worker", wrote to complain that Lenin wanted to turn the party into an "immense factory". Yes, replied Lenin, (See *One Step Forward, Two Steps Back*,) in a sense that is just what *is* intended. It is intended to build a factory which will turn out a product labelled "working-class power", and to do so by means of rational, consciously co-operative labour, just as a well-organised modern factory turns out its characteristic product. It is only the intensely individualistic bourgeois intellectual, wrote Lenin, who will be afraid of this idea.

"For it is precisely the factory, which some seem to regard as a bogey, that is the highest form of capitalist co-operation, which has brought together and disciplined the proletariat, taught it to organise and placed it at the head of all other sections of the toiling and exploited population. It is precisely Marxism, as the ideology of the proletariat trained by capitalism, that has been teaching unstable intellectuals to distinguish between the factory as an instrument of exploitation (discipline based on the fear of starvation) and as a factor in organisation (discipline based on collective work, united under conditions of technically highly developed production). The discipline and organisation, which it is so difficult for the bourgeois intellectual to acquire, are easily acquired by the proletarian precisely because of the factory "school" he goes through. Mortal fear of this school and complete inability to understand its importance as an organising force are characteristic ways of thinking which reflect a petty-bourgeois mode of life."

What immense importance Lenin attached to the question of keying up the level of organisation of working-class political parties to a far higher pitch than they had hitherto reached is shown in the passionately worded final paragraph of *One Step Forward, Two Steps Back*.

"In its struggle for power the proletariat has no other weapon but organisation. Divided by the rule of anarchic competition in the bourgeois world, ground down by slave labour for capital, constantly thrust back to the "lower depths" of utter destitution, savagery and degeneration, the proletariat can become, and will inevitably become, an invincible force only when its ideological unity round the principles of Marxism is consolidated by the material unity of an organisation, which united millions of toilers in the army of the working class. Neither the decrepit rule of Russian tsarism, nor the senile rule of international capital will be able to withstand this army."

There we have it. Ideological unity is the first essential of parties of the new type. But in itself it is not enough. They must express this unity of idea by the material unity of an organisation of a far more highly developed type than anything that has hitherto existed.

Fifthly, and finally, a political party, if it is to qualify as genuinely built upon the new model, must possess a special quality of leadership. This quality has two aspects; the one aspect is internal to the party, the other concerns the quality of leadership displayed by the party to the working class, and ultimately, as we shall show, to the community as a whole. In the first place the party must develop a small corps of fully qualified men and women who are really capable of leading it. The first part of this book contained much criticism of some of the leaders of the British Labour movement. They were criticised as unqualified for their jobs. They had never made a study of Socialism as a science. Hence they had almost no understanding of the nature of capitalism and were unable to foresee its developments. This in turn caused them to impose upon the movement a hand-to-mouth policy of doing what seemed easiest and least likely to cause trouble, at the moment. In contemporary conditions this meant a policy of accommodation to the ever growing demands of a capitalism which was in irrevocable, if unevenly developing, decay. Such a policy must, unless and until it is reversed take the movement backwards through the successive phases of its development. At the end of that journey lies the death of the movement.

But to point this out is not to deny for one second the need for leaders and leadership. It is a demand for qualified leaders, not for no leaders. It is important to point this out because there developed, as an inevitable reaction to the existing type of leadership, in some sections of the left wing of both the British and American Labour movements, a bitter hostility to leaders of all kinds, a demand that the movement should do without leaders, or should circumscribe and tie down what leaders it did appoint to such an extent as to make them virtually powerless. Now the main body of the British and American working classes are rightly exceedingly hostile to this attitude. There is nothing which most normal, experienced British Trade Unionists (and I imagine this to be true of American Trade Unionists also) more dislike than an embittered, narking, up-against-everything-and-everybody attitude on the part of critics of the leaders of the working-class movement. For such shrewd judges know perfectly well that leaders are a necessity for any movement, and that whatever may be the faults of their present leaders, critics who display an unreasoned hostility to them are constitutionally incapable of taking their place. Again and again during the past twenty years criticism of the leaders of the movement, which events have subsequently proved to have been only too well justified, has had no other effect than to rally the mass of the movement to the criticised leaders. For it has incurred the suspicion that it was infected with this ungenerous, narking, anti-leaders-in-general attitude of mind. Hence it is vital for every member and supporter of the new model to make it unmistakably clear that his view is that what the movement needs is not less leadership but, in one sense, actually more leadership. *Only this leadership must be a qualified leadership.* Socialism is now a science and only those who have mastered this science are qualified to have a decisive voice in the leadership of a Labour movement. For experience has shown only too plainly that catastrophe inevitably descends upon every movement which is led by men and women who understand neither the nature of capitalism nor the measures necessary for achieving Socialism.

This conception of leadership, as a function that can only be undertaken by persons who have qualified themselves for it, is inseparable from the claim that Socialism is now a science which has objective laws of its own which cannot be infringed with impunity. From this claim comes also a particular view as to the right and the wrong way of establishing unity amongst Socialists. The wrong way to unity is to attempt to reconcile Socialists holding different views on basic questions *without attempting to modify their respective views in any way.* Lenin engaged Trotsky in a sternly fought controversy on this question in the dark days of reaction in 1910. This was a moment when the Russian Labour move mentwas apparently hopelessly split into a dozen wrangling fragments. Lenin, however, protested with all his strength against the attempt to get unity within the ranks of the conscious Socialists in the above superficial, unscrupulous way. He said that Trotsky was simply trying to play the rôle of "matchmaker" between these warring groups. Such attempts must fail, he said, because they were not based on any effort to get at what were the real points at issue. He characterised the false way to unity thus:

"One view on unity may place in the forefront the 'reconciliation' of 'given persons, groups and institutions'. The identity of their views on Party work, on the policy of that work, is a matter of secondary importance. Differences of opinion must be hushed up, their causes, their significance, their objective conditions should not be elucidated. The principal thing is to 'reconcile' persons and groups. If they do not agree upon the carrying out of a common policy, that policy must be interpreted in such a way as to be acceptable to all. Live and let live. This is philistine 'conciliationism' which inevitably leads to narrow-circle diplomacy. To 'stop up' the source of disagreement, to hush it up, to 'adjust' 'conflicts' at all costs, to neutralise the conflicting trends—it is to this that the main attention of such 'conciliationism' is directed."[1]

The only result of trying to get unity between conscious Socialists in this sort of way would be, said Lenin, to expose

[1] Lenin, *Selected Works*, Vol. IV, p. 41

"the falsity, the hopelessness, the wretchedness" of the point of view of a "matchmaker" such as Trotsky. The only true road to unity between conscious Socialists lay, on the contrary, in the thrashing out of all differences in the most open, clear, and if need be ruthless, way, so that at last the truth should be apparent to all. This way of achieving a united leadership of a working-class movement is, it is clear, dependent on the aforementioned conviction, that there does exist a definite, wholly objective and ascertainable truth in the political, economic and socio-logical sphere; a truth which sufficient discussion will reveal, and which when revealed will command the allegiance of all genuine Socialists.

This was Lenin's conception of the only worth-while kind of unity between conscious Socialists. He had, however, what was in a sense an opposite conception of the broad kind of unity which was possible for the Labour movement as a whole. He was not so naïve (he was the very reverse of naïve) as to suppose that the unity of the movement had to wait until every one of its members had reached this degree of scientific clarity. He knew that at particular times and places what he called "a number of profound objective causes" must force a movement into unity, on pain of its extinction, and in spite of all sorts of remaining disagree-ments between its members.

Thus there must be two kinds of unity within a working-class movement. Amongst the conscious Socialists there must be unity based on a profound knowledge of scientific Socialism. But the movement as a whole can only be united on the general basis of a united resistance to the attacks of the capitalists upon the working population. Such an all-inclusive unity brings together millions of men and women, many of whom will have mutually contradictory ideas on all sorts of political, social and religious questions. They unite because they feel the need for self protection. They unite on the basis of what Keir Hardie called "Labourism". As Keir Hardie said (see p. 52) Liberals, members of the Labour Party, and, he could now add

Communists, can all unite on that basis. This is the basis of that movement towards progressive unity, which will be discussed in the last part of this book. It is a principal criticism of the members of the British National Council of Labour that they departed from this basis, which is the only one upon which such a broad, federally built organisation as the Labour Party can be built.

But within such a broad movement it is indispensable that there should be a party built upon the new model, working towards an ever greater and more conscious degree of unity upon essentials in the movement as a whole. And within the ranks of this party there must be the incomparably higher and more difficult form of unity to which Lenin refers. There must be ideological unity based upon a mastery of the principles of scientific Socialism.

The second aspect of the question of leadership is concerned, not with the ability of a party to throw up men qualified to lead it, but with its ability to lead the working class. Now to lead something or somebody you must be in advance of them. You cannot merely reflect their ideas and opinions. If you do this you will in fact be following them, however much you give it out that you are leading them. From the very foundation of the first example of the new model this was one of the questions which most sharply divided Lenin and his supporters from the other Russian Socialists. The latter regarded it as presumptuous on the part of Socialists to do more than voice the point of view to which the workers had spontaneously arrived. Lenin called this "bowing to spontaneity" and disrespectfully described those who advocated it as being content to contemplate the posterior of the Russian working class. He emphasised nothing more strongly than the right and the duty of Socialists to lead the workers—to aid them, that is to say, to give fully conscious, rational expression to the things which they had been able merely to sense more or less unconsciously. Above all, it was the duty of Socialists to enable the workers to see all the implications which putting forward their demand for tolerable living conditions must ultimately have.

We have already discussed the basis of this question in Chapter IV, when we established the right of Socialists to provide a Labour movement with an ideology. But it is an essential characteristic of the new model to go further than this. It is a leading principle of such parties that it is their duty to tell the workers frankly and clearly the truth, and the whole truth, about their position, the prospects of their movement, and the measures which it is necessary for them to take if they do not wish their movement to be destroyed. Socialists must do this even when the workers as a whole have by no means fully faced the facts of the situation; when they still retain deep illusions about the position of their movement, and even when telling them the truth may give opportunities for the enemies of the new model to attempt to discredit it with the workers.

"A party," said Lenin, "is the vanguard of a class, and its duty is to lead the masses, not to reflect the average state of mind of the masses."[1]

Experience has shown that it is difficult to exaggerate the importance of working-class parties accepting this duty of leadership. In Britain, in particular, the leaders of the Labour movement have again and again made it an excuse for inaction, or for some piece of accommodation to the policy of the governing class, that the workers were not sufficiently educated to support or even to understand anything else. It is rather as if, seeing a blind man step out into the road where he will shortly be run down by the traffic, a group of onlookers, in whose care he is supposed to be, should remark reflectively that after all the poor fellow would not see the need for pulling him back onto the pavement. But the analogy is inadequate. For the relative blindness of the workers (imposed on them by the whole conditions of their life under capitalism) to the full implications of the struggle in which they find themselves engaged,

[1] *Selected Works*, Vol. VI, p. 44

is curable. It is a prime duty of those who take on the heavy responsibility of leadership in a working-class movement to take off the bandage with which capitalism blinds the eyes of the workers. But, instead, the existence of that bandage is made the excuse for every inadequacy, for every inaction and for every surrender.

This is the most disastrous of all the self-justifications by means of which leaders of Labour movements have explained their failure to lead. They are ever ready to blame the "apathy" or "backwardness" of the workers for everything, while never lifting a finger to remedy this alleged backwardness. It is hardly too much to say that the very conception of active leadership, in the sense of implanting new ideas into the minds of the workers and, if need be, strenuously fighting the prejudices that capitalism has instilled into them, is wholly absent from the minds of many British and American Labour leaders. They recoil in horror if ever they realise that parties built on the new model regard this as part of their task. They evidently feel that to ask them to attempt to do more than to reflect the minds of the workers, just as they are, is to impose on them a task of which they are totally incapable.

And it is true that only leaders who have genuinely raised themselves to a higher level of comprehension of the whole world-wide struggle can even attempt to raise the level of comprehension of their supporters. No man, however talented, can to-day hope to achieve unaided and in isolation an adequate comprehension of the enormously complicated world situation which confronts the working-class movement. That can only be done by the collaboration of many men working in a well-knit organisation such as a party built upon the new model.

It is, then, the supreme task of new model parties to provide leadership, in the precise sense in which we have just defined that term, to the working class in its struggle. But, it may be objected, is there not a danger that if new model parties attempt this responsible task of leading the workers, in the sense of consciously combating their prejudices, they will run so far ahead as to break the link between themselves and the vast majority of men, and so end in the impotence of a sect? Undoubtedly there is such a danger. And newly emerged new model parties have not always escaped it. But the besetting sin of the immense majority of the leaders of the British and American Labour movements has been exactly the opposite. Far from running too far ahead of their movements they have done absolutely nothing to raise the level of comprehension of their supporters. Then they have sheltered behind this backwardness, for which they themselves have been primarily responsible, as an excuse for inaction, retreat and surrender. Hence for us, in Britain and America, to stress the danger of running too far ahead would be grossly inappropriate. To do so would be to say something which is in itself true enough, but is entirely misleading in the given circumstances. It is like the Russian folk story, of which Lenin was so fond, of the fool who seeing a funeral procession shouted loudly to the mourners "many happy returns of the day". To warn the leaders of the British and American Labour movements of the danger of running too far ahead of their supporters is to wish ourselves many miserable returns of the days of prostration, defeat and humiliation. For nothing is more certain than that victory will not come to the British and American Labour movements until they find leaders who will lead, even if that leadership may involve temporary unpopularity.

Such are the main distinguishing characteristics of the new model. It may be that some British and American readers will feel that these characteristics are somewhat startling. They may even feel that their enumeration tends to confirm the familiar accusation that such parties are over rigid, over disciplined, autocratic bodies which seek to regiment their members into an impossible orthodoxy. The mental climate in which the upper and middle classes of Britain and America (and this mental climate has affected the rest of the population also) have been brought up is inimical to any such organisations as these, which seek to achieve an agreed unanimity amongst their members on all essential matters. For British and American capitalist society has grown up in the contrary tradition of the fight for the right to diversity of opinion, long denied by semi-feudal, ecclesiastical or monarchic authority. Moreover, the conditions produced by the successful development of British and American capitalism have been, for the favoured sections of the population, so easy and stable that the need for scientific, consciously achieved agreement on fundamentals has fallen out of sight. Thus the parties of the new model will inevitably seem rigid, massive, formidable organisations to many British and American observers. And no doubt new model parties, when compared to the loose, vague, political organisations which have hitherto sufficed for the working class, are rigid, massive and formidable. It is not, however, irrelevant to ask whether, in the conditions of the modern world, there may not be a need for organisations of just this character.

The contemporary world is a bloody flux. Nothing in it remains stable, fixed or safe. Alike in the sphere of moral values, beliefs and ideas, and in the material sphere of kingdoms, empires, states and principalities, "the eternal altars tilt and tumble". Men have few remaining unshaken beliefs, loyalties, or traditional principles upon which to base their actions, and their lives. In periods such as this, social regression is only too likely to occur. Men, lacking any moral or social principles whatever, run amok, living lives wholly egocentric, regressing to the primal jungle fight. Or, more deadly and more frequent still, they fall victims to the nearest demagogic enchanter, himself the hireling of the rich and the powerful, seeking nothing but the preservation of their privileges. This, though we favoured Anglo-Saxons may not yet fully realise it, is the kind of world in which we live. Is there not in such a world something to be said for a strongly built, massive, formidable, association of well-instructed men and women, who know precisely what they want and how to get it?

Moreover, the human associations in question, the new model parties, are built in such a way; are so morticed and dove-tailed into the very body of the people itself, that they have, and can have, no other interest than the salvation and development of human society. The unanimity of opinion which they enforce as a condition necessary to their effective existence, is based not on some myth, irrational tradition or supposed revelation, but on the discoveries of sociological science, and is itself constantly developing and changing as experience accumulates. Is it not a thousand times well for man that in this *dies irae* he has developed this new type of human association? Do we not need, in order to withstand the roaring tempests of our days, just this kind of association, by means of which, we may clasp the hands of our fellows, pool our knowledge, skill, and resources, and so triumph over the chaos that has been loosed upon the world? For in isolation and without such association we shall infallibly perish one by one.

It is true that such a highly developed form of association as the new model parties attempt to be, raises difficult problems of human relationships, not all of which have been perfectly solved. Moreover, this degree of association cannot be achieved without a sacrifice of that complete independence, in the intellectual, moral and material sphere, which those who come from the favoured classes in Britain and America enjoy so fully and prize so much. But is this sacrifice too high a price to pay for the salvation of human society? After all, men have always found some of their deepest and highest joys in this very sacrifice. The gains which a man (or a woman) may make by accepting such an association; the intellectual, moral and material aid which it can bring him or her, far outweighs the initial sacrifice, which is often far more imaginary than real, which he or she must make to enter it.

The same type of consideration should surely be borne in mind when we hear the accusations that parties of the new model regiment their members. In one sense the accusation is true. Such parties do make their members into regiments; into regiments, brigades, divisions and armies for the accomplishment of the mission of the working class, for the creation of the new Socialist form of human civilisation. In Lenin's words they perform the essential function of "gathering, organising and mobilising permanent troops."[1] In time of peace a regiment may be an irksome thing. There may be, there will be, a time when this particular type of closely knit human association, designed expressly for winning the social struggle, will be no longer necessary. But to-day there is a war on. We did not make that war. We strive with all our might to end it in the only way in which it can be ended, namely by eliminating the social relationships which are continuously generating it. But if we refuse to recognise its existence, we reduce ourselves to futility. And in time of war there is a great deal to be said for belonging to a regiment. The cohesion, and power of resistance and manœuvre, which can alone be displayed by such disciplined bodies, will again and again prove to be the one thing which can save each and all of their members from destruction. Where a mob will be annihilated, a regiment will conquer.

It may be that there are, however—indeed these inevitably must be—many profoundly sincere members of the British and American Labour movements who do not yet, and may never, feel the need or possibility of accepting the obligations and advantages (and both are heavy) involved in membership of parties of the new model. Not every one can be a regular in the struggle to remake the world. But that does not mean that they cannot play an active part in that struggle. As we shall describe below, a new model party can in British and American conditions be but one of the organisations of the working-class movement. The Trade Unions, the Co-operatives, the older and looser working-class political parties (for, as we shall see, such parties are indispensable) must necessarily claim the membership of millions who have not reached the point at which they feel the need to join a party built upon the new model.

[1] *Selected Works*, Vol. II, p. 182

It is a purpose of these pages to show, however, that the history of the world during the past thirty-five years leaves no room for doubt that new model parties are instruments indispensable to the victory of the wage-workers in their struggle against the conditions of their life under capitalism. Such parties, acting within a wider Labour movement, are the means, long sought and now discovered, by means of which the capitalist epoch may be closed, the ownership of the means of production transferred from a small monopolising class to the whole community, and a way opened for a new, Socialist type of human civilisation.

CHAPTER XVII

THE NEW MODEL IN BRITAIN AND AMERICA

How much has been done in Britain and America towards the development of political parties of the new type? In 1920 the Communist Party of Great Britain was founded in order to provide the British working-class movement with a party built upon the new model. In 1919 the Communist Party of the United States was founded with the object of performing the same function in America.

The men and women who founded both these parties had come to the conclusion reached in our last chapter. They had concluded that the contrasted experiences of the Western and Russian Labour movements proved that this kind of party was indispensable to the success of a working-class movement. This conclusion was the subject of hot international controversy in the immediately post-war years. As we have seen, the first reaction of the Socialist and Labour leaders of Western Europe, when they saw the new model taking shape under Lenin's hand, was to condemn it unequivocally. Its form of organisation and its ideology alike repelled them. In 1914 they were just about to pass judgment and sentence upon it. In the post-war period, when the new model had actually led the Russian workers to power, such wholesale condemnation did not seem possible to one group, at any rate, of European Socialist leaders. (The main body of European Socialists, led by such representative figures as Kautsky, MacDonald and Vandevelde, continued, however, to condemn the new model and all its works as roundly as ever.) This minority group of Socialists took up the position that the development of a new kind of political party with the characteristic features described above; the development, that is to say, of a coherent and easily recognisable body of political theory and practice which has come to be known as Leninism had been a perfectly legitimate and correct thing *for Russia*, but that no such development in the theory and practice of the Western Labour movements was either desirable or possible. The supporters of the new model had, therefore, as almost their first task, to prove that Leninism in general, and the characteristics of the new model in particular, did apply to the conditions of the Western capitalist democracies; that although it was perfectly true that the new model had been built in the conditions of a capitalist autocracy, yet the Labour movements of the capitalist democracies could not dispense with this new type of weapon.

Every year of the post-war history of the world has held its demonstration that the supporters of the new model were right. The existence of political democracy in a capitalist society does not, it is now clear, change the very nature of that society, as, for example, Mr. Sidney Webb supposed that it did. The ownership of the means of production by a small class is a fact anterior to, and more fundamental than, a universal franchise. In order to change the very nature of human society an organisation far more formidable than the old type of exclusively parliamentary, vote-gathering parties is necessary, whether or not that society already possesses political democracy. Until and unless Labour movements equip themselves with such parties, and with the ideology of scientific Socialism which such parties incarnate, they are condemned to frustration, futility and defeat.

In the nineteen-twenties it was necessary and inevitable to lay almost the whole stress upon maintaining this claim that Leninism did apply to the Western democracies. For it was precisely this claim which was so hotly denied. This claim is, of course, still denied by the leaders of the Western Labour movements. Hence it is still necessary to demonstrate it tirelessly. It is, however, now possible to begin to make the assertion of the applicability of Leninism to the

West more precise and, therefore, more convincing. For the lesson of experience is that while Leninism most certainly does apply to the capitalist democracies it does not do so automatically or mechanically. The struggle of the wage-workers against the conditions of life imposed upon them by capitalism is fundamentally the same struggle whether the particular capitalist state which faces them possesses democratic institutions or not. But the forms which their struggle takes in States possessing democratic institutions are different, and are, in particular, more varied and more complex.

In general, we may say that in capitalist democracies a greater part of the workers' struggle takes place in the realm of ideas. Once the workers have succeeded in getting a universal, or nearly universal, franchise, and until and unless they allow that franchise to be taken away from them again, the capitalists must rule by managing to persuade a majority of the population to support them; they must succeed in enslaving the minds as well as the bodies of the wage-workers. In such conditions a primary task of the Labour movement is to free the minds of the workers; to exert so profound an educational influence upon them that they become immune to the vast and powerful capitalist ideology with which their environment is necessarily saturated. It is just this function which, as we have seen, the British Labour movement so signally failed to accomplish. Its failure was inevitable. For before you can free the minds of the working class from the domination of capitalist ideas you must first free your own mind from this domination. And this the British Socialists of the past fifty years have never done. Even when they thought that they were most advanced they rarely succeeded in freeing more than a mere corner of their minds from the all-pervading influence of capitalist ideas.

This failure has been attributable, to a predominant extent, to the lack of a party built upon the new model. It is only by the mutual support of a "compact group" of this kind that it is possible for men and women to achieve a new ideology. To escape from the influence of the all-pervasive ideas of a dominant social class is a task beyond the powers of all but the most exceptional individuals. Hence work in the realm of ideas was and is of prime importance for parties of the new kind working in the conditions of the capitalist democracies. The early years of the history of new model parties in both Britain and America were chiefly occupied by the difficult search for the right form and style of work for their particular environment. That search was not easy; for they had both to insist upon the complete applicability of Leninism to British and American conditions, and in actual practice to find the particular, definite way to apply it. There is nothing to wonder at in the fact that they have only gradually and over a number of years begun to succeed in this double task.

Nor must we be surprised that the creation of parties of the new kind has proved a slow and laborious business, and that they remain small. The individual members of such parties are the bricks out of which the whole edifice must be built. And it is not too much to say that each brick has to be individually laid. It is only in exceptional circumstances, therefore, that such parties can grow with great rapidity,[1] nor will they ever, in capitalist conditions, count their numbers in millions. If they did they would run the risk of ceasing to be parties built upon the new model. For a mass influx of millions of members, in a short period, would inevitably mean that the party had ceased to have the characteristics of high organisation, strict discipline, conscious and universally understood identity of outlook, and capacity for any kind of activity, which we described above.

The building up of a political party of the new kind is an incomparably difficult, incomparably important enter-

[1] The growth of the French Communist Party in the past two years provides an instance of such rapid growth in exceptional circumstances. It is, however, certain that the French party has now an enormous task of assimilation and self-education before it.

prise. It is, to return to Lenin's words, "gathering, organising, mobilising permanent troops" who alone can win, not this or that engagement, but the whole world-wide, century-old struggle for Socialism. It is by the successful accomplishment of this work that the face of the world can be changed. We deceive ourselves if we suppose that such a job can be done easily or quickly. It can only be done over the years, bit by bit, with infinite patience and pertinacity. For it involves the creation of a higher type of human association than anything which mankind has hitherto succeeded in evolving. It involves finding in each major capitalist society, not millions—that is impossible— but tens of thousands, and ultimately hundreds of thousands, of men and women capable of being transformed, or rather of transforming themselves, into an association at once more disciplined, more conscious of its purpose and of its methods, more flexible, more tightly knit, and yet more closely linked with the rest of the population, than anything hitherto conceived of. All this is not done in a day.

It is interesting to observe what size experience indicates such parties can attain to under capitalist conditions. The original example of the new model had a most chequered history in this, as in every other, respect. Various figures of its membership are given by different authorities, and it may well be that in the conditions of Tsarist persecution the size of the party was often in doubt. I know of no figure for the initial period between 1903 and the two years of semi-legality (1905–7) during the 1905 revolution. Popov, in his *Outline History of the Communist Party of the Soviet Union* states that the peak figure of membership reached in this period of legality was 150,000. With the crushing of the revolution and the driving of the party underground, the membership rapidly dropped. Popov records that by 1908 it had shrunk to "a few hundreds or, at best, thousands". In the period of revival the membership rose again slowly but steadily. At the moment of the February revolution (1917) it is variously estimated at 30,000 and at 75,000. By the time of the October revolution, membership had grown greatly from this figure, but was still under 250,000. These approximate figures give us a sense of scale as to the possible size of a new model party under capitalist conditions. Seven months before it commanded a clear majority of the votes of the working class, the original new model party had much less than 100,000 members. Thus we must not think that the majority of a working class, numbering many millions, will ever, while capitalism lasts, join parties built upon the new model, or that it is necessary that they should do so in order that such parties shall accomplish their mission. What is necessary to the success of such parties is that they should gradually come to command the *support* of a majority of the workers. Without this they can do nothing.

The Communist Party of Great Britain numbers at the moment of writing (the figure was given at the May 1937 Congress of the party held in London) some 12,500 members. The Communist Party of the United States of America has some 54,000 members.[1] It is important to realise two things about these figures. In the first place, this membership is inadequate to the tasks of these parties, so that one of the main things which requires to be done for the general development of the new model in Britain and America is greatly to increase this membership. In the second place, we have to think in terms of a membership first of tens of thousands and then of hundreds of thousands—and not of millions—so that the present membership of these parties does represent a real beginning in the building of the new model.

It is necessary to say all this, because the whole conception of a party of the new kind is so strange to most people in Britain and America that they easily become confused and suppose that, because, for example, there are only 12,500 members of the Communist Party in Britain, this

[1] See W. Z. Foster's *From Bryan to Stalin*. This figure includes the membership of the Young Communist League. 4,000 must be added to the figure of British Party membership if the membership of the British Young Communist League is included.

means that only 12,500 people support Communism. How very far from the truth this is may be seen from the fact that in the two constituencies contested by the British Communist Party at the 1935 General election (Rhondda East and West Fife) 13,655 and 13,462 people, respectively, voted for the Communist candidates. Thus in two small areas with a combined electorate of only 90,514, out of a total electorate of over thirty millions, nearly twice as many people voted Communist as belong to the Communist Party in the whole country. It would, of course, be quite fallacious to generalise from these figures and to suggest that if Communist candidates had contested all the 612 parliamentary divisions, even 10,000 Communist supporters, giving a national total of over six million votes, would have been found, on the average, in each of them. For in the two constituencies fought support for the Communist Party was, naturally, much above the average. Still, the figures give some idea of the inevitable disproportion between the actual membership of a party built upon the new model and the number of supporters and the degree of influence which it acquires. Indeed it is probable that before the Communist Party of Great Britain has raised its membership to the neighbourhood of 50,000 it will have acquired sufficient influence to transform, and so save, the British Labour movement.

It is equally important to emphasise that, just because the growth of any new model party must be a slow and difficult business, its members must make continuous and pertinacious efforts to increase the size of the party. So long as the party is not diluted with members who have not grasped, or are not able or willing to learn, the principles upon which it is founded, the larger the party, the better. There must not be the slightest suggestion that there is any virtue in smallness for its own sake. For that way lies the most sterile and pernicious sectarianism. Determined efforts to increase the size of the party by every kind of activity must be made; indeed, the one and only means to this end that must not be used is to allow the organisation

K1

to degenerate into a party of the old type, containing members who hold diametrically opposite views on basic questions of theory and practice; to degenerate into a party which is little more than an exclusively parliamentary or vote-gathering organisation, and has not learnt the many-sidedness of political activity.

Again a danger arises that just because parties of the new model require far more of their members than other political parties have ever done, people may feel that if they join them they must cut themselves off from all other types of association. But in the conditions of contemporary Britain and America new model parties cannot, we repeat, be the sole, or even the sole political, organisations, of the wage-workers. We shall discuss in detail in the next chapter the place of new model parties in the complex series of associations with which the British and American workers are equipped. Suffice it here to say that every member of a new model party, far from cutting him- or herself off from other associations and contacts, should strive to increase and deepen them in every possible direction. Parties of the new model are not exclusive sects, trying to find a personal salvation for their members, and condemning the rest of the world to outer darkness. They must link themselves, by means of the other associations of their members, with the everyday life of everyday men and women at thousands of points. Far from being, because of the higher degree of political consciousness which they require in their members, further removed from the lives of the politically unconscious or semi-conscious mass of the population, they should be much nearer to them. For it is by broadening and deepening the conception of what politics are; it is by showing men that political activity is not mere vote-gathering, but is the collective pursuit of ever better conditions of life for the whole working community, that politics can be brought back to the non-political man and woman.

We have left to this chapter the discussion of a characteristic of new model parties which is sometimes regarded as their most prominent. There are now sixty-eight such parties in existence in the world. These parties are in various stages of development; some are no more than small, nuclear groups; others, such as the French Communist Party, for example, are powerful organisations which play an important part in the political life of their states. All these new model parties are closely linked together in an International Federation, known as the Third, or Communist, International.

The principle of international federation does not, of course, differentiate the new type of working-class political parties from the old. All working-class political parties have felt the need of such international federation. The original small revolutionary groups of the mid-nineteenth century united themselves in such an organisation, which has come to be known in history as the First International. Then, when the larger Socialist and Labour parties were formed towards the end of the nineteenth century, or, as in the case of Britain, in the early years of the twentieth century, these parties also united into another, or Second, International. The war destroyed this organisation, but it was reconstituted after the war, and the British Labour Party unhesitatingly re-affiliated to it, and is to-day its dominant organisation. Hence the necessity of international organisation is not a matter of dispute between the different kinds of working-class parties, whether they are built on the old or on the new model. What does distinguish the new kind of parties from the old, however, is that the principle of international federation has in their case been pushed much further than ever before. We may describe the essential difference by saying that the decisions of the Second, or Labour and Socialist, International are not in practice binding upon its member parties, while the decisions of the Third, or Communist, International are so binding. Thus the International Federation of the new model parties is by far the tighter, more highly unified, body.

This degree of internationalism on the part of the new model parties has been felt by many of the older Socialist leaders, and, of course, by every spokesman of capitalism, to be as great an outrage as their insistence on unity of ideas, on discipline, on democratic centralism, or on any other of their new and disturbing characteristics. Moreover, the most familiar accusation which is aimed at the new model parties, namely that they are mere "tools of Moscow", is based upon this fact of their tight international organisation. In principle it would not seem apparent why the fact of closely knit international organisation should make, say, the British Communist Party a tool of the American Communist Party, any more than it would make the American party the tool of the British party or both, or either, of these parties the tools of the French or the Russian parties. Effective international organisation in one sense renders, it is true, every party the tool, or instrument, of every other; or rather it renders all these parties instruments of the international organisation as a whole, and of the social philosophy which it serves. Naturally, opponents of that philosophy, and of Socialism in general, object to such a super-national allegiance. For the capitalist system of economic organisation is inseparably associated, both historically and at the present time, with nationalism as the highest form of human allegiance.[1] But no one who professes a belief in Socialism can surely subscribe to that argument? The truth is that many Socialists have so far failed to free their own minds from the dominance of capitalist ideas, that they are still sincerely and profoundly shocked by the existence of supernational links of more than a tenuous and superficial kind. They still feel, at heart, and in spite of sincerely favouring a Socialist organisation of society, that national allegiance must come first and that, if the needs of the struggle for Socialism conflict with that allegiance, they must give way to it.

Moreover, colour is lent to the attack on the closely-

[1] Historically, capitalism to a considerable extent developed out of the successful struggle to disrupt one such supernational allegiance, namely the Roman Catholic Church of the Middle Ages. For the Church was the elaborate expression, in the field of ideas, of that feudal society which capitalism had to break up.

knit character of the international federation of the new model parties by the fact that one, and only one, of these parties has actually led the working class to power and carried through the transference of the means of production to the community. Hence that party, the Communist Party of the Soviet Union, is disproportionately large and strong in relation to the other new model parties. Moreover, since the Soviet Union is the only place in which it can be free from molestation, the international federation perforce meets in Moscow in its periodic congresses, and has there established its permanent offices and its administrative machine. Again, the Communist Party of the Soviet Union is not only the largest and strongest, but is also the original, new model. Thus it is by nearly twenty years the oldest of the federated organisations. It is much the best equipped with thinkers and social scientists, and it inevitably possesses all the immense prestige of unique success. Hence, during its early years, the Communist Party of the Soviet Union inevitably exercised a predominant weight in the International. But this is not the least inherent in the principle of effective international organisation, and the cure for it lies in the development of the new model parties of other countries to the point at which they are fully adult organisations, undeniably capable of taking their due part in reaching the common decisions of the International.

Indeed, it will be found upon examination that almost every one of the difficult problems which face the working-class movements in the capitalist democracies will become susceptible of solution when their new model parties are adequately developed, but not till then. This is not to say that the development of these parties should be the be-all and end-all of working-class political activity in, for example, Britain and America. This would be to over-simplify the position. On the contrary, the adequate development of these parties is the key which can alone unlock the door to the accomplishment of all those other vitally necessary tasks which may be summed up as the general development of every part of the working-class movement. The fact remains, however, that the development of parties built upon the new model is an inseparable part of the regeneration, or, in the case of America, the crystallisation, of the working-class movement. The Communist parties of Britain and America are, as yet, little more than the foundation stones of the organisations which are needed for this purpose. Our attitude to these parties will depend upon whether or not we have grasped the fact that these are parties of a new type, striving to make themselves into organisations of a more highly developed kind that anything which the world has so far known.

Unless we have comprehended the lesson of what happens to Labour movements which are confronted with decisive struggle before they have developed a party of the new kind, we may look with indifferent eyes upon the attempts of the small group of men and women who have striven to provide the British and American working-class movements with such parties. We may assume an attitude of disastrous impartiality to their desperate efforts; we may condescendingly point out their inevitable mistakes, without reflecting upon whether we, if we had faced their problems, should not have made far greater mistakes ourselves. We may stress the partial character of the success of their efforts to develop new model parties in the particularly difficult conditions of Britain and America, and generally tend to belittle, and in the end to turn away from, these parties and to go back, in spite of their proved political bankruptcy, to the old model of working-class political organisation. But if we have once grasped, *in principle*, the indispensability of an adequately developed party built upon the new model, then the difficulties and inevitable setbacks of those who are striving to develop them in our countries will act merely as a powerful incentive upon us to aid them with all our strength to overcome these difficulties.

That is why I have approached the problem of the political organisation of a modern working-class movement in the particular way which has been attempted in these pages. After surveying the consequences for the British Labour movement of its rejection of the ideology of scientific Socialism, we have discussed, in principle, the character of the new form of organisation which is inseparable from that ideology. If we become convinced that the development of a party built upon the new model is an indispensable step towards the evolution of a Labour movement genuinely capable of setting up a socialist society, then the question of the extent to which such parties have been created up till now will fall into its proper perspective. We shall see the work that has already been done in building up the British and American Communist parties, not as an attempt, or experiment, which may or may not succeed, and with which we will only associate ourselves if we approve of everything that has been done and is being done, but as the early, difficult stages of the creation of the one type of organisation which can enable the Labour movements to save us from the oncoming night of social reaction and war.

For, again, the building of such new model parties is indispensable, but not enough. In highly developed capitalist societies, such parties operate in an environment already modified by the existence, not only of a rich tradition of political life, but of widespread, fully legal, and potentially extremely powerful, Labour movements. In simpler, more autocratic, capitalist societies the question at issue may be largely one of the relationship of a party built upon the new model to the class, or coalition of classes, which it seeks to lead. (Though even in such societies some embryonic parts of a Labour movement, Trade Unions, Co-operative Societies, etc., usually exist.) But in British and American conditions the relevant question is of the relationship of the new model party to the Labour movement, and only indirectly, through the medium of that movement, to the class, or coalition of classes. We shall discuss this highly complex and highly important question in the next chapter.

CHAPTER XVIII

THE NEW MODEL AND THE MOVEMENT

IN THE CONDITIONS of British and American political
life the creation of a new model party provides one indispensable feature of the Labour movement.

It is necessary to emphasise and re-emphasise this fact,
for politically inexperienced persons have sometimes conceived of new model parties as organisations which would
immediately supersede the old kind of working-class political
parties, or would even replace the other fundamental organisations which make up a working-class movement, namely
the Trade Unions and the Co-operative Societies. It is, I
hope, needless to repeat that, on the contrary, parties built
upon the new model regard, and always have regarded,
the maximum development of the Trade Unions and Co-
operative Societies as an absolutely essential part of their
work. At first sight, however, it is by no means so obvious
that new model parties will not wish to supersede the older
type of working-class political organisations; it is by no
means so obvious that there is room for two different kinds
of political parties in a Labour movement at any given
time and place. And, in fact, in certain circumstances and
places, particular Communist parties have either attempted
to draw all the politically active workers out of the older
parties and into themselves, or have advocated a fusion of
themselves and the existing, old model, working-class party.[1]

In the existing (1937) circumstances of both Great
Britain and America, however, an indispensable function
exists for working-class political parties of the older type.

---

[1] For example, the French and Spanish Communist parties are advocating
fusion with the French and Spanish Socialist parties at the moment.

This circumstance arises, in Britain, partly from the fact that in the shape of the Labour Party there exists a party of the old type, which has been the essential vehicle of the efforts and aspirations of many millions of British workers over the past forty years. It is quite idle to suppose that a working-class which has with the utmost difficulty (as we have seen) created this large-scale political instrument, will be suddenly willing, as a whole, to abandon it and to turn to another. Any attempt to induce it to do so would be likely to result in the disintegration of the old working-class party without achieving a commensurate growth of the new. It is only too easy to disgust a large section of only semi-politically conscious workers with political activity; to drive them, disillusioned and bewildered, out of political life altogether. And this, experience indicates, is likely to be the result of an attempt suddenly to replace an old model by a new model party as the largest political instrument of the wage-workers.

But the case for the co-existence, in the contemporary conditions of Britain and America, of both a large, loose, mainly electoral, old model party, and a new model party, does not rest on the existence of an historic, deeply rooted party of the old type. For in the case of America an existing new model party is at present actually engaged in trying to create, in the shape of a Farmer-Labour Party, an old model party, although nothing of the kind exists at present. (At the same time there is no reason why a future American Farmer-Labour Party should fall into the theoretical and practical errors which we have discussed in earlier chapters.) This shows that in the political conditions created by the British-American type of capitalist democracies, there is an inherent need for a broad, loosely organised, federally built working-class party, based upon the Trade Unions and mainly designed for electoral purposes. It shows that far from the British Labour Party being indispensable merely because it has an historic tradition behind it, it would be necessary to attempt to create such a party in Britain if none existed.

It is, in a word, Utopian to suppose that great masses of workers, brought up in the mental climate of a highly developed capitalist democracy, can adequately develop a new model party without resorting to the intermediate step of creating a working-class party of the older type. To make the same point in another way, there must be, in Britain and America, at any rate, mediating links between the new model party and the working-class as a whole. It has, I repeat, always been recognised that the Trade Unions and Co-operatives formed links of this sort and that they were indispensable. In the simpler, though far more severe, conditions of capitalist autocracy they were sufficient, and were indeed the only links which could be created.[1] The main lesson of recent experience is that in capitalist democracies another link is necessary—the link of a working-class political party of the older, looser, electoral type. It is, then, of prime importance, that it should be understood that far from the Communist Party and the Labour Party being in competition, or opposition, to each other, the growth of the Communist Party is a pre-requisite for a proportionate, and far larger, growth of the Labour Party. Every man and woman who reaches the degree of political consciousness at which they feel the need to join the Communist Party, should (and, as a matter of fact, they mostly do) make it their first business to draw at least ten others, who have not got so far, into the wider, looser association of the Labour Party.

The British Labour Party affords, in its general structure, a good example of what such a party should be like. It should be federally built so that all working-class organisations of no matter what type, be they Trade Unions, Co-operative Societies, Socialist Societies or political parties of the new model, can affiliate to it. The British Labour Party, however, not only excludes the British Communist Party from affiliation, but strives to exclude individual Communists from membership of any of its

[1] In Fascist-capitalist autocracies these links exist only in the form of the Fascist Trade Union. It is in these bodies that a wholly illegal and secret new model party has to work.

local constituency organisations. Moreover, though it cannot exclude Communists from membership of the Trade Unions, it deprives them of the right to represent Trade Union organisations at its Conferences. Thus it does everything in its power to prevent itself from acting as the link between the new model party and the working class as a whole. If and when, however, working-class unity is achieved in Britain, by some form of the inclusion of the new model party within the wider movement, the British workers will possess a Labour movement extremely well organised for the present phase of the working-class struggle in Britain.

It must not be supposed that it is suggested that all the blame for the present division of the British Labour movement can be laid upon its leaders. A share of the blame rests upon those of us who have opposed the policy of accommodation. We have made it easy, by committing the historic sin of the Left, the sin of sectarianism, for our opponents to exclude us from full participation in the life of the Labour movement. It is not, after all, easy for men and women, living in the midst of stormy political events, simultaneously to grasp and adopt the ideology and principles of organisation which the new model parties incarnate, and yet draw nearer to, instead of farther away from, the main body of the Labour movement.

When we first begin to shed the illusions of non-scientific Socialism—such as those discussed in the earlier chapters of this book—we are apt to attack those who still hold these illusions with peculiar venom. We do so just because these illusions have been, till very lately, a part of ourselves. When we first realise what terrible disasters these illusions have led the movement into, we are naturally inclined to an extreme vehemence of denunciation of those who hold them—forgetting, perhaps, that they are to-day just as sincerely convinced that they are right as we were yesterday when we too held these very opinions. A double process is required of those who would participate with real efficiency in the present phase of the struggle of the British and American wage-workers. In the first place, it is necessary to cut oneself off from a thousand ties and influences which prevent anyone brought up in the British and American environment from becoming a scientific Socialist. And yet at the same time it is almost useless to become a scientific Socialist if in the process one cuts oneself off from full, effective participation in contemporary life in general and the life of the Labour movement in particular. Therefore, this difficult, double process of simultaneous parturition and reunion is indispensable. If either, opposite, aspect of it is slurred over; if the individual fails genuinely to revalue his values; if he fails to become, in full, a scientific Socialist, then his participation in the Labour movement, however close it may be, will be useless or actually pernicious. But on the other hand, if he loses touch with the outside world, no degree of cloistered perfection in his self-development will be worth anything. In practice people can only hope to approximate to the ideal of a full mastery of scientific Socialism without any tendency towards cutting themselves off from the movement as a whole. Hitherto, at any rate, the two parts of the development of almost every individual have been more or less discontinuous. First they have made themselves, more or less completely, into scientific Socialists, cutting themselves off, more or less seriously, from the movement in the process. Then they have had to turn round and attempt to recreate the contacts which they themselves had severed. Some tendency towards this sort of thing is no doubt inevitable. But as the roads towards a mastery of scientific Socialism become easier to find, and as the enormous importance of refraining from self-isolation becomes fully understood, this tendency can be enormously minimised.

Sectarianism has been, I repeat, the historic sin of the Left. The formation of the new model parties marked a great step away from sectarianism. For hitherto most Socialists had belonged to small societies, which were in many cases almost literally sects. Some of these societies, as for instance the Socialist Party of Great Britain, or the Socialist Labour Party of America, survive to-day. Anyone who wishes to see how far sectarianism can go should study these societies. They neither attempt, nor wish to attempt, to work in the Labour movement. They are not really designed to do anything—to have any objective effect upon the outside world. They are much more analogous to religious bodies, the purpose of which is to provide subjective comfort and consolation to their own members.

From their foundation all parties of the new model have repudiated this outlook. From the first they have attempted to work actively both in the wider Labour movement and directly amongst the mass of the population.

But the left wing of the Labour movement was by no means the only section to suffer from sectarian tendencies. To-day in Britain, for example, it is especially the more conservative of the leaders of the movement who suffer from this disease. For to-day it is they, and not the left, which rejects co-operation with the liberal and progressive forces outside the Labour movement.

We have already seen what are their reasons for so doing. The purpose of a "People's Front" movement is to erect an impassable barrier against the capitalists' counter-offensive. Such resistance will undoubtedly involve very severe political struggles. But such struggles are the only alternative to the policy of retreat, surrender and disin-tegration, down which the British Labour movement has, for the past five years, been propelled. Hence in reality the refusal to form any kind of alliance, or People's Front, with the progressive forces outside the Labour movement, far from being an expression of militancy and full-blooded Socialism (as is sometimes pretended), is a logical part of a studied refusal to fight, not merely for Socialism, but for democracy. Thus the sectarian inclinations of the movement are traded upon in order to avoid attempting to build up that democratic alliance or People's Front which is the need of the hour. The British Labour Party has succeeded during recent years in getting the worst of both worlds. While repudiating any open or admitted alliance with any non-working-class progressive organisation, it none the less accommodated itself to the dominant capitalist forces to such an extent that it became in many cases a less resolute opponent of reaction than the very non-working-class organisations with which it would have nothing to do.

Mr. Attlee, in his *Labour Party in Perspective*, repeats the argument that the Labour Party can have nothing to do with non-Socialists, but then qualifies it as follows:

"I would not myself rule out such a thing as an impossibility in the event of the imminence of a world crisis."

Thus we may hope for a modification in Mr. Attlee's attitude if and when he considers that a critical world situation approaches. Would he consider, for example, that crisis had become "imminent" if Spain, all China and Czechoslovakia had followed Abyssinia as victims of Fascist aggression? Or would he not consider that a critical situation was imminent until, for instance, Europe as a whole had been similarly conquered?

The question of a People's Front raises the problem of the relationship between the working-class movement and that politically important middle class of professional, commercial, scientific, salaried, men and women which exists in every highly developed capitalist society. In Britain it has been an axiom of the leaders of the Labour movement that the only possible way of winning the middle class is to steer well to the right, to stress heavily the gradualistic note, and above all to damp down, and if need be to suppress, any vigorous or militant form of working-class activity. If a section of the working-class movement refused to abandon militant activities, then it must be formally expelled from the main body "so as not to antagonise the middle class". The Left of the British and American Labour movements, in the period before parties built upon the new model came to maturity, tended to reply to this attitude by asserting that the middle class was not worth winning anyhow; that the working class must keep itself pure and undefiled by any such contacts.

It is now clear that both these attitudes were disastrously mistaken. There is not the slightest doubt that whole sections, at any rate, of the middle class can and must be won as allies of the workers in the struggle against capitalist reaction. But it is equally clear that the method of toning down the theory and practice of the Labour movement, and excluding its militant section, in an attempt to curry favour, far from achieving this purpose, will in the end result in losing almost the entire middle class. The contrasted experiences of two major Labour movements of Continental Europe are, surely conclusive on the point. In Germany the leaders of the main body of the Labour movement carried the policy of attempted conciliation of the middle class as far as it could conceivably be carried. They became, in the admiring words of a leading German middle-class writer, Mr. Emil Ludwig,[1] "the real conservative party" of Germany. Their one object, for which they were willing to sacrifice, and for which they sacrificed, everything, was to preserve the then existing system of capitalist democracy in Germany. They suppressed ruthlessly, repeatedly using armed force, that section of the German workers which would not abandon all militant forms of activity. Above all, they refused, even in the hour of maximum common danger, to have anything to do with the Left of the German movement, led by the large and influential new model party which had been built by the German Communists. All this they did very largely in order to win the German middle class. And with what result? The overwhelming mass of the German middle class was utterly lost. It was precisely this class which streamed over to Hitler and formed the very core and heart of the Nazi movement. If ever men died of unrequited love, the

[1] In conversation with the writer.

German Socialists died of unrequited love of the German middle class.

Now take the experience of the French Labour movement, which was faced in 1934 by a situation similar, in one respect, to the German situation in, say, 1930. A quickly rising Fascist movement was threatening to gain the support of the middle class. After great difficulty, and in the face of the strong opposition of the Socialist leaders, who foretold the alienation of the entire middle class, the Communist Party succeeded (to a considerable extent) in uniting the working-class movement. The movement naturally became far more vigorous and militant than ever before. A breath of self-confidence passed through it. Its Socialist character was deepened and reinforced. Exactly those conditions which, the British, French and German leaders had endlessly reiterated, must drive every member of the middle class into the arms of the capitalists, had arisen. What happened? Within just six months of the achievement of the unity of the French working-class movement, the great, historic party of the French middle class, the Radicals, formed a close alliance with the working-class movement. The middle class had been won for the Left, with results which have transformed the whole political situation in France, and may yet transform Europe.

There is no doubt about the conclusive character of these contrasted examples. It cannot any longer be said that the unity of the working class, with the increased militancy which that unity must involve, will frighten off the middle class. But what is the explanation of this? The middle class certainly does not consist in advanced Socialists, or militant rebels. The view that it will be frightened off by any working-class movement which looks too much as if it meant business is highly plausible. How is it that experience indicates that this view is quite false? The explanation is, I think, as follows. In ordinary times, in times, that is to say, of social and international relaxation, when the economic system appears to be functioning smoothly and efficiently (such times will in future be most extraordinary) it is perfectly true that the middle class, which receives appreciable crumbs from the rich man's table, will be frightened off by a militant and formidable Labour movement. But we do not live in such times. The crises, caused, in the last resort, by the disintegration of capitalism, follow each other without appreciable intermission. It is true that they change their form. Acute economic crises, with their accompanying terror of widespread personal starvation and ruin, are succeeded by international crises with their accompanying terror of war. But crisis itself is chronic. In these periods every section of society, except the small, very rich, class of large-scale owners of the means of production at the top, is seeking a way out. The question at issue is not whether something should be done; the question is: What is to be done? Above all, the struggle between the two main forces in society, between the Right and the Left, which are themselves the expression of the capitalist and the working classes, begins to stand out inescapably. The middle class lies between these two forces. To-day its private inclinations are to the Left. For, however much it misunderstands and fears Socialism, it sees that the three great popular interests of peace, democracy and the national standard of life are threatened from the Right. This is the basis of that strong and deep, if confused, anti-Fascist feeling which undoubtedly pervades all but the highest sections of British and American society to-day.

But as the struggle grows deeper the members of the middle class have to think of other things as well as their preferences. Not to put too fine a point on it, they have to begin to consider which side is going to win. Now there is no need to sneer at such an attitude. It is not a pleasant thing to be on the losing side in the class struggle. For people who, because of their intermediate position in society, can choose, it is quite inevitable that in the end the dominant consideration when they come to choose sides will not be exclusively "which side do we want to win?", but "which side is going to win?" Once this situation has arisen, members of the middle class will look at the working-class movement with new eyes. What will matter to them now will not be whether that movement is quiet, nicely spoken and inoffensive; what will matter will be whether that movement is strong and united. If the Labour movement is, on the contrary, weak and divided, the middle class will not be attracted, no matter how "sane", "moderate" and "reasonable" Labour leaders show themselves to be. If the Labour movement looks incapable of winning the power to impose its solution of the social crisis, then nothing on earth will prevent the middle class from passing into the camp of reaction. This is why the unity, strength and militancy of the French Labour movement won the French middle class; that is why the conservatism, division and weakness of the German Labour movement repelled the German middle class.

This is not to say, however, that the British and American Labour movements will win their respective middle classes by proposing a programme of the immediate and universal expropriation of the capitalists. In any event, and whatevery any of us may wish, that is not the subject which history has to-day written upon our agendas. In both countries the next thing to do is to prevent the already firmly united reaction from destroying the three basic interests of the mass of the population. It is, fundamentally, for the purpose of the defence of those interests that a united Labour movement must appeal to the forces of the middle class for an alliance. But, I repeat, the defence of the three great interests can never be a passive one. Peace cannot be defended except by organising a force which can make aggressive war impossible. Democracy cannot be defended except by using every one of the rights and liberties of the subject, and by making the existing constitutional system an effective vehicle for social amelioration. Above all, the national standard of life can only be defended by continual activity. In every boom it is eaten into by rising prices, which can only be offset by the Trade Unions securing increases of wages, by reforms such as the abolition of the Means Test, and by the continual improvement of the social services. In every slump it is certain to be directly attacked by attempts to cut wages and unemployment relief. Its active defence is the basis of a programme for a united Left.

A final question must be discussed. What will be the ultimate effect of a successful and active defence of the three great popular interests? It has been repeatedly emphasised that the state of contemporary capitalism is such that a condition of its existence is that it must wage war, destroy democracy and degrade the national standard of life. If we prevent it from doing these things, shall we not make it impossible for capitalism to continue to function? In the long run that is so. That is why the successful defence of the three popular interests opens up a straight road to Socialism. For if we determine to preserve peace, democracy and the national standard of life, we shall find, not as a matter of theory, but in actual practice, that Socialism is the only economic system which can serve our purpose. For the same reasons, moreover, any Government which has successfully defended the three popular interests will be forced by circumstances to pass very rapidly on from that defence to a progressive transformation of the economic system. And such a transformation will inevitably involve trenching deeply upon powerful vested interests. But what, it will be immediately asked, will be the position in all this of the non-Socialist allies, which you have suggested the Labour movement can rally to the defence of the popular interests? Are you not attempting to trick them into attacking capitalism by making them do things which you know capitalism cannot tolerate?

On the contrary, there is no element of trickery or concealment about our proposed alliance. The Socialist element in the alliance, or People's Front, declares clearly and at the outset, as I have declared here, that in our opinion it will be found that capitalism has become incompatible with the preservation of even elementary popular interests, so that their effective defence will involve us all in the progressive modification of capitalism. But we know that non-Socialist democrats do not agree with this. They believe, on the contrary, that it is possible permanently to preserve peace, democracy and a decent standard of life while leaving capitalism in existence. That is why they are not Socialists. I am sure that if they believed that capitalism had become inseparable from open tyranny, war and a coolie standard of life they would be the first to demand its abolition. But as it is they do not at all admit that a joint and successful defence of our three popular interests will bring us to a critical point of conflict with a capitalism whose means of existence that defence is cutting off. They believe, on the contrary, that the preservation of peace, democracy and the national standard of life will provide ideal conditions for the smooth functioning of the capitalist economic system (suitably revised and reformed from time to time). They believe, as did, and do, all the adherents of Fabian or British Socialism, that the general line of development of capitalism is still upward, as it undoubtedly was in the last century; that once we can rid ourselves of the reactionaries who (presumably for their own perverse purposes) are dragging us back to war, tyranny and coolie conditions, we shall find that the ordinary forces of economic competition will carry us all rapidly forward again upon the road of progress.

"Very well, then," we Socialists may reply, "let us assume that you are right. No one is suggesting that we should face a contest with the formidable forces of capitalism, if we can get peace, democracy and progress, without so encroaching on capitalist interests that such a contest became so inevitable. We Socialists are convinced, however, that you are mistaken; that you have misread the nature of the capitalist system and that you will find that it has become incompatible with all the good things which we both want. But for heaven's sake don't let us stand here arguing about that. *Let us put the matter to the test of experience.* For we have only to carry our joint defence of peace, democracy and the national standard of life to a successful

conclusion to discover beyond doubt whether the preservation of these things is permanently possible under capitalism.
If things turn out as you say they will, then our successful
defence will terminate our joint work. If, on the other hand,
things turn out as we Socialists say they will, and we discover that contemporary capitalism simply will not work
if it is forced to maintain a decent standard of life, to keep
the peace and to tolerate democracy, then we ask you to
join with us in the job of so altering the economic system
as to make it compatible with these three great interests
of all of us. For, in that event, it is clear, we shall all have
to choose between peace, democracy and a decent standard
of life and leaving the economic system as it is. And we
would not dream of insulting you by suggesting that in
such circumstances you would hesitate for a moment. We
know that, faced by the inescapable choice of beginning
the job of seriously modifying the structure of capitalism
or deserting your defence of peace, democracy and a decent
standard of life, you will choose to come with us. We
know also that you do not believe that any such choice will
arise; but we ask you just to bear in mind that we think
it will."

Is not this the basis of a fair and frank alliance between
Socialists and non-Socialists for the defence of the three
great popular interests? I believe that it is. It is an agreement to unite for the defence of certain very precious
things, which are only too obviously threatened, without
waiting to argue out why they are threatened, or what
will be the consequences of preserving them. French
experience has shown that an alliance can be formed on
this basis and that it can do great things. There remains
the question of the type of programme which such a popular
alliance, or People's Front, should seek to implement
to-day.

PART III

TOWARDS A UNITED LEFT

CHAPTER XIX

TOWARDS A PROGRESSIVE PROGRAMME

THE CONCLUSION OF the first part of this book was that the British Labour movement was in peril of decline and ultimate disintegration.

In the immediately post-war period, the ideology of Fabian or British Socialism proved a disastrously inadequate guide to action. The movement's failure to exploit its strength in relation to capitalism, then pinned upon the defensive, led, around 1930, to a new situation in which it was capitalism's turn to attack; to a situation in which Labour found itself everywhere on the defensive. But just as in the 'twenties the Labour attack was never pushed home, in order to avoid, at all costs, serious conflict with capitalism, so in the new period, and for the same reason, no unyielding defence, even of the most precious popular interests, has been made. Instead, a policy of retreat before, and accommodation to, the ever more exigent needs of capitalism was, in 1933, embarked upon. This policy, if it is now abandoned, will kill the movement.

The disintegration of the British Labour movement is, in the present world situation, an event too appalling to contemplate. In the modern world the forces of progress have no other rallying point than the industrial, co-operative and political associations of the wage-workers. The disintegration of these associations would leave reaction unchallenged and omnipotent, to wreck the world. For, let us not deceive ourselves, the dominant capitalists have to-day interests which are flatly incompatible with the maintenance of human civilisation. The capitalist class can nowhere permanently remain in power without racking the world with Fascist tyrannies and ever more frequent wars. It is true that very few individual members of the capitalist class realise this fact. They do not even consciously turn to Fascism, much less to war, as their salvation. War almost always presents itself to a capitalist class as a disastrous necessity, forced upon it by an unkind fate or a dastardly enemy. And so it is—war is the disastrous necessity of capitalism. Towards Fascism the members of the capitalist class feel far less hostile, but even in this case they do not take to open tyranny until they feel that they have no alternative way of rule. They simply do what they see will alone enable them to keep their power. The consequences they leave to look after themselves. But, beyond possibility of doubt, those consequences would be, if the capitalists were to have their way, our enslavement, and, sooner rather than later, our physical destruction in war.

Hence the Labour movements of such communities as Britain and America must at all costs accomplish their historical task of changing the world. They can only do so, let it be repeated, by acquiring a knowledge of scientific Socialism. For this alone can enable the organised wage workers to see where they are in contemporary society; to realise the general drive towards social disaster of contemporary capitalism; to grasp their movement's historic mission as the one force which can arrest that drive and put society back on to the road of progress. We saw also, however, that it was not enough for a Labour movement to acquire this new ideology. A new form of organisation, as a vehicle for that new ideology, was likewise indispensable. This new form of organisation has been developed in the shape of working-class political parties built upon a new model. We analysed in detail the difference between such parties and the older type of working-class parties. We concluded that the new parties attempted to be a much more highly developed form of human association than anything which the world had hitherto seen. We suggested that once the gigantic nature of the task of social transformation which faces a working-class movement has been realised, the need for some such new model party simply leaps to the eye. It followed that the most rapid possible development of a party built upon the new model was an indispensable means to the revival and salvation of the Labour movement as a whole.

All this involved a process of differentiation and even, in a sense, of division. It necessitated the emergence out of a Labour movement of a highly organised, integrated and disciplined body of men and women, who, equipped with a mastery of scientific Socialism, could provide an indispensable core to the movement, and indeed to the working class as a whole. But we immediately went on to point out that we must on no account think of the development of a party built upon the new model as, in itself, the whole task before us. A new model party, in the political conditions which exist in highly developed capitalist democracies, can be only one of the organisations which go to make up a Labour movement. Moreover it replaces none of the existing organisations. Its mission is, on the contrary, to aid and develop every one of the existing organisations of the movement to the maximum possible degree. Finally, we saw that the need of the hour in both countries was not merely for a united Labour movement, containing an adequately developed new model party, but for an alliance of such a movement with all the progressive and democratic, but non-Socialist, forces.

Hence we see that the activity of scientific Socialists must to-day be two-sided. On the one hand they must differentiate themselves from the movement as a whole by so deepening and completing their mastery of scientific Socialism that they gain perfect confidence in their ability collectively to see the right road forward. And they cannot do this without building up their own tightly integrated organisation. Yet at the same time they must unify and consolidate, by bringing together first the entire Labour movement, and then the entire progressive, popular forces of the community. Precisely in order, that is to say, to build the unity of all the forces of progress, those who have grasped the full nature of the situation which confronts the world must come together into one nuclear organisation.

We have now reached the question of the specific programme upon which all the forces of progress can unite. In principle their programme, I repeat for the hundredth time, can only be the defence of peace, democracy and the national standard of life. But this is the framework for a programme, not a programme itself. Nor is it possible in a book of this character to attempt to write such a programme. Such a programme must necessarily be written by the leaders of the different bodies which come together to form the democratic alliance or People's Front. It must deal, to a considerable extent, with the issues of the precise situation in which that alliance is formed. It may be useful, however, to examine somewhat more closely the conditions which should govern the writing of any such programme.

Such a programme will inevitably be in fact a list of suggested measures of reform. For neither peace, democracy, nor the national standard of life can be defended passively. Peace can only be preserved by an almost exact reversal of the present (1937) foreign policy of Great Britain; democracy can only be preserved by using it; the national standard of life can only be preserved by continual efforts to raise it; by the most active steps of social reform and economic re-organisation. For the general tendency of any capitalist system is to exert heavy pressure upon the standard of life of the 85 per cent of the population which has no appreciable ownership of the means of production, continually forcing it towards the subsistence level. The programme will then be a programme of reforms. But this statement will at once bring a question into the reader's mind. Is it not the case that left-wing Socialists and Communists disapprove of reforms? Are they not whole-hoggers, neck-or-nothing men, who wish to achieve their whole ends in one fell swoop? Do they not actively oppose any compromises or half-way houses? No, that is not the case. Nor has it ever been the case. Lenin, for example, wrote an amusing and enlightening passage in this connection:

"The term compromise in politics implies the surrender of certain of one's demands, the renunciation of part of one's demands by agreement with another party. The usual idea of the man in the street regarding the Bolshevists, an idea fostered by the systematic calumniations of the Press, is that the Bolshevists are opposed to all compromises, no matter with whom and under what circumstances. That idea is flattering to us as the party of the revolutionary proletariat, for it shows that even our enemies are obliged to admit our loyalty to the fundamental principles of Socialism and the revolution. Nevertheless, the truth must be told: this idea does not correspond to the facts. Engels was right when in his criticism of the manifesto of the Blanquist Communists (1873) he ridiculed their declaration, 'No Compromise!' 'That is a mere phrase,' he said, 'for compromises are often unavoidably forced upon a fighting party by circumstances, and it is absurd once and for all to refuse to stop at intermediate stations.'"[1]

Socialists and Communists, like other people, are only too pleased to gain a yard, or even a foot, of ground, in the course of the long struggle of the working class, if they cannot gain more. Immediately beneficial reforms will be achieved precisely by means of the more effective and resolute waging of the general, many sided struggle of the working class. Sometimes they will be achieved through the agency of progressive or Labour Governments which have been placed in office by means of successful electoral struggles; sometimes they will be achieved by ever-increasing pressure upon unwilling, reactionary Governments. The final objective of the struggle is power. But during the course of the struggle for power valuable reforms can undoubtedly be won, and every Communist is determined that they shall be won.

I think it must be admitted, however, that Socialists and Communists have brought some of the above misunderstandings upon themselves. All through the period of the working-class offensive in the nineteen-twenties a

[1] *Selected Works*, Vol. VI, p. 208.

favourite term of opprobrium levelled at the then leaders
of the Labour movement by their left-wing critics (especially
in Britain) was that these leaders were "reformists". This
phrase had accurately described the leaders of the Labour
movement in the previous period. It had suggested an
essential criticism which had to be made of their policy,
namely, that they had abandoned the struggle of the working
class, and had diverted the political side of the movement
into the attempt to get reforms by means of collaboration
with the capitalist class. But when the pre-war leaders
were stigmatised as "reformists", this did not mean that
their critics were opposed to the workers getting reforms.
What was meant was that the only way to get both reforms
immediately, and full power for the working class ultimately, was the steady, resolute, unflinching prosecution
of the struggle of the working class against the conditions
of life imposed upon it by capitalism. What was meant
was that not the achievement of reforms, but the disintegration of the movement, would result from attempts
to damp down and stifle that struggle in order to make
possible co-operation with allegedly beneficent elements in
the ruling class.

In the post-war world the term reformist became open
to grave misinterpretation. It could be, and was, represented that those militant critics who used it were against
the achievement of partial reforms for the benefit of the
workers. But so far from this being the case, the real position
was that the Left was endeavouring to point out that leaders
of the movement were failing, time after time, to achieve
most important reforms, precisely because of their repeated
damping down of the independent struggle of the workers,
in the hope of conciliating and co-operating with the
representatives of the ruling class. Indeed, it is hardly
too much to say that the real trouble with the "reformist"
leaders of the British Labour movement, in the post-war
period, was that they never reformed anything! In the
circumstances the continued use of the word "reformist"
as a term of opprobrium by their critics seems to me to

have been too open to misunderstanding and misrepresentation. It would have been better, surely, to say roundly that the charge was that our leaders were failing, not only to get power, but also to get reforms, by stifling the workers' struggle, in the vain, and ultimately treacherous, hope of conciliating the ruling class.

If, for example, the two British Labour Governments had actively pressed on with a programme of reforms, they would have had the whole British working-class movement behind them, almost to a man. What destroyed the confidence of the workers in these Governments, and especially in the second Labour Government, was that so soon as they discovered that British capitalism was in no condition to grant reforms or concessions they abandoned their whole programme of reforms, first stood still, and then actually began to withdraw reforms which had already been made. For to have implemented any programme of reforms in the conditions of the great slump of 1929–1932 would have meant grave conflicts with the dominant capitalist interests. It would have meant nothing less than attempting to impose the workers' solution of getting out of the crisis at the capitalists' expense. And for such a conflict the leaders of the Labour Party were totally unprepared.

This is the real criticism of the MacDonaldite leadership of the British Labour movement. It was not that the Labour Governments which it controlled did nothing more than enact reforms. No Governments in their positions could have done more, and any government which had done so much would have shown itself to possess bold and resolute leaders. A determined attempt to begin the enactment of its programme, as laid down in *Labour and the Nation*, by the second Labour Government, in particular, could have taken the movement forward to the point at which it could have begun to acquire the power to abolish capitalism altogether. But that Government, far from pressing on even with the most moderate reforms (and these in the conditions of 1929 and 1932 would have sufficed) began the process of repealing existing reforms (their basic step in this direction was the Anomalies Bill of the summer of 1931). Hence the proper name for them would have been, not "reformists" but "counter-reformists" or "repealists".

This view has been confirmed by the experience of the French Socialist Government of 1936–1937. In internal, as opposed to foreign, affairs this Government did carry out a considerable part, at any rate, of its programme. And in doing so it received the enthusiastic support and co-operation of the whole French Labour movement, including the powerful French Communist Party. If the British Labour Governments had tackled their tasks in the same spirit as did the Blum Government during the first six months of its period of office (and the Blum Government was also a minority government, let it be remembered) they would also have been actively supported by every section of the British Labour movement.

There is, however, an ambiguity about this word reform. I am here using it in the sense of the granting of concessions of one kind or another to the working class; the increase of this or that social service, increased maintenance for the unemployed (the abolition of the Means Test, for example), the passing of minimum wage legislation, legal protection of Trade Unionists exercising their right of association, the free distribution of some commodity (as milk for school children), the provision of state-assisted housing accommodation, etc. etc. All such measures are definite gains to the working class; they strengthen the workers and proportionately weaken capitalism. (As to the consequences of this much more below.) Every Socialist and Communist who knows his job works wholeheartedly for them.

But there is another kind of "reform". A whole category of measures, of which tariffs, subsidies to particular groups of capitalists, the compulsory cartellisation of an industry, the compulsory destruction of "redundant" means of production (e.g. the activities of the National Shipbuilders Security Company Ltd., or The Woolcombers Mutual

Association Ltd.), and the devaluation of a currency, are examples. Such pseudo reforms are designed to restore or to increase the profitability of capitalist industry. They have an exactly opposite effect to the former category of genuine reforms. Far from strengthening the working class at the expense of the capitalists, they strengthen the capitalists at the expense of the working class. For the increased profits which these measures bring to particular capitalist industries all come, in the last resort, out of the pockets of the workers. In the cases of the devaluation of the currency, or tariffs, the workers pay for them by way of higher prices. In the case of the compulsory cartellisation or rationalisation of an industry, or the compulsory destruction of redundant means of production, they pay for them in unemployment (and often by way of higher prices as well). The inhabitants of whole towns (of which Yarrow is merely the most famous example) may be thrown out of work. The production of wealth is deliberately curtailed, so that the very attempt to use our copious modern means of production to meet the still gross poverty of the population is abandoned. The familiar claim that such reforms are desirable and necessary because of the "efficiency" which they produce in the industry so reformed is quite inadmissible. The only efficiency which they produce is the more efficient production of profit by the larger dominant firms in the industry. For what, from the point of view of society as a whole, could be more fantastically inefficient than the deliberate curtailment of the output of some bitterly needed commodity, such as fuel, for example? Naturally, Socialists and Communists who know their business oppose this whole category of "reforms" as strongly as they support the other category.

Endless misunderstanding was caused within the British Labour movement during the nineteen-twenties by confusion between these two kinds of measures. The Left sometimes accused the Right of desiring to "bolster up capitalism" by proposing a programme of reforms, regardless of whether the measures proposed were in the nature

L1

of genuine concessions to the workers, which the capitalists would have to pay for, or were measures for the reorganisation of capitalist industries on a more profitable basis, which the workers would have to pay for. Since these two opposite kinds of measure were confused by the Left, the Right felt that the Left was denouncing any definite programme for the satisfaction of the immediate demands of the workers, and, not without some justification, did not see how they could co-operate with people who seemed so unreasonable as that. But the Right confused the two kinds of measures just as badly themselves. Labour ministers, for example, genuinely supposed that they were carrying out a reform, in the sense of a measure benefiting the workers, when they passed measures like the Coal Mines Reorganisation Bill of 1930, which greatly benefited the larger, dominant coal owners at the expense of the miners, who paid by way of increased unemployment, and of the general public, who paid by way of a higher price for coal. If only the Left had distinguished between the two kinds of reforms, it could not have supposed that there was the least danger of real reforms, of concessions to the workers, that is to say, "bolstering up capitalism". On the contrary, the real effect of such measures is to weaken capitalism. Indeed they tend to create reactions amongst the capitalists which, as we have already seen, may soon produce a situation in which such measures must either be carried much further or abandoned.

All this refers, it should be noted, to the post-war period. It would need serious qualification before it could be applied to the pre-war period. At that time capitalism was undoubtedly in a position to make considerable concessions to the workers (e.g. the 1906–1914 British programme of Social reforms) without feeling any serious strain. Hence the objective effect of such reforms was, in the short run at any rate, to stabilise the system.

But to-day, the urgent question which faces the British, and to a hardly lesser extent the American, Labour movements is whether the capitalist system is not now so far gone that it is congenitally intolerant of any substantial reforms or concessions to the non-capitalist classes. Will the attempt to implement a programme of such reforms immediately produce a situation in which either the reforming Government must press on at once to the abolition of capitalism or abandon its programme in the face of symptoms such as rapidly rising unemployment? As will be shown below, the answer to this question depends upon several secondary factors connected with the time, place, and conditions under which such a programme of reforms is initiated. But, in any case, the right policy for a Labour movement is in all circumstances to put forward a programme of practical reforms designed to meet the most bitterly felt needs of the working population. Even if it were clear that the initiation of such a programme would soon produce the above situation, the Labour movement should take its stand on such a programme, and a Labour or progressive Government should proceed inflexibly to put it into operation. For then Socialism itself would emerge as merely a necessary means to get the much needed reforms—a necessary means to the highly practical ends of higher wages, shorter hours, better social services, more democracy and secure peace. And this is as it should be.

A Labour movement should never put forward the demand for Socialism as an abstraction. The movement should continually voice and struggle for the simple, and extremely definite, demands of the workers for reform and improvement in their way of life, while never ceasing to explain that, at a certain point in the satisfaction of these demands, it will be necessary to take the power out of the hands of the capitalists and to reorganise the entire economic system on a new basis. Men who are by no means Socialists will support a socialistic measure—as, say, the nationalisation of the mines, or the compulsory acquisition of slum property for giant rehousing schemes—if it has become plain, by the logic of events themselves, that this is the only way of securing a decent standard of life for the miners, or of simultaneously abolishing the slums and finding real work for the unemployed. Thus, in all circumstances, and even when engaged in the most intensive propaganda for Socialism itself a Labour movement should put forward a programme of demands for definite, simple, limited reforms or concessions to the working class. This raises the question of the difference between propaganda and agitation. Propaganda was defined by Lenin as the bringing of many ideas to a few people, agitation as the bringing of a few ideas to many people. Thus the *agitation* of a Labour movement must always be for the most immediately and desperately felt wants of the population (e.g. Lenin's demand in 1917, not for Socialism, but for bread, peace and the land). Its *propaganda*, on the other hand, must be directly for Socialism. It must strive to make the very maximum possible number of people understand so much about the whole situation of the world that they will know both precisely what Socialism is, and why Socialism alone can make it possible to satisfy the demands of the population for bread, peace and the land, or whatever their immediate necessities may be. Let us first consider the character which such a programme should have in Britain to-day. Then we can consider the question of the complex struggles which its implementation must, sooner or later, involve.

A programme for any progressive government will to-day inevitably fall into the framework of the promotion of our three great popular interests of peace, democracy and a satisfactory national standard of life. Let us briefly enumerate the kind of measures which, according to current circumstances, will be necessary under each head.

The measures necessary to save the peace of the world are, in 1937, familiar enough. To-day the only way to prevent the Fascist Powers from plunging the world into war is to rebuild some system of collective security. It must be made apparent that any State attacked by a Fascist aggressor will be unhesitatingly succoured by the full strength of the armed forces of all the democratic States. If that is done in time to save Spain and China, and before the Fascists commit their next major act of aggression, there need never be another world war. If it is not done, there certainly will be. To-day (1937) the position is as simple as that. But the simplicity of the measures which could alone bring peace must not blind us to the extremely drastic, almost revolutionary, character which the implementing of a programme of rebuilding the League and collective security would have in the contemporary world.

Mr. Attlee in his book, *The Labour Party in Perspective*, declares that there is universal agreement within the Labour movement on such a programme, and no doubt he is right. He writes:

"If the Labour Party came into power now in this country, there would not, I think, be any division as to what policy should be followed. A Labour Government would at once take action to rebuild the League of Nations and the collective system."[1]

We can all agree to that. But have Mr. Attlee and his colleagues fully realised what are the practical steps necessary to the rebuilding of the League of Nations and the collective system? Have they fully faced the fact that the League and the collective system cannot be rebuilt unless, for a start, the States members of the League give Italy and Germany, say, two weeks in which to withdraw their armed forces from Spain? For nothing on earth is more certain than that no one will even take into account a League of Nations which allows one of its member States, such as Spain, to be invaded by between 70,000 and 200,000 troops of another member State, Italy, without taking any action whatever. To re-establish the League and the collective system means to-day the coercion of Italy and Germany. And this must now be a tough business, involving some risk of war. But there is no other way. For a failure to rebuild the League and the collective system means the certainty of war. If this fact has not been faced it is a foolish

[1] P. 224.

deception to talk of rebuilding the League and the collective system. It may be, I trust it is, that Mr. Attlee and his colleagues have fully faced these simple facts.

I am acutely conscious, however, that even by the time this book is published the world situation may have been transformed either for good or ill. The worst may have happened. The collective peace system may have been finally disrupted. Spain, China or some other State such as Czechoslovakia, may have joined Abyssinia in the list of victims which the Fascist States have been allowed to conquer, while the pusillanimous democracies looked on. In that event, we can expect nothing but a world war, in which the Fascist States will have been enabled to gain an enormous initial advantage. Or again, the collective system may not have been rebuilt before the Fascists strike, but, in sheer self-defence, the democratic States may have come together, too late to avoid war, but soon enough to ensure that they will crush the Fascist States in a short conflict. For the combined power of Britain, France and the Soviet Union, plus their potential allies, could undoubtedly do this. Or, third, a collective peace system may actually have been rebuilt, by the adhesion of Britain (it lacks only that) in time to save Spain and to make it impossible for the Fascist States to strike down another victim. In that case disintegration within the Fascist States will begin at once. In such a situation it is clearly impossible to say more, in advance, than the above sentence that peace can to-day be saved by rebuilding the system of collective security, and in no other way.

Nor can we say very much to-day on the measures necessary to the defence of democracy in Britain. For the existing system of capitalist democracy has been, so far, encroached upon rather than frontally attacked. It will be important, however, for any Labour or progressive Government to repeal the three main anti-libertarian statutes of recent years, the Sedition Act, the Public Order Act and, more important than either of these, the Trade Union Act of 1927.

It may well be still more important, however, to deal with the related questions of parliamentary procedure and the relations of local authorities to the Central Government. We must, however, make one distinction on this subject, analogous to the above distinction between true and false reforms. There is to-day a perpetual anti-democratic under-current in governing-class circles. One of the expressions which this tendency takes is to suggest all sorts of methods for "speeding up" parliamentary procedure. This is to be done by decreasing the opportunities of discussion and criticism in Parliament and by increasing the powers of the Cabinet. A second tendency (which has at times been carried out) is to curtail the power of local authorities, in case these fall into Labour hands and begin to frame policies opposed to the Central Government. To both these tendencies the Labour movement and its allies must be relentlessly opposed. The "efficiency" in the name of which they are both advocated is merely a more efficient conduct of the capitalist State machine; of a machine, that is to say, of which the essential purpose is to provide a framework within which the owners of the means of production can extract their unearned incomes. In general the more "efficient" such a machine is made, the worse it will be for the wage earners.

At the same time any Labour or progressive Government is certain to be faced from the outset with innumerable forms of the most extreme obstruction both in and outside Parliament. The very men who, when they are in office, were all for efficiency, political speed-up, and the curtail-ment of the powers of local government, will emerge, under a Labour or progressive administration, as the champions of the most extreme doctrine of the right of Parliament to endless debate and obstruction, and of the right of re-actionary local authorities to sabotage (for instance) the Central Government's housing or public works programme to any extent. A Left government must not be taken in by this familiar *volte face*. Just because one of its main objects is the defence of democracy, it must make democracy work. An essential part of its task is to show that tangible benefits can emerge from the election of a progressive administration. In order to prevent parliamentary obstruction, or the sabotage of local authorities, such an administration is unlikely to need new legislative powers. There are plenty of powers already on the Statute Book by which Governments can put legislation through the House of Commons in a matter of days instead of months. Where reactionary administrations have really wanted particular measures they have repeatedly done so. The two Labour Governments were too irresolute to use such powers. It might be, of course, that a future Labour or progressive Government, resting on a composite majority, would be defeated when it attempted to put essential measures through without delay. If so, this would be a thousand times better than to stay in office without accomplishing anything while the apathy, disillusionment and finally despair of the Government's supporters accumulated.[1]

Democracy is not, however, merely a matter of parliamentary procedure—though it is often in Britain regarded in this grotesquely narrow way. Democracy is a question of the whole structure of the community. This is why in the final analysis it is inseparably bound up with the question of who is to own the means of production. Nonethe-less a progressive Government which cannot deal directly with this basic issue, can (and it is imperative that it should) begin to democratise those great State institutions of which the most important are the armed forces. The British armed forces are organised on an almost pre-capitalist, semi-feudal, basis. Their commissioned ranks are the almost exclusive preserve of the governing classes. It is imperative that any progressive Government should tackle the job of democratising them. And it is profoundly encouraging that the official short programme of the Labour

[1] Mr. Attlee tells us that "A Labour Government will not allow its programme to be wrecked by factious obstruction, but will not trample on the rights of a minority". Does not Mr. Attlee find, however, that what one man calls overcoming factious obstruction another stigmatises as trampling on the rights of a minority?

Party (issued March 1937) refers to this question in the following words:

"Throughout the services" (the armed forces) "promotion to commissioned ranks will be open to all, and will depend on merit alone, and no longer on wealth or class privilege. Conditions of service will be improved and, so far as possible, employment on the termination of service will be guaranteed to all. A bill will be passed enabling the Government to take over any undertaking manufacturing munitions of war."

These sentences, as was perhaps inevitable in a short programme, may mean much or little. (It is very much to be hoped that an explanatory statement or pamphlet will be issued on this point in the programme.) But it is much that this extremely important and highly controversial matter has found a place in the short term programme.[1]

Again this is almost all that can be usefully said about that section of the programme which must deal with the defence of democracy. It may, however, easily be that by the time a progressive administration comes into office this section of its programme will be the most important of all. The incipient capitalist attack upon democracy is in Britain merely suspended during the period of the boom. It may well be renewed in an extreme form to meet the social conditions created by the next slump or, still more, the next war. It may well be that the first task of the next progressive administration in Britain will be to sweep away a whole series of anti-democratic measures and to restore, against legal and administrative encroachments, the traditional liberties of British subjects.

[1] Mr. Attlee has an excellent passage on the matter.

CHAPTER XX

TOWARDS A PROGRESSIVE
PROGRAMME (*cont.*)

THE THIRD PART of any progressive programme must be devoted to the active defence of the national standard of life. It is possible to say a good deal more as to the nature of this part of the programme and of the probable consequences of carrying it out.

The measures which must make it up have been familiar features of Labour, and to some extent Liberal, programmes for many years. They fall into three overlapping but distinguishable groups. In the first place, there is a group of measures consisting in improvements and enlargements of the social services; the abolition of the Means Test; increase of unemployment benefit scales; retirement pensions; free milk for school-children; raising the school leaving age with maintenance allowances, and many other kindred measures. Included in this group are measures designed to raise wages; the extension of Trade Boards to particularly sweated industries; the imposition of statutory minimum wages, or statutory limitations of hours, or compulsory holidays with pay, and the support and encouragement of the Trade Unions' activities. All such measures, of which the above are merely examples, aim at distributing increased purchasing power amongst the wage-earning population—the money being found either by the employing capitalists by way of an increased wages Bill, or out of taxation imposed by the Government on this same class.

The second group of measures aims at providing work, and therefore wages, for the mass of workers which the capitalists never now find it profitable to employ. It is proposed to do this by means of public works of one kind or another—road building, bridge building, land drainage, railway development, afforestation, etc. etc., with the addition to this otherwise somewhat uninspiring list of housing and slum clearance. These two groups of immediate measures are intended to lead on, in all Labour programmes, to a third group of measures. These are measures of economic reorganisation, such as the establishment of a national investment board, the control or nationalisation of the central bank, and of the joint-stock banks, the nationalisation of the mining and armament industries, etc. etc. However, the programmes are written, and whether they be short programmes or long programmes, these are the measures which they all contain.[1]

What are we to say to such programmes as practical measures for the defence of the national standard of life to-day? The first thing to say is that they are perfectly correct in themselves. The enactment and carrying through of such a programme would have immeasurably beneficial results for the whole 85 per cent of the population which, in Britain, has no appreciable ownership in the means of production. To increase wages and social services, to limit hours of work, especially for young workers, to produce the conditions necessary for an immense growth in Trade Union membership, to provide for universal annual holidays with pay; to abolish the Means Test and the semi-starvation of the temporarily unemployed; to provide work for the permanently unemployed, especially in the depressed areas, to begin the extension of public ownership, to save democracy and peace—all this would transform the lives of tens of millions of British citizens.

Why is it, then, that nobody feels any particular enthusiasm for such a programme? We all know the answer to that question only too well. It is because these are just the measures which have been promised by the Labour

[1] Almost all these measures found a place, for example, in both the official Labour party programme and in the manifesto issued by the Committee of the Unity Campaign in the winter of 1936–7.

Party, and in many cases by the Liberals, too, ever since the war. It is because parliamentary majorities have twice been elected which were pledged to carry them out, and on neither occasion was anything appreciable accomplished.[1]

But why did neither Labour Government do anything appreciable to carry out a programme of social reform for which both had clear mandates from the country and a clear majority in Parliament?[2] It was not original sin on the part of the Labour leaders. *It was that they had never faced the consequences which the enactment of such a programme as this must have in the conditions created by contemporary capitalism.* Those consequences will vary widely according to the circumstances in which the enactment of the programme is begun, above all according to whether the trade cycle is in its upward or downward phase. For it is perfectly true that during periods of marked recovery, British and American capitalism can still stand the burden of increased wages and social services without an appreciable slowing down of economic activity. But the main point remains. When all is said and done, increased wages and social services, holidays with pay and shorter hours—all sorts, and any sort, of improvements in the conditions of life of the wage-workers—throw a burden of one kind or another, on the rent, interest and profit derived from industry by the capitalists. In so doing they decrease the demand for Labour at the margin of profitability. It is perfectly true that even in times of depression there are thousands of companies which could easily carry the increased burden and still retain thumping profits. That is not the point. The point is that, under a competitive system, there must always be other less efficient or less fortunate companies working at a margin of profitability

[1] The Wheatley Housing Act of 1924 was the most substantial measure of social reform enacted during the nineteen-twenties.

[2] Of the second Labour Government Mr. Attlee, the present (1937) leader of the Labour Party writes: "There was therefore a clear mandate from the country for a programme which would be generally to the left." (*The Labour Party in Perspective*, p. 55.)

which the increased burden will extinguish. And since the extraction of profit is the purpose for which capitalist production is carried on, these companies, if the burden is imposed on them, will cease, or decrease, their operations and their workers will become unemployed. (It is worth while to point out that this consequence will follow to the same extent if the wage-workers are benefited by the free distribution of some commodity, such as milk.)

It is true that this is only one side of the picture. The basic difficulty from which contemporary capitalism suffers is its inability to sell the final product of the industrial system; to dispose of the total flow of consumers' goods at prices which will yield a profit to their producers. There is, notoriously, a chronic, and periodically catastrophic, tendency for the purchasing power of the mass of the population to fail. Hence any such programme of social reforms as that sketched above, with its measures for the all-round increase in the purchasing power of 85 per cent of the population, will, it may be argued, actually benefit the capitalists by helping to solve their chronic problem of how to sell their products. Will not, it might be, and has been, argued, a programme of social reform, far from tending to depress capitalism, help it enormously by expanding the market? The answer is: So it will, *but only at the cost of imposing a lower general rate of profit and interest on the class which owns the means of production.* If the capitalists are willing to accept a lower rate of interest or profit on their capital, then undoubtedly social reforms, by increasing the purchasing power of the masses, will help them to keep their system going; will stave off an approaching slump or help recovery. But will the capitalists be willing to settle down to the prospect of receiving a generally lower rate of return on their capital? It is the *rate* of return, I must emphasise, that is here in question. For it is quite possible that social reforms by widening the market and so making it possible for the capitalists to use all their capital would actually increase the total *amount* of profit and interest which the capitalists would receive, in spite of lowering the rate. All experience indicates, however, that the capitalists will not (except in certain circumstances to be discussed below, p. 359) be willing to take a lower rate of return on their money. Increased wages, social services, etc., inevitably appear to them in the first instance as increases in their *costs*. The fact that they are also an increase in their *market* will always appear as a dim, questionable, theoretical sort of consideration which no practical man would be willing to take into account. For the increase in costs inevitably comes first. The employer is faced with the necessity of producing more money to pay out to his workers and for his raw materials at the end of the week. He will not be in any mood to listen to arguments about this money flowing back to him by way of an increased demand for his goods. How does he know that it will not flow back to one of his competitors, anyway?

Here we touch on the heart of the dilemma of capitalism. The incomes of the whole non-capitalist part of the population, of 85 per cent of the population, that is to say, are at one and the same time the capitalists' costs and their market. Hence in order to make their system work profitably they continually strive to lower them. But in doing so they inevitably destroy their own market. Hence for practical purposes we must recognise the fact that a programme of social reforms, in spite of the undoubted fact that it will increase the purchasing power of 85 per cent of the population, and so greatly widen the market, will exercise a depressing tendency upon capitalist industry.

Now this proposition has always been a commonplace, and, we may be sure, a most heavily stressed commonplace, of capitalist economic thought. Why, then, did the Fabian Socialists, who were steeped in capitalist economics, refuse to recognise it? (For it was the refusal to recognise this fact which led to the painful surprise always felt by Labour ministers when economic conditions became unfavourable for carrying out their programme.) The Fabians refused to face these facts, first because in its hey-day British capitalism had such an immense margin of profitability that it could afford to pay—and to some extent actually did pay—increased wages and social services with only negligibly adverse affects on the demand for labour. Secondly, the capitalist spokesmen put forward the view that any increased burden on capitalism would produce a crisis in so grotesquely exaggerated a form that the Fabians were always easily able to refute them. But to-day this tendency is unquestionably there, and any Labour movement which refuses to face it is simply blinding itself to facts.

Moreover, the real situation is by no means that the capitalists will go on smoothly working their system until the rate of return on their capital begins to approximate to zero. Except in the period of rapidly rising profits during a recovery (when they will probably be willing to put up with a lot, even now) they will deliberately use the *tendency* of a programme of social reform to curtail economic activity, to create a panic, in which great sections of the economic system, which are still making substantial profits, will be dislocated and hundreds of thousands of men will be thrown out of work. For this is the obvious way of discrediting any progressive Government and so preventing the carrying through of its programme of social reforms. Hence the much canvassed question of whether the economic and financial crises which have struck down progressive Governments (as in 1931 in Britain or in 1937 in France), and one of which the Roosevelt administration is now (1937) facing, are genuine or are put-up jobs on the part of the capitalists is not susceptible to a direct yes or no answer. They are always both. They are the result of the inner group of finance capitalists using the tendency of social reform programmes to depress capitalism, or, as was predominantly the case in 1931, the inherent tendency of contemporary capitalism to run into crisis on its own account, to discredit a progressive Government and stop its social reforms.

To speak of the certainty that the dominant capitalist groups will make this form of attack upon any progressive Government is to incur extreme unpopularity amongst many of the leaders of the British Labour Party. Sir Stafford Cripps, for example, was bitterly attacked for suggesting that a future Labour Government would have to face a struggle with the ruling class, intent to wreck its programme of social reforms. These Labour leaders evidently believe that it is bad electoral tactics even to hint that there may be any difficulties in the way of carrying out a programme of social reforms. To suggest so much as the possibility of resistance by way of economic sabotage on the part of the ruling class is supposed to be disastrously foolish. Well, we have twice now got progressive majorities by this method of promising a delightfully easy, effortless progress towards all-round social amelioration. And the result has been that when the inevitable difficulties arose no one was ready to face them. Hence the disillusionment and scepticism which everywhere surrounds us. Would it not be better this time to warn our supporters that we shall not accomplish much without facing serious opposition, and so come to the struggle prepared for it? If we have to point to a single factor as being more responsible than any other for the contemporary difficulties of the Labour Party, we must point to this refusal to face up to the inevitable struggle which the enactment of any programme of social reforms must produce.

But how, the reader will ask, can even the best prepared Labour or progressive Government overcome the weapon of economic sabotage, the strike of capital, with which it will be faced? In the first place, that depends very largely upon whether such a Government comes into office in a period of depression or of recovery. If it has the good fortune to take office in a period of recovery, then it should undoubtedly press on rapidly with the first group of social reform measures, which bring immediate, direct, tangible benefit to tens of millions of people. In these circumstances the Government will not be faced with an economic crisis before, at any rate, it has been able to give these millions enough to have immensely consolidated their support, so that when the crisis comes it can be surmounted.[1] If, on the other hand, the progressive Government comes into office in a time of depression, then the part of the programme to concentrate upon is the provision of work for the great mass of unemployed workers which will exist at such a time. For the provision of vast work schemes, financed by loan, will, at any rate at first, have a strongly stimulating effect on the economic situation. Here the problem is to find suitable work schemes.

This problem itself is again only too familiar. But in this case, also, the nature of the problem has been most imperfectly realised. Clearly there is never in any capitalist society any dearth of work, in the sense of things needing to be done, or goods needing to be produced. Eighty-five per cent of the population of Britain needs, with varying degrees of urgency, an increased supply of almost every kind of commodity. Why not then put the unemployed on to producing clothes, boots and shoes, food and fuel, or to providing, in a word, all the things of which there is a frightful lack? The answer is, of course, that it is the prerogative of private profit-making capitalist industry to produce all these things; that the capitalists own the land, the factories and the mines without which they cannot be produced; that no Government which is unwilling to dispossess the capitalists can turn the unemployed directly on to producing these necessaries. That is why Governments always try to put the unemployed on to all sorts of "made work", from road building, which may be socially necessary, though it often is not, to afforestation, levelling pit dumps, and the usual dreary and ineffectual list of "schemes". There is, in principle, no way out of this dilemma. There is, in principle, no way of putting the unemployed on to work worth doing without invading the sphere of

[1] M. Blum's Socialist administration in France came into office in such a period of recovery and had a year before the inevitable crisis broke. Nor did it fail to carry through a notable programme of social reforms during that period, and these reforms secured it wide mass support. But when the crisis came M. Blum preferred to resign rather than use this mass support to attempt to overcome the strike of capital and the resistance of the Senate. (See below, p. 358.)

production hitherto reserved to the capitalists. There is, however, one point at which this invasion can be undertaken immensely more easily, with far greater public support, and with greater economic effect, than at any other. That point is slum clearance and rehousing.

Anything up to half the wage-workers of Britain may be reckoned as extremely ill-housed. The provision of decent houses for them, which will involve the rebuilding of whole sections of almost every city in Britain, plus the building of many hundreds of thousands of extra houses, over and above those replaced (for there is still an acute absolute shortage of shelter, apart from the grossly unsatisfactory character of much existing shelter)[1] would provide almost any amount of highly necessary work. Why, then, has this supreme important job never been seriously undertaken by any progressive Government? The answer is, of course, that the provision of dwellings, and even more the letting out of existing dwellings, is an important sphere of capitalist profit-making enterprise, and that, therefore, there is always a formidable resistance to the State undertaking it. Still a beginning has, in Britain, been made. Public authorities have since the war built between 900,000 and 1 million houses and have in almost every case retained these houses, becoming the landlords of the housing estates which have thus been created. Hence it is considerably easier to enlarge this breach in the monopoly of capitalist production than it would be to start out, for example, on the creation of Government owned and operated boot and shoe producing works.

A progressive Government coming into office during a depression should, therefore, concentrate its main effort upon putting many hundreds of thousands—eventually

---

[1] In 1933 a careful investigation conducted on behalf of the Architects Journal by Mr. Philip Massey showed that there were at that time some seven and a half million people in Great Britain living in vilely overcrowded conditions. Some housing progress has been made since that date, but it is still (1937) safe to assume that several million British subjects ought to be provided with new houses before we can concentrate upon improving the quality of existing houses. For the present policy of pulling down houses, however dilapidated, while there is still gross overcrowding is open to the gravest criticism.

over a million, perhaps—unemployed workers directly or indirectly to work on rehousing from a quarter to half of the population of Britain. No doubt other public works schemes could and should be devised. For example, while secondary and local roads are in Britain probably already over-built, a great deal of work is still genuinely needed on the twenty or thirty main trunk arterial roads of the country in order to fit them for modern traffic needs. Again railway development, electrification, afforestation, the creation of public parks, water supplies, land drainage, reclamation schemes, and all the other old favourites of the nineteen-twenties, might still supply some genuinely useful work. But none of this work even begins to compare in social usefulness to the building of dwellings. Rehousing is immeasurably the best form of public works.

In order, however, to get a rehousing programme going on an adequate scale in anything like the time which is likely to be available for a progressive Government, before it must show tangible results, quite new methods will have to be used. Hitherto successive Governments have got houses built by paying subsidies to the local authorities in the hope that these authorities would be induced to buy the necessary land (sometimes using certain compulsory powers) and would then employ building contractors to build the houses for them. No really rapid expansion of building to the point at which it will suffice to meet a serious depression can possibly be got by these methods. (A scale of house-building comparable to the present (1937) scale of armament building (in which anything up to £300,000,000 a year will be spent) is here envisaged. For the suggested rehousing programme would to a large extent have to replace the present armaments programme.) The Treasury has always worked upon the basis of the calculation that each £1,000,000 spent will provide 4,000 men (2,000 directly and 2,000 indirectly) with work for a year. Hence, if the population of Britain were rehoused at the rate of £300,000,000 a year, 1,200,000 workers would be employed.

The only way, I am convinced, by which work on anything like this gigantic scale could be initiated is for the Government to establish a National Housing Corporation (on the lines of the Central Electricity Board, but with far wider powers). This corporation must be given the use of the proceeds of the housing loans which the Government will raise.[1] It must be equipped with compulsory powers for the acquisition of land and existing house property of an incomparably more drastic kind than those possessed by the local authorities at present. It will pay compensation to existing landowners and house-owners at existing market values, but it must have unquestionable power to acquire compulsorily all land or buildings which it needs, at a price fixed by specially appointed valuers, against whose valuations there must be no right of appeal either for the land-owner or the corporation (or there will be insufferable delays).[2] The corporation, if it is to move swiftly, will not be able to organise building operations itself on an adequate scale and should therefore employ the existing building contractors—though no doubt it should build some houses (and produce some building materials) itself by direct labour as a check on its contractors. In order to make a considerable effect on the economic situation, the corporation will have, I repeat, to work on a scale comparable to the present rearmament programme. This will mean (and why not?) rebuilding the slum areas of every great city. Moreover, the appearance of the corporation in the

[1] We are still envisaging a progressive government coming into office during a depression. In these circumstances the raising of a great re-housing loan would be the correct way to finance the building programme. It is clear of course that many formidable problems, as for example, the re-training of much labour for the building industry, by agreement with the Trade Unions, would have to be faced in any such scheme. But no action on a scale sufficient to affect the situation can possibly avoid such problems. Moreover they are all perfectly soluble, given the degree of determination with which, for instance, the National Government has tackled its armaments programme. (For example, Mr. Wheatly had no difficulty in coming to an agreement with Building Trade Unions in 1924.)

[2] The Labour Party's official Short Programme proposes this. It states that "A short Bill will be passed enabling the Government and other Public Authorities to acquire such land as they need for any purpose without delay and at a reasonable price."

field will undoubtedly have a tendency to decrease the amount of house building being undertaken by the local authorities and by private enterprise. It will have to be prepared to become the main provider of dwellings for the wage-earning population. But granted the above powers and finances there is no reason why a National Housing Corporation should not in from one to two years get building operations under way on such a scale as profoundly to affect the economic situation.

This is an example of the necessity of the progressive forces thinking out, to a considerable extent, and especially in regard to their initial measures, not only what they want to do but how they mean to do it. For such a drastic housing programme as this would be opposed not only by the property owners but by the Civil Service. There is no need to enter into the question of the motives and ultimate loyalties of the upper Civil Servants. Suffice it to say that the whole tradition of the British Civil Service is rigidly opposed to large-scale Government schemes of this sort. Hence a progressive Government can expect no assistance whatever from its technical advisers, in such matters. It must, on the contrary, know so well what it wants to do, and how it means to do it, that it is able to force its plans through against their passive resistance.

It is a commonplace that the recovery of 1932–37 was largely based on the boom in the building, for profit, by private enterprise, of houses for the middle class and best off wage-workers. The vast Government armaments programme is at present (1937) sustaining the building boom. But when armaments expenditure itself has passed the peak will come (if the armaments have not been used in the meantime) the slump. There is no reason, however, why a progressive Government, coming into office at such a juncture, should not enormously improve the general economic position and re-employ over a million workers by replacing the armaments boom by a new, but this time publicly conducted, building boom, based on nation-wide slum clearance.

Nothing, however, will get done, either in house-building or anything else, unless we face the fact that the opposition which a progressive Government acting in this kind of drastic, effective way will produce, will be extremely formidable. In order to rehouse substantial sections of the working population the existing urban landlords will have to be dispossessed (with full compensation, but with a compensation which they will howl to heaven is inadequate) and the initiative for house-building taken out of the hands of the private builders though these can still be employed (and in many cases, no doubt, be far better off) as contractors to the National Building Corporation. All this will mean an invasion of property rights and an extension of public enterprise which will be ferociously opposed. Anyone who does not realise this is deluding himself. But the point is that far more formidable forces still can be mobilised behind such a programme. A Government which shows itself determined to rehouse the vilely housed part of the British population, to employ over a million men in doing so, and thus to produce general economic recovery, and which has a definite, simple plan (such as the above) for doing it—a plan which can be expounded on one side of a leaflet—can overcome such opposition.

I have presented the situation as if a future progressive Government had to choose between the application of the first two groups of measures listed above; as if it had either to enact measures for the direct monetary benefit of the wage-earners, or to create employment by public works such as rehousing. But the choice will be one of emphasis. Even if it comes into office at the height of a boom such as the present (summer 1937) a progressive Government will be lost if it does not begin at once to prepare public works schemes, to organise its National Housing Corporation, and endow it with adequate powers in order both to provide work for some of the million and a half workers still unemployed and as preparation against coming slump. But at such a moment its main, immediate legislative effort should be directed towards the provision of higher wages, increased social services, shorter hours, holidays with pay, etc. etc., which, in 1937, British capitalism could well afford to pay, and is probably too busy making gigantic profits to engineer a financial panic against. Similarly, if the Government comes into office in a time of depression, it should concentrate upon the provision of work, chiefly by a gigantic housing programme; but it cannot possibly fail to begin applying its general programme of social reforms; it must at the very least at once abolish the Means Test, increase rates of unemployment benefits, force up wages in the grossly sweated industries, enact holidays with pay, and shorten hours of work.

The above two groups of measures—social reforms and public works—are thus but two sides of the same programme, each side of which should be emphasised in different circumstances. Moreover, the whole programme, whichever side is emphasised, and whatever the economic circumstances in which it is begun, will certainly lead to a struggle with the dominant capitalist interests as to who is to be the master—they or the legally elected progressive Government. This is really the single, simple conclusion which I am attempting to establish in these two chapters. *For if this fact is not faced, and to-day it is deliberately glossed over, there is no hope of a future Labour or progressive Government avoiding the fate of its predecessors.*

Both in the execution of public works, involving, as they must, if they are not to consist in worthless made-work, encroachments on entrenched property rights, and in the carrying through of social reforms, which will all increase the cost of labour, a point will come when the capitalists will say that they have had enough of all this sort of thing. Then the financial counter-attack will occur. It is not suggested, of course, that a progressive Government should deliberately provoke such a crisis. On the contrary, it should do everything in its power, *short of failing to carry out its programme*, to postpone it. For only so can it gain time to show results which can win the support it will need in the crisis. But all reason and all experience combine to

show that sooner or later the struggle will come. A point
will arise, just as it arose in 1931, for the second Labour
Government, and in the summer of 1937 for the Socialist
Government of M. Blum in France, when the biggest
capitalists, who have large disposable hoards of liquid
money capital, will begin exporting them, and a gold drain
on the central bank will set in. This financial crisis may
or may not be superimposed on a genuine economic crisis,
which the leading capitalists did not create but are using.
It was in Britain in 1931, it was not in France in 1937. But
in either event the financial crisis is intended to break the
progressive Government, to force it either to drop its programme and actually to begin imposing cuts on the workers,
or to resign office. *And hitherto all Labour and progressive
Governments have been destroyed by this simple, if drastic, device;
this stay-in strike of capital.*

They have either dropped their programmes of social
reforms, hung about miserably for months on end, begun
to reverse their programme and impose cuts, and then
have broken up, as did the second British Labour Government, or have resigned straight away, as did the French
Socialist Government. In one way or the other (though the
second way is far less damaging than the first) they have let
themselves be beaten. *For they have been led by men who were
acting on the assumption that no struggle would occur.* They have
been led by men who were either Fabian, British or
Revisionist Socialists; by men who had staked their whole
political careers on the view that the interests of the workers
and the capitalists were somehow fully reconcilable; that
the carrying out of a great programme of social reforms
would somehow benefit the capitalists almost as much as
the workers. Accordingly, when even the first stages in
the application of such a programme began to reveal the
irreconcilable and inevitable opposition of the dominant
forces within contemporary capitalism to any form of social
advance, they always felt that there must have been some
mistake; that a sufficiently eloquent appeal to the better
natures of the capitalists, and to the patience of the workers,

would get over every difficulty. In a word, the leaders of all recent progressive Governments have been committed to the attempt to carry through their programmes by securing all-round agreement on them. When the capitalists signified their dissent by actions more eloquent than even the best of speeches, they could do nothing but give up the attempt.

The British Labour Party is, moreover, still led by a man who firmly adheres to this general view. Mr. Attlee has been at pains to put on record that "The Labour Party believes that, when it has obtained the support of a majority of the electors for its policy, it will secure the acquiescence of the greater number of its opponents in the changes that will be brought about."[1] The point could hardly be put more clearly and strongly. It is evident that Mr. Attlee sincerely believes that just as he and his colleagues acquiesced (see p. 199) in denying arms to the Spanish Government, while maintaining its right to them, so the capitalists, while maintaining their right to retain the industries of the country, will acquiesce in a Labour Government nationalising these industries. To anyone who knows something of the British ruling class, this belief in its acquiescence would be very humorous, if it were not so overwhelmingly sad. Mr. Attlee goes on to contrast his belief in the acquiescence of the capitalists, with the view that "Socialism will never be introduced without a violent struggle". He evidently supposes that Communists, for instance, envisage the ruling class as rising in armed rebellion soon after a future Labour Government takes office. But this is not in the least likely, and no one supposes that it is. The capitalists will neither acquiesce nor rise in armed revolt if they are faced by the prospect of the enactment of a progressive programme. They have a dozen methods of resistance short of the attempted use of armed force. The first of these is the precipitation of financial crisis, the second would probably be the use of the House of Lords (possibly in co-operation with the use of the monarchy) to block all Labour Bills.

[1] *The Labour Party in Perspective*, p. 113

MD

It is out of this combined economic and constitutional struggle that the decision as to who was to be master would emerge. Mr. Attlee (and in this his treatment is exactly typical of British Socialist thought on the matter), in oversimplifying the problem to the alternative of acquiescence or direct armed resistance on the part of the capitalists, misses the real nature of the issue. The issue is simply this. Shall the British Labour movement face the impossibility of capitalist acquiescence, and the inevitability of capitalist resistance—that resistance being of many kinds, of which armed rebellion against a legally elected Labour or progressive Government is only the ultimate one?[1]

A frequent reaction to a realisation of the inevitability of capitalist resistance on the part of the Left of the Labour movement has been to conclude that it is useless to put forward any programme of social reforms; that the movement ought to demand Socialism or nothing. But this is a wholly unjustified conclusion. What experience has shown is that, in contemporary conditions, it is impossible to carry through a programme of social reforms, *without a severe struggle with the dominant capitalist interests*. But this fact must certainly not be allowed to prevent the movement putting forward its programme of social reform, *and carrying it through in the face of that opposition*. To confine the movement's propaganda to the bare demand for Socialism, without voicing, and being absolutely determined to satisfy, men's simple demands for a decent standard of life, for democracy and for peace, would be to reduce ourselves and our movement to sterility. For Socialism is an abstraction. And men, in the million, do not fight for abstractions. The way to Socialism must be made concrete by being translated into a clear programme of social reforms. A thousand men will support a Government which is giving them better wages, shorter hours, and decent houses for one that will support a Government which is talking about Socialism. The

[1] And, I repeat, a sufficiently resolute progressive Government will be able to prevent any opportunity for that ultimate form of resistance arising.

Labour movement must choose the most favourable ground on which to fight the inevitable struggle with those who rule society to-day; and the most favourable ground is precisely the struggle for the simplest, most elementary, social reforms and ameliorations. For events will show fast enough that even those reforms and ameliorations to-day involve a large measure of Socialism.

Socialism must emerge, not as a theory, not as something which people called Socialists and Communists happen to prefer, but as the inevitable and indispensable means of getting simple, concrete benefits, such as decent houses, a living wage, tolerable hours of work, democracy and peace. A progressive Government, even in the unlikely event that it, and its parliamentary majority, are exclusively composed of declared Socialists, must set out, not to introduce Socialism for its own sake, but to get tangible benefits for the population as a whole. In the process of getting those benefits, events themselves (which of course must be tirelessly explained and demonstrated) will show that measures of Socialism are necessary. For example, the Government will not set out to socialise the building and ownership of dwelling-houses. It will simply set out to get decent shelter for those many millions of British citizens who are to-day extremely ill-housed. But it will all too soon appear that the very substantial capitalist interests which are based on real estate in house property, passionately oppose the provision of adequate shelter for all. After all, their ability to draw rent from their slums depends on the perpetuation of the housing shortage and their monopoly of the land (sufficiently near places of work, etc.) necessary to build new dwellings on. It will emerge that nothing but the socialisation of house property can possibly give the workers decent houses.

To take another case, a progressive Government should take office determined to secure decent wages, hours and, above all perhaps, safe conditions of work for the miners. But, again, it will emerge that it is quite true that by and large, and within the present structure of British capitalism, the mine-owners cannot give the miners decent wages, hours and conditions. Or, rather, they cannot do so without closing down many marginal pits and so throwing many thousands of miners out of work altogether. So once again nationalisation will emerge, not as something which may or may not be theoretically desirable, but as the one way to get something done the necessity of which all democrats are agreed on—namely, a square deal for the miners. Again, the armament industry should certainly be nationalised—but not on general Socialist principles, but because of the obviously appalling scandal of giving a body of shareholders a vested interest in war.

These are particular instances. But this principle of what we may call pragmatic Socialism has a wider application. For this is the type of measure which must necessarily be resorted to by any progressive Government to meet the financial and economic assault which will be launched against it as its programme of social reforms is applied. The progressive Government will in all probability consist, either in itself, or, as in the case of the two British Labour Governments, in its parliamentary majority, of a coalition of Socialists and non-Socialist liberals and democrats. Such a Government will come into office pledged to carry through the programme of social reforms sketched above, nothing less and nothing more. It will proceed with its task. It will be faced, either almost immediately, in six months, in a year, or in two years, according to circumstances, but certainly sooner or later, with a struggle with the dominant capitalist interest, who will be using the weapon of financial or economic crisis. If such a Government, in the face of this crisis, begins to complain of the difficulties of its situation, yields, gives up its programme of social reform, and imposes cuts on the mass of the population, it will be irretrievably lost. Reaction will be restored to power for decades. What then must it do? It cannot simply go on with the programme of social reforms as if nothing had happened. For tens of thousands of workers will be being thrown out of work every month. What such a Government must do, if it is to survive, is to proceed to the third group of measures indicated above (p. 339)—the measures of economic reorganisation which have been agreed to in its original programme. These measures will inevitably be of a socialistic character. They may involve such things as a national investment board, national ownership of the central bank, control of the joint-stock banks, control of the exchanges, and the prohibition of the export of liquid money-capital. They may involve, though probably not quite so urgently, the nationalisation of the mining and armament industries.

In such circumstances a Labour or progressive Government will of course pay full compensation for the means of production taken over. There could be no question of a mixed Government, or indeed of any Government in such circumstances, confiscating property. Confiscation of means of production can, in the nature of things, only occur in a revolutionary situation, after, say, a capitalist Government has been defeated in war and the existing social and economic system has almost completely broken down. There is no objection (as indicated in Part I of this book) to compensating dispossessed capitalists for their industries, and raising the money to pay the interest on the resulting increase in the National Debt out of taxation from the rich. The objection is to the illusion that this will reconcile the capitalists to Socialism, and so avoid the necessity of overcoming their resistance, which they will certainly attempt (though they need not be allowed to succeed in this attempt) to make into violent and armed resistance.

Thus a Labour or progressive Government will undoubtedly find itself proceeding with socialistic measures. But they will be measures of a kind which many non-Socialists now support. They will have been included in the Government's original programme. Moreover, the Labour or progressive Government will only proceed to them as the sole way of securing those measures of social reform which it has already enacted. This will, of course, be the critical point. No previous progressive Government, when it has been faced with the capitalists' economic counter-attack, has ever yet taken up the fight. The second British Labour Government first arrested, and then began to reverse, its programme of social reforms. In so doing, it almost destroyed the British Labour movement. In France in 1937 M. Blum, faced with the same situation, did much better. He actually asked for powers adequate to deal with the situation. But when the Senate refused to give them to him, he resigned. Hence a progressive Government which showed fight would be a new phenomenon. At the time of writing (Nov. 1937) Mr. Roosevelt's administration is clearly just about to be subjected to the test. It remains to be seen whether or not it will fight.

It is of course quite impossible to say what the course of events would be. A constitutional crisis would almost certainly impose itself upon the financial and economic crisis. For the existing ruling class has in every country (less so in America than elsewhere—more so than anywhere else in Britain) reserve forces, of which a second Chamber, indirectly elected (as the French Senate) or not elected at all (as the House of Lords), are the chief examples, which can be used to block legislation. The crisis might well be long-drawn-out. It might be that during the course of it the popular forces would suffer many set-backs. The Labour or progressive Government might be forced to fight one or more elections (as even the Liberal Government of Mr. Asquith was in 1910). But such set-backs would not matter—so long as the popular forces kept fighting. It is surrenders, not set-backs, which discredit and destroy popular movements. The struggle would itself temper and harden the popular movement—would create a movement capable of victory.

It might be, however, that a Labour or progressive Government which showed that it meant business would not after all face a very long crisis. The stay-in strike of capital, by which such Governments have hitherto been broken, are extremely expensive things from the capitalists' standpoint. Just as a workers' strike imposes bitter sacrifices on the workers, so also a strike of capital, or even a refusal to co-operate with a progressive Government in measures designed to get out of a depression, is an extremely expensive business. The capitalist class is not a homogeneous mass. The great bankers and finance capitalists who to-day rule the class can, it is true, usually save themselves from any serious losses during a self-created or self-prolonged slump. But they can only do so by pushing the full weight of it onto the mass of smaller capitalists. If the progressive Government, by means of the type of measures of financial control indicated above, showed that it was determined to master these central financial interests, it might subsequently receive an unexpectedly large measure of co-operation from the medium and smaller capitalist interests. After all, they would not be threatened by its measures of social reform or economic reorganisation. If the Government made it perfectly clear that it was creating a new framework of conditions (rates of wages, hours, social services, etc.) within which profit-making enterprises could alone be carried on, but within which they definitely could and should be carried on, it might well be that the strike of capital would collapse very rapidly. Then, but not till then, the positive side of a programme of social reforms; its actually beneficial effect on capitalist industry by way of widening the market—though at the expense of the rate of return on capital—would have a chance of showing itself. But, let it be repeated, the smaller capitalist interests will always follow the lead of the dominant central banking and finance interests, unless and until these have been got under effective control. It will not be until a progressive Government has shown that it is master in its own house that it can have the slightest hope of this kind of co-operation.

It may be suggested that this prospect of a prolonged and complex struggle, which will involve both an economic and a political crisis, is not a very pleasant one. Cannot we promise, on the contrary, that a progressive Government will be able to carry through a great programme of social reforms, benefiting and reconciling all classes, and so ushering in a period of uninterrupted social tranquillity, harmony and progress? Oh yes, we can promise all this. In fact, this is what we always have promised. This is what Mr. Mac-Donald promised. This is the prospect which was always held out to us by the exponents of British Socialism—till lately the almost undisputed ideology of the British Labour movement. We have been promised, and some of the leaders of our movement continue to promise, just this delightful prospect. But no one—not even they themselves, I think—believes in it any longer. That is why the programmes and policies and manifestos which the movement issues tend to fall on deaf ears.

Even from an electoral standpoint the British Labour movement will never conquer until it frankly faces the prospect of a complex political, economic, and constitutional struggle in order to achieve even its minimal programme. It must continue to put forward that programme, but it will never get serious attention till it does so in a new spirit. Let it tell the British people that here are enormous benefits which could be theirs. But let it tell them also that nothing will be accomplished, and indeed everything that we have now which makes our lives worth living will be lost, unless we are prepared to face a struggle to overcome those forces of reaction which are leading us straight towards the pit. When it speaks like that the Labour movement will again be listened to. The British people has never been a cowardly one. We are not children to be fed on pap. We can see the realities of the grim world in which we live. And we now say to our leaders: Give us hope of escaping from catastrophe, even at the cost of prolonged and complex struggles, and we shall show what we are made of. But stop telling us that you can set everything right without injuring anybody's interests, or causing any disturbance, or having to overcome any serious opposition—for so long as you talk like that we know that you are frauds and will not follow you an inch.

There is no need, on the other hand, for a Labour movement to give a handle to its opponents by talking of a crisis arising if and when a Labour or progressive Government comes into power, and thereby laying itself open to the charge that the advent of such a Government would *cause* a crisis. For this is not the case. Such a Government will not cause a crisis. What will happen is that the resistance of the present ruling class to the will of democracy will cause a complex and prolonged struggle. Nor need the Labour movement be for ever talking of the prospect of such a struggle to the electorate. What is indispensable is that *the movement itself, from top to bottom,* should have become convinced of the inevitability of such a struggle; of the inconceivability of capitalist "acquiescence" in the will of a legally elected progressive Government. For once the movement has faced the fact of inevitable struggle, the whole character of its propaganda, its whole approach and attitude to the questions of the day will change and will begin once again to carry conviction.

In fact the prospect of a prolonged and complex political, economic and constitutional struggle is by far the best prospect which anyone can honestly hold out to the peoples of the remaining capitalist democracies. To confine, by means of the type of the policy and programme indicated above, the struggle to the purely political and constitutional field; to prevent it breaking through into violence will be an enormous achievement. This is what we must work for by every means in our power. I am convinced that it can be done. But it can only be done by facing the facts; by realising the full desperation of the resistance of the great dominant capitalists to social change. It can only be done by the mobilisation of such overwhelming popular forces on the side of steady, step by step, but cumulative, social advance, that at no point does the opportunity for a violent counter-attack arise.

A second question inevitably arises at this point. Will any such People's Front as we have envisaged as the necessary force to carry through a programme of social reform in the conditions of to-day, hang together during a period of economic and political crisis? Will not the liberal, middle-class, non-Socialist part of the alliance turn back when the necessity of serious measures of economic reorganisation, if the social reform programme is not to be abandoned, becomes obvious? I confess that I feel some diffidence in even suggesting this possibility. The record of our Labour movement in facing up to the necessity of serious struggle to get its programme carried through is not such that we can afford to begin to question the toughness of others. Experience has unfortunately shown that there is nothing in the label Socialist which ensures that a man is willing to face the issue when the testing time comes. Similarly, because a man has called himself liberal, or non-party, that is no reason to suppose that he will be willing to abandon his sincere fight for social reform, democracy and peace when he sees that measures of economic reorganisation, and consequently severe struggles with vested interests, are necessary to the success of that fight. There is a tough, non-Socialist, radicalism still current in Great Britain which should not be underrated. If the Labour movement has the capacity to give the popular forces the leadership which they must have, there is no reason to suppose that the alliance will not hold to the end.

Finally it may be suggested that in admitting that the dominant capitalist forces will not acquiesce in the programme of a Labour or progressive Government, I have admitted that progress is to-day very difficult. That is so. Social progress, or even the arrest of social decay, to-day involves swimming against the current. It will continue to do so until the capitalist system no longer exists. For the general tendency of the system is now unmistakably downwards towards social degradation and disruption. To reverse that tendency, and to do so without grave social violence, is no easy matter. It can only be even attempted by the policy of aligning the widest popular forces possible behind a simple programme for the defence of our three great interests; peace, democracy and the national standard of life. Then the logic of that programme, the very obstacles which will arise against the attempt to carry it out, will demand that we shall overcome the forces which stand in the way of economic reconstruction.

To carry such a policy through to success cannot be other than a most complex, difficult and many-sided task. That is why, side by side with the mobilising of the very widest possible forces, on the very simplest possible programme, an equal, opposite yet complementary, process is indispensable. The core of the forces of progress must be got together into the highly organised, integrated and disciplined form of a political party built upon the new model. All those whom luck or skill have enabled to see into the nature of contemporary social reality must come together in this way, in order to pool their experience and knowledge, to teach and to be taught, and to receive the thousand-fold reinforcement of a closely organised association. If they lack such an association, or new model party, they will dissipate their separate, individual influence, and never succeed in permeating the whole of the democratic forces. If, on the other hand, in coming together in their new model party, they cut themselves off from the Labour movement, or from the mass of the population generally, they will, equally, destroy their influence. It is certain that the struggle cannot be won along the lines indicated in these chapters —and this is incomparably the best prospect for peaceful progress—unless a new model party develops adequately in size, and becomes a part of the flesh and blood of the Labour movement. For only then will there be a never-tiring, never-failing centre of energy and faith within the movement, capable of carrying it through the great and unavoidable difficulties which lie ahead.

It is only recently, however, that in Britain and America parties built upon the new model have reached the point at which they could begin seriously to fulfil what is, I am convinced, their destined task of setting, first the Labour movement, and then the progressive forces as a whole, upon this one hopeful road of advance. For, difficult and rocky as is the road of advance which starts from the point of the united defence of peace, democracy and the national standard of life, it is the only road open. If we cannot push forward along this road, then the British and American Labour movements, in their present form, cannot be saved. If we cannot lead the popular forces in unity along the path of social reform and the defence of peace and democracy, though a serious, but foreseen and therefore prepared for, struggle with the dominant capitalist interests, to a substantial measure of economic reorganisation, then there is no way forward. Then the dark forces of reaction must have their way. Then the Labour movements of Britain and America, impotent, torpid and divided like the German Labour movement, will go down in ruin. Then the popular, democratic forces, leaderless, with their central pillar knocked away, will count for nothing. Then a period of bitter social reaction, capitalist-Fascist tyranny, rapidly falling standards of life, and major wars, lies ahead of us.

That would not mean the end of Socialism. On the contrary, such Fascist-capitalist reaction is above everything else self-destructive. We may implicitly rely on a group of Fascist-capitalist empires to shatter themselves to bits in an unending series of wars. Socialism will come. But if we let reaction triumph first, it will come by blood and iron. If Fascist reaction has been allowed to triumph, Socialism will come by the revolt of desperate, famished peoples against a social order almost completely destroyed by war; by the mutinies of broken troops; by civil war and all its attendant horrors. That is the prospect to which we condemn the world if we refuse to face the certainty of a prolonged and complex economic, political and constitutional struggle to overcome the stubborn resistance which will be offered to even the mildest programme of social reforms.

Here, it seems to me, a special responsibility lies on those leaders of the non-Socialist progressive forces, which to-day hold a key position. Let them be assured that no Communist is seeking a trial of strength in civil war. It is precisely in order to avert such a catastrophe that Communists are seeking to unite the entire progressive forces of the community. If the non-Socialist section of those progressive forces refuses its co-operation it will produce what it most dreads, namely, the opportunity for the reaction to resort to violence. If, in a word, we pretend to ourselves that we do not face any kind of struggle; that everybody will "acquiesce" in a programme of social reforms, then we shall certainly get armed, physical, struggle. But if we face the certainty of serious, complex, prolonged political and constitutional struggle, then we can do much to confine it within limits which will not half destroy human civilisation itself. If we go forward, as Labour and progressive Governments have always hitherto done, believing what it is nice and comfortable to believe, refusing to face the fact that the forces of reaction will attempt to use all means against us, we shall go through hell itself before we reach our goal. If, on the contrary, we go forward, prepared for every form of struggle, economic, political, and, if need be, armed, then it may be that the struggle will after all be by no means so grave as we had feared. If we can win the first round of that struggle, in which every Labour or progressive Government has so far been ignominiously defeated; if we can beat off the inevitable economic and financial counter-attack, the strike of capital, which is certain to be launched against us; if we can assert once and for all that the legally elected Government is master, we shall be able to build something in the nature of a transitional economic system, which will work reasonably well. If we can once do that, we shall have opened the door to a future which, though it will be stormy and difficult enough, will enable the world to avoid traversing a hellish period of Fascism and war.

It may be objected that all these speculations as to what will happen if and when a progressive Government begins to put through its programme are very academic and hypothetical. That is true. It is impossible to foresee the future. The position which will face such a Government may well be very different from anything here envisaged. The one thing that is certain is that no such Government can put through its programme without having to face a prolonged and complex struggle. And it is necessary to emphasize this one certainty, and then to re-emphasize it. For it is just this that the British Labour movement has never faced and does not fully face even now. And until this cold fact is soberly faced, not only will future progressive Governments go down to ignominious defeat, if they are elected, *but there will be no future progressive Governments*. For until the necessity of struggle, in the first place here and now against reaction in full power, and then against the vicious counter-attack which will be made on us after any electoral victory, is realised, we shall win no victory. Until men hear in the voices of the spokesmen of Labour a clearer, harder, sterner note; until, by facing facts ourselves, we make men feel that we mean business, they will not give us their votes—even if we promise them all a thousand a year for the asking.

The programme indicated in these chapters is almost identical with the official programme of the British Labour Party. But such a programme can be either the rallying cry of millions or a series of lifeless paragraphs, which no one troubles even to read, according to the spirit in which it is approached. If it is approached and popularised as something which will reconcile all classes by benefiting every one at nobody's expense, the British people will show no interest in it. They know all about such programmes already. They have had some. But if it is presented as something behind which so vast a mass of popular support can be mobilised that a determined Government can impose it upon the great vested interests, then it will begin to live. We shall indicate to the world how we regard our policy more by what we do than by what we say. If we go on talking of admirable social reforms, of peace and of democracy, while all the while we yield, with only mumbled protests, to measures which we know must lead to war and tyranny (such as the attempt to stifle Spanish democracy), or lift no finger to help men struggling desperately against a frightful degradation of their standard of life (as were the unemployed in 1934–5–6), then no one will even begin to listen to us. But if we fight with the whole strength of a united movement against reaction now, then our programme will begin to live and grow, till it becomes something behind which the strength of tens of millions is ranged.

The carrying out of such a programme will not indeed take us all the way to our goal of a satisfactory economic and social system. But it is the door to the future.

CHAPTER XXI

THE ROAD FORWARD

IT WOULD BE futile to discuss what would happen next after the carrying through of an effective programme of social reform by either a Labour Government, or a Government based upon a People's Front.

There remains, however, one question with which we must deal, for it has been made into a burning issue upon which attempts have been made to divide the movement. It is the question of whether general democratic rights and liberties can be maintained in full force, for the capitalists and ex-capitalists, during the transition from capitalism to Socialism.[1] Now, I repeat, it is impossible for any one to foresee the duration, or even, except in the most general terms, the character, of that transitional period. Lenin, speaking after the experience of the Russian revolution, said that in his view it would occupy a whole historical epoch. Moreover, this period will have a different character in different countries. It will be largely conditioned by the character of the capitalist society out of which Socialism is developing. Its character will partly depend upon whether the old society was a traditional, semi-feudal autocracy, a capitalist democracy, or a newly established Fascist-capitalist tyranny. But, even apart from this, it is quite impossible to foresee the nature of the transitional period. For example, if, in the case of a capitalist democracy, the members of the old ruling class at some point in the transition succeed, as the Spanish ruling class has done, in plunging their country into civil war, but are then defeated,

---

[1] In Chapter X we briefly defined the position of Communists in regard to democracy. But it will be worth while to return to the question in the light of the discussion of the intervening chapters.

it will clearly be quite impossible to restore to them their democratic rights. Imagine, for example, the feelings of the Spanish Government if, after defeating General Franco, it was asked immediately to restore full civil rights to him, to Señor March and their fellow mutineers! On the other hand, if the popular forces in any society achieve so high a degree of unity, political consciousness, and resolution that they manage to carry through the whole transition without the reaction being given any opportunity for violence, then the possibility of maintaining existing democratic institutions for all will naturally be much higher.

One would have thought, then, that it would be foolish for the progressive forces to commit themselves in advance to any particular policy for dealing with this future situation, the character of which none of them can possibly foresee. And one would have thought it downright insane of them to split themselves into two warring camps on this only too hypothetical question of what their attitude should be to the capitalists, if and when they had got the forces of the State out of the capitalists' hands and into their own! And yet this is precisely what we have done. The leaders of the British Labour movement have declared that they will never have anything whatever to do with persons so abominably wicked as to suggest that after, or during, the passage of State power from the hands of the capitalists to the Labour movement and its allies, the rights and liberties of the capitalists might have to be curtailed in order to prevent them plunging their country into civil war. Not content with committing themselves to the wildly optimistic view that the capitalists will "acquiesce" in the policy of a democratic Government, they attempt to excommunicate any one who even questions that view.

In the history of the international Labour movement this controversy has been waged over the doctrine of the dictatorship of the proletariat. No phrase has been more misunderstood, nor more misrepresented, than this one. One of the best definitions of it occurs in the original draft programme (it was written by Lenin and Pleckanov) submitted by Iskra to the inaugural Congress of the Russian Social Democratic Party. The dictatorship of the proletariat, this programme states, amounts to the assumption by the working class of such power that the capitalists cannot prevent the abolition of capitalism and the introduction of Socialism.[1] Thus correctly defined the doctrine of the dictatorship of the proletariat becomes the very linchpin or cornerstone of scientific Socialist theory.

As we saw in Part I of this book, a central error of the Fabian, British and revisionist Socialists was that they all ignored, or at best slurred over, this question of State power. We saw, that abundant experience has shown that until and unless the working class and its allies are able to take power; until, that is to say, they are able to assume the same dominating political relationship to the capitalist class as the capitalist class now assumes to them, all hope of achieving Socialism is vain. In this exact sense the dictatorship of the proletariat is an absolute prerequisite of Socialism.

But this conception of the absolute necessity of the rule of the working class (and its allies) as a condition precedent to Socialism tells us nothing whatever about the way in which that rule is to be exercised. For every class that has ever ruled society has exercised its rule in different ways according to time and place. In general if its rule has been precarious it has had to be autocratic and dictatorial; if secure it has often (though not always) tended to become democratic and libertarian. We must ask those who are seeking to divide, and so wreck, the working-class movement on this issue, the following question. Do they admit the necessity of the rule of the working class and its allies, if capitalism is to be even modified, let alone abolished? If they do not, if they reject the basic truth that Socialism,

---

[1] The text of the programme reads:
". . . the dictatorship of the proletariat, i.e. the conquest by the proletariat of such political power as will permit it to suppress all attempts at resistance on the part of the exploiters." (Quoted by Popov, *Outline History of the C.P.S.U.*, Vol. I, p. 104.)

and indeed social progress, to-day, can find no other champions but the popular forces, and will be bitterly opposed by the existing ruling class, then all rational political discussion between us and them becomes impossible. But, whatever they may sometimes say, they do not of course, in practice reject this view. For if they did, they would not have built up a Labour movement and would not be attempting to place a Labour Government into office.

If, then, this political axiom is accepted, we can come on to the question of how the working class and its allies are to exercise their rule. Will they, or will they not, even as they labour at the tremendous task of carrying through a programme of social progress in the conditions of to-day, find that the opposition which they excite in the old ruling class transcends the boundaries of ordinary democratic criticism and so, whether they like it or not, forces them, if they are not to give up their programme, to give their rule an authoritarian character? I say that we *can* pass on to this question, but quite frankly it seems to me almost useless to do so. For none of us can possibly foresee the conditions of such a period. Some of us may be much more optimistic than others about the possibility of over-coming the capitalists' resistance without resort to authoritarian methods. But to split now on the question is, surely, insane? For the one thing which creates this split is the extraordinary pronouncement by the majority of the leaders of the Labour party that they *know* that the Capitalists will acquiesce; that therefore no authoritarian measures will be necessary to the working class and its allies, and that any one who even suggests such a thing is a malefactor who must be drummed out of the Labour movement.

On the other hand any rigid dogmatism on the part of left-wing Socialists and Communists as to the forms which working-class rule will take in Britain would be quite misplaced. We, no more than anyone else, can foretell what the conditions of such a period will be. They may be the very favourable conditions envisaged in the two preceding chapters. They may be the conditions created by a progressive Government elected in a period of relative social stability. But we should be blinding ourselves to the facts of the world situation if we ignored the possibility that the forces of progress will not be in power again in Britain until after a world war has been fought and the whole social structure of both Britain and every other European country has been shattered. Very different forms of the rule of the working class and its allies will clearly be necessary in the two different sets of circumstances. If reaction has had its way and the world has plunged into war again, then the question of preserving democratic methods of rule is only too likely to prove a wholly academic one.

It may be well in this connection to say something about the situation which will arise if, before an effective People's Front has been formed, the British governing class turns Fascist in fact, if not in name, and attempts to suppress the British Labour movement, thus making its rule as absolute as that of the German capitalists and landlords. No one can pretend to foretell anything as to the course of the struggle which such an attempt would provoke. But it is possible to foretell this much with certainty, namely, that there would be a struggle, and, if need be, a long, bitter, stubborn and violent struggle. Before the British Labour movement could be suppressed, as the German Labour movement has been suppressed, the British workers would go to any lengths of resistance. Social classes learn from the fate of the same classes in other countries. And this, at any rate, the members of the British working-class movement have learnt from the fate of the German workers under Hitler: we have learnt that, no matter what the difficulties, no matter what the contemporary leaders of the Labour movement may do, no matter what the desperation of the situation may be, a working class must fight rather than see its essential organisations, its Trade Unions, its Co-operative Societies, and its political parties, suppressed by force.

Therefore let our rulers not deceive themselves. They have not the slightest chance of repeating the almost effortless victory of the German ruling class in 1933. If they attempt to suppress the British working class movement by force; to ban the British Trade Unions, to dissolve the Co-operative Societies and to declare the Labour Party, and the other working class parties, illegal, they will plunge Great Britain into a social cataclysm, the result of which no man can foresee. For this lesson is burnt into us by the Italian, the German and the Austrian experience. A working class which allows its movement, consisting of its Trade Unions, its Co-operatives and its political parties, to be suppressed becomes hopelessly enslaved. It suffers anything and everything at the hands of the ruling class.

Therefore, if their Trade Unions, their Co-operatives and their political parties are touched, the British workers will fight. They will use any and every weapon, of which the general strike will be but the first, to prevent the introduction of any form of Fascist dictatorship into this country. The British governing class would do well to remember this. British Imperialism is to-day faced with increasingly menacing rivals. At any moment she may be called upon to fight to protect some vital imperial interest. How can anyone doubt that if our rulers, by trying to suppress the British Labour movement, were to plunge Britain into a violent social conflict, of which a prolonged general strike would be but the opening phase, Japan, Italy and Germany would each and all seize their opportunity to dismember the British Empire? The British workers are thus in an impregnable position. They have only to make it unmistakably clear that they will fight rather than let their movement be suppressed (as everyone who really knows them, knows that they would) in order to make an attempt to destroy that movement impossible. For even though the British governing class might feel confident of its ultimate ability to crush all resistance, it dare not precipitate civil conflict, for it knows that in so doing is would deliver itself into the hands of its Imperialist rivals.

If, on the other hand, we manage to build a British People's Front of all the forces of progress in time to avert social and international catastrophe; if a progressive Government comes into power in Britain in more or less normal circumstances, then the question of the methods of its rule assumes much greater importance. In no circumstances would such a Government deviate from constitutionalism, unless it was subjected to unconstitutional sabotage and attack by the forces of reaction. Nor is it unimportant for Labour to make it perfectly clear that it accepts the democratic machinery of existing society (in spite of the gigantic bias against it which the privileges of wealth give to that machinery), and pledges itself not to depart from its use, *so long as its antagonists leave it there to use*. For by so doing Labour can avoid giving to the reaction any opportunity for using the endlessly repeated libel that it is the Left which stands for disturbance and civil conflict.[1] We know how grossly disingenuous that accusation is. But that is no reason for giving our opponents the opportunity to use it. On the contrary we must fling this accusation back in their teeth. We must show, as we can from a dozen historical examples, from the Curragh to the 18th of July 1936 in Spain, that it is always the reaction which does not hesitate to use violence if it feels that violence will benefit its case. This is a lesson which it is necessary for us tirelessly to teach. For we cannot possibly let the accusation of incitement to violence pass unanswered. In British conditions it is a very formidable accusation. Chiefly because of historic circumstances; because in particular of the uniquely favourable conditions under which British capitalism developed, hatred between the different social classes has in Britain been less intense than in most other capitalist

---

[1] The profound tragedy of a divided Labour movement is poignantly illustrated by the fact that many of the leaders of the movement have not hesitated to repeat this monstrous slander of the spokesmen of capitalism, in respect of the Left section of their own movement. Thus, by being repeated from within the movement, it is given incomparably greater currency and strength than the spokesmen of capitalism could give it. There is literally no hope for a movement so long as it continues to indulge in such horrible self-mutilation.

communities. We have been so rich that there has been in Britain, for the past seventy or eighty years, a certain ability to give and take between rich and poor, owner and non-owner, which has perceptibly mitigated the ferocious social antagonism which any class divided society must otherwise breed.

This social tolerance has had its thoroughly bad side. It has led to tolerance, both by those who suffered from them and by those who benefited by them, of some of the most horribly degrading conditions of life, for substantial sections of the population of the great cities of Britain, which the civilised world has ever known. But it has had its advantages also. Mr. G. D. H. Cole in his recent book "*The People's Front*" has well expressed the mood which these conditions have created.

"Now we in Great Britain want, I hope, to hurt one another as little as may be. We want to build upon the past, and not to pull down all that we have built in order to begin building afresh. We value the tolerance and the half-democracy that we have succeeded in creating under capitalism, even while we are fully conscious of their limitations. We want to adapt our economic system, and our ways of living together, to the new needs of the twentieth century with the minimum of destruction of what is good. Some things we must set out to destroy, because they are evil and stand definitely in the way of democratic advance. But there is also a great deal that we wish to preserve; and not least among the things we should like to save is a habit of living together without too much hate."

We wish to live together without too much hate. It is an admirable wish. If we can succeed in doing so during the period of the transition from capitalism to Socialism, we shall have accomplished much indeed. But we stand no chance of doing so if we blind ourselves to the lesson of history, which is that such periods have never yet been traversed without a sharp growth in the mutual hatred of social classes. It is not by ignoring the causes of inter-class hatred in such periods that we can hope to minimise them. The mood, which, very rightly in itself, regards the avoidance of any such growth in social hatred as an evil to be avoided almost at all costs is a very real one—nor is it confined exclusively to the middle strata of society, though it is strongest in this section of the community. We shall ignore this, in itself, admirable sentiment at our peril. If we give any grounds for the suspicion that we do not realise, just as clearly as everyone else, the frightful consequences of a growth of social hatred; if we do not make it clear that it is precisely because we too long for a community free of class hatred that we are determined to root out its cause —which is nothing but the existence of human exploitation; if we fail to make all this clear, we shall not be listened to by our fellow-countrymen.

What we must do is, first, to demonstrate tirelessly that the one infallible way of making social hatred grow to monstrous proportions is to leave things as they are. If we attempt to go on living indefinitely under our present disintegrating and decaying economic system, which suddenly withdraws the very means of life from one section of the population, while it piles meaningless wealth on to another, we shall in the end produce a paroxysm of social hatred such as we have witnessed in Europe. But we must also make it clear that in our insistence on the necessity of changing that economic system by the socialisation of the means of production, we are not careless of the conditions and methods under which that change may be effected. We must convince men that we really care for those democratic elements in our national life which three centuries of popular struggle have won; that we will resolutely defend those rights, and that when we are undertaking the essential work of social transition not one of them shall be infringed, until and unless they are destroyed by reaction in revolt.

More than this we cannot say. For we should be frauds if we pretended to know the conditions and necessities of the period of the transition to Socialism. After all we are here dealing with a situation for which there is no precedent. The working class has not yet got power in any State which has been previously a highly developed capitalist democracy, such as Britain or America. Almost the only thing which we can say about such a period is that it will be as different in character from the period of transition which we are actually witnessing to-day in the Soviet Union as British capitalist democracy is different from the semi-feudal autocracy of the Tsar. This is not to say that the transition will necessarily be easier in our case. It is simply to say that it will be different. All we know of it is that it will be a period of political struggle, complex, prolonged, arduous; and that that struggle will need many different forms of working class rule,[1] just as to-day our struggle against capitalist rule needs many different forms of working-class resistance and activity.

It may be for the convenience of the reader to summarise the series of propositions which have been put forward in this book.

(1) Capitalist societies spontaneously generate a social phenomenon called the working-class, or Labour, movement.

(2) These Labour movements are always in the end driven, by the conditions of life which capitalist relations of production impose on their members, to aim at the establishment of a new form of human society, which they call Socialism.

(3) But the Socialism which these movements are bound to acquire may be of different sorts. It may be Fabian, British or Revisionist Socialism, or it may be scientific, or Marxist, Socialism.

(4) The experience of the British Labour movement shows that any kind of Socialism other than scientific Socialism fails the movement as a guide to action, both in the movement's periods of strength and in its periods of weakness, in relation to the strength of capitalism.

(5) Labour movements as they grow in size, and as they become more conscious of their aims, inevitably reach a

[1] The rule of the working class and its allies in the Soviet Union has already taken three distinct forms (or will have done so by the time this book is published), each represented by a new constitution.

point of development at which they become incompatible with the existing capitalist, social system, which is itself becoming more and more unstable. When this point has been reached, the movement must either begin rapidly to modify its environment, or that environment must begin rapidly to destroy the movement. No Labour movement which has not grasped the essential principles of scientific Socialism (of which this is one) can hope to succeed in saving itself by changing its environment.

(6) The ability of a Labour movement to modify its environment instead of being destroyed by it will depend upon its steadily and resolutely prosecuting the struggle of the wage workers against the conditions of life imposed upon them by capitalism. If, instead, it attempts to stifle that struggle in the hope of accommodating itself to the existing ruling class, it will wither and die. This, and not loosely and emotionally formulated questions of "evolution versus revolution," is the supreme issue before a Labour movement. For the prosecution of the struggle of the workers will have to be undertaken by all manner of means, from the most constitutional to the most desperate, according to time and place. Nor will the question of what means are to be used be left, primarily, in the hands of the workers or their movement.

But what is in our hands is the decision to prosecute or abandon that struggle itself. The unmistakable lesson of the fifty years history of the British working-class movement is that whenever our movement has abandoned the struggle and accommodated itself to capitalism, it has begun to die; that whenever it has resisted the will of the ruling class, and resolutely defended the interests of the working class, it has lived and grown.

(7) But the acquisition of scientific Socialism as the ideology of a Labour movement, and the resolute prosecution of the workers' struggle, will not in themselves suffice. Or rather they involve a profound change in the structure of the movement. They involve the emergence of a working-class political party built upon a new model.

(8) In the political conditions created by highly developed capitalist democracies of the British and American type these new model working-class political parties should replace no existing part of the Labour movement. Their function is to add an indispensable and hitherto lacking part to these movements.

(9) In the same way the Labour movement is only a part, though it is the principal part, of the entire popular forces which have emerged within such capitalist societies as Britain and America. The next step in the struggle of the Labour movements of such communities is to gather all these popular forces round them in some form of progressive alliance or People's Front.

(10) Such a democratic, progressive alliance has an indispensable function to perform in implementing a programme for the defence of the three supreme popular interests, peace, democracy and the national standard of life.

The answer to our initial question of what are we to do, is then as follows:

(*a*) Provide the British Labour movement with the ideology of scientific socialism.

(*b*) Develop, as an integral part, as indeed the core and heart of the movement, a party built upon the new model.

(*c*) End the policy of accommodation to the needs of a declining capitalism. In order to do this unify the movement by one means or another. Put into effect a policy of the united, active, defence of peace, democracy and the national standard of life.

(*d*) Gather round this policy the very widest possible alliance of all the popular and progressive forces in the country.

These four closely interrelated things are what we have to do. They involve a two-sided, opposite process. On the one hand the movement must deepen and intensify itself; must differentiate out of itself a hard yet flexible core in the shape of the new model party. On the other hand the movement must broaden itself, so that it can unite with the whole popular and progressive forces of the community. Its growth must be both intensive and extensive. For, to borrow a biological image, the organism will not have the vitality, the energy or the necessary nervous structure, to grow extensively to a size adequate to its historical function, until and unless it produces an adequately developed nucleus consisting of tissue of a much more highly developed type than that of the organism as a whole. This is what has to be done. By means of this two-sided type of development, and by means of it alone, the British Labour movement can rise to the height of its historical opportunity in the twentieth century, and save the world.

But can it be done? Are there forces, or can forces be created, which can overcome the obstacles which have hitherto prevented any such development as this? Let us not deceive ourselves as to either the size of the obstacles or the inherent difficulties which confront those who attempt to bring about these developments in the British Labour movement.

To take inherent difficulties first, the discredit which now attaches to the Labour Party and, to a lesser extent, to the Trade Unions, in the eyes of a considerable section of the working population is very serious. A Labour movement cannot go through the events of 1926 to 1931 unscathed. There is a deep impression in the minds of many workers, who have never been closely attached to the movement, that during those years the present Labour movement was tested and found wanting. If this was the only mood of the people of Britain it might be thought better to attempt to create a new movement than to attempt to restore the old. But unquestionably there is a still deeper contrary feeling amongst the several millions of workers who actually compose the Labour movement. These vitally important workers still feel the intensest loyalty to their movement. And this intense loyalty exists in the hearts of the very finest members of the British working-class. They

are depressed and shaken by the defeats which the movement has suffered. But they and their fathers built this
movement with toil and sacrifice. The question of deserting
it simply cannot arise in their minds. Let us never forget
that in the hour of the Labour Party's greatest humiliation
and disgrace, in 1931, six million British workers tramped
sadly but steadfastly off to vote for it. The existence in the
British workers of this enormous and unshakable loyalty to
the movement of their making renders it utterly impossible
to attempt to do the job by the creation of a new movement.
And for that matter, whatever the circumstances, and
however far the discrediting of the Labour movement had
gone, it is always impossible to create another Labour
movement. Such a second movement would always be an
artificial, inorganic, feeble thing. A class has only the
creative energy to give birth to one movement in any
historical period. If that movement fails, and is destroyed,
the class lies fallow for a whole period, as the British working-
class lay fallow between the fall of Chartism in the 'forties
to the beginning of the modern Labour movement in the
'eighties.[1]

There is no other way but the revival of the real, existing
British Labour movement. Nor is such revival psychologically
impossible. The discredit of the movement is not irreparable.
Nothing comparable to the irredeemable betrayals which
the German workers suffered from their movement between
1918 and 1933 has happened in Britain. The British
working class has not yet despaired. It cannot be denied,
however, that with every month that the policy of accommodation to the needs of capitalism was continued the moment
of ultimate, and irreparable, despair came nearer. Had it
not been for the desperate efforts of those gathered round
the British Communist Party to keep alive some struggle;
had it not been for the Communist led struggles of the
unemployed in 1934, 1935, and 1936; had not the British
Communist Party organised the sending of the British

---

[1] Though in modern conditions a new movement would undoubtedly arise
far more rapidly.

Battalion of the International Brigade to Spain in 1936, when the National Council of Labour was actively supporting non-intervention, that moment of despair, which is final, might have been near indeed. As it is the movement has only to begin to fight again for it to regain its health. The British workers have only to hear a new note in the voices of the spokesmen of their movement for them to take heart again. If once those spokesmen come to believe again in themselves and their cause, they can lead the movement, neither easily nor quickly, but yet certainly, to victory.

In order that this may happen renewed vitality must sweep through the movement. This revival has to be produced in spite of all that has happened. This is the difficult, but yet possible, task which faces all those who would revivify the British working-class movement. Forces for the accomplishment of this talk are now emerging. The Communist Party of Great Britain, the new model party, grows slowly but steadily. Its influence, as measured by the circulation of its periodicals, and the sale of its literature, grows much more rapidly. Striking evidence of the possibility of the sudden emergence of forces which can save the British Labour movement is the growth, far more rapid than anything hitherto known in Britain, of the Left Book Club to 50,000 members, with over 700 discussion groups, in a year and a half. Nothing comparable to the appearance of a nation-wide educational and propagandist organisation of this sort in anything under ten years—and far more usually thirty years have been required—has ever been seen before. These forces are already sufficient to revive the movement. If the Labour Party accepted the affiliation of the Communist Party, or even achieved the unity of the movement in a less direct way, the movement would be making rapid progress again within three months.[1]

---

[1] Though, of course, it would, in this case, be facing the embittered attacks, instead of the contemptuous tolerance, of the ruling class. It is perfectly true that a united movement would excite far more vicious opposition from this quarter—but it is only when they are being attacked by the spokesmen of capitalism that Labour movements live and grow.

We know, however, that a stubborn fight lies ahead of us before the unity of the movement is formally and officially recognised. But the revival of our movement cannot wait for this final victory in the struggle for unity. Hence, while not for one moment slackening the fight for officially recognised unity, it is the duty of every man and woman who comes to an understanding of the present situation to build unity, and to reverse the policy of accommodation to capitalism, here and now by active work within the Labour movement. We must not for one moment stand about bemoaning the refusal of the National Council of Labour officially to recognise the unity of the movement. For the ability of the majority of our leaders to prevent the achievement of a large measure of actual unity, effected by means of every individual supporter of the policy of united resistance joining, and actively working within, one or more units of the Labour movement (local Labour Parties, Trade Union branches and Co-operative Guilds) is very limited. If every reader of the *Daily Worker*, every member of the Left Book Club, every supporter of the recent unity campaign, became an active, efficient member of his or her local Labour Party (and if possible Trade Union branch or Co-operative Guild), a measure of unity, which would not indeed be nearly so good as an officially recognised unity, but which would be enough to save the movement, could be achieved to-morrow. *And it is not the National Council of Labour which is preventing this degree of unity. On the contrary, it is our own failure to use our undoubted rights and opportunities.*

This failure is perfectly comprehensible, but it is none the less disastrous. On a rough computation there are a quarter of a million members of what may be called the "Left" of the Labour movement in Britain. All of them to a greater or lesser extent understand the essentials of the present political situation. If they were all fully active within the Labour movement they would represent an irresistible force, intent on its transformation and revival. But it is just these 250,000 or so men and women who have felt the profoundest disillusionment with the Labour movement as it is to-day. It is just these poeple who have been profoundly "put off" work in the movement by all that has happened in the last ten years. Their first reaction (I should say our first reaction, for my own case is an excellent example of the general rule) was, almost universally, to sever, to a greater or lesser degree, their connection with the main, official, part of the movement. Moreover, many of them now feel that this part of the movement has continued to go from bad to worse. If they left it some time ago, they fail to see why they should go back to it now, Hence, they are often unresponsive, or even hostile, when it is suggested to them that their first duty is to get back into the appropriate local Labour Party, Trade Union branch or Co-operative Guild.

But however natural our first reaction away from the Labour movement may have been, and however natural a lingering reluctance to work within it may now be, it is high time that we overcame these emotional reactions. It is time that we faced the imperative necessity of universal and full participation in the life of the official sections of the movement. For imperative necessity it is. We may depend upon it that we shall accomplish nothing, and that moreover we shall have only ourselves to blame for it, if we do not immediately and entirely overcome this attitude of withdrawal from the full life of the movement as a whole. Surely the idea that the very desperation of the position of the Labour movement, the very straits into which the policy of accommodation has led it, is an overwhelming reason, not for sectarian withdrawal from it, but for tireless participation in the life of any and every part of it, in order to transform and revive it—surely this idea is not too subtle for everyone of us to grasp? The Left in Britain is young. But it must now put away childish things and begin to play the part which only it can play in the life of the British working-class movement. No doubt the hard, unthanked job of transforming the Labour movement by full participation in its work, combined with steady, tireless, explanation of why the policy of accommodation is disastrous, is more difficult than to stand aside and criticise. But it is also a hundred times more fruitful. Millions of members of the movement are waiting for those who can show them, clearly, soberly, sensibly, why their movement has not for eight years made any progress and what has got to be done to save it. The British working-class movement contains some of the noblest natures and stoutest hearts of the world. These hearts are to-day filled with depression and with bitterness, for their movement has been let down. But they have only to find out why and how, and what to do about it, for them to take fire again.

When once that has happened nothing can stop the root and branch transformation of the British Labour movement. It is true that some, but not all, of those who at present control the movement are not susceptible to argument on the basic questions discussed in these pages—we deceive ourselves if we think that they are. But they are susceptible to the conversion of the movement beneath them. They have been able to carry the movement with them because the decisive majority of the active, organised workers who constitute its effective core have had no adequate opportunity to hear the case against the policy of accommodation; the case for united resistance; for the inclusion within a united movement of a party built upon the new model; for the creation of the widest possible People's Front for the defence of peace, democracy and the national standard of life. *And to an appallingly large degree this is our own fault.* Only too often we have stated our case in the worst possible way. Only too often we have been strident, abusive, dogmatic, supercilious—all the things which the shrewd, practical workers of the movement hate, and rightly hate, most. Again we have attempted to create organisations when we should have attempted to mould opinion. The British working class, with its genius for organisation, has plenty of parties, unions, leagues, groups, committees and movements already. The job is not to create any more, but to fill the existing ones with a consciousness of their historical purpose.

ND

The new organisations which the Left has founded have almost always been destroyed by the deadly accusation that they were disruptive and disloyal. Disaffiliations, excommunications, boycottings, ruthlessly employed, have shattered these organisations one after another. But there is one type of left-wing activity which cannot be so destroyed. And that is the steady exposition of scientific Socialism; the quiet implanting of the idea of united resistance as the salvation of the movement. For you cannot disaffiliate an idea. And an idea, the idea of scientific Socialism, with everything that it involves, is what the British Labour movement lacks.

The situation of our movement is very critical. No one who faces facts can honestly deny that if no change had been wrought in it in 1937, the British Labour movement would soon have become sick unto death. The point of depression in the fortunes of the British Labour Party reached in the series of twelve by-elections which took place in the summer of 1937 forced every single member of the movement, from the top to the bottom, to admit, either privately or publicly, that something was gravely amiss. Since that time the beginnings of struggle have led to the beginnings of revival. The advocates of united resistance have now both a supreme opportunity and a supreme responsibility. They and they alone, have a rational, coherent, effective diagnosis and remedy to offer. Nothing can stop our policy being adopted—unless we prove unworthy exponents of it. We have only to convince the decisive majority of the members of the movement of our sobriety and our integrity to win them. Our road forward is straight and open. Let us tread it confidently, and we shall not fail.

BIBLIOGRAPHY

ATTLEE, C. R.: *The Labour Party in Perspective.*

BEER, MAX: *British Socialism.*

BLATCHFORD,
  ROBERT: *Merrie England.*

COLE, G. D. H.: *Self-government in Industry.*
  „   „   *The Condition of Britain.*
  „   „   *The People's Front.*
  „   „   *The World of Labour.*

FOSTER, W. Z.: *From Bryan to Stalin.*

HOBSON, J. A.: *Imperialism.*

HUTT, ALLEN: *The Post-War History of the British Working Class.*

JACKSON, T. A.: *Dialectics.*

LEAK, H. AND
  PRIDAY, T.: *Migration from and to the United Kingdom.*

LENIN, V. I.: *Selected Works. Vols. I. to VI.*

PEASE, EDWARD: *The History of the Fabian Society.*

POPOV, N.: *Outline History of the Communist Party of the Soviet Union.*

SHAW, BERNARD: Appendix to *The History of the Fabian Society.*
  „   *Fabianism and the Empire.*

STRACHEY, J.: *The Theory and Practice of Socialism.*

TAWNEY, R. H.: *Aquisitive Society.*

WEBB, SIDNEY   *A Constitution for the Socialist Commonwealth of*
  AND BEATRICE: *Great Britain.*
    ,,   ,,   *History of Trade Unionism.*
    ,,   ,,   *The Decay of Capitalist Civilization.*

WEBB, SHAW,
    ETC., ETC.   Fabian Essays.

Labour and the Nation.
Report of the 1933 Labour Party Conference.
T.U.C. Report, 1933.
T.U.C. Report, 1935.
Democracy versus Dictatorship.
Dictatorships and the Trade Union Movement.

INDEX